P9-DER-763

Contents

SEXUAL ASSAULT
ON THE
COLLEGE CAMPUS

SEXUAL ASSAULT ON THE COLLEGE CAMPUS

The Role of Male Peer Support

Martin D. Schwartz
Walter S. DeKeseredy

SAGE Publications
International Educational and Professional Publisher
Thousand Oaks   London   New Delhi

For information address:

 SAGE Publications, Inc.
2455 Teller Road
Thousand Oaks, California 91320
E-mail: order@sagepub.com

SAGE Publications Ltd.
6 Bonhill Street
London EC2A 4PU
United Kingdom

SAGE Publications India Pvt. Ltd.
M-32 Market
Greater Kailash I
New Delhi 110 048 India

Printed in the United States of America

Library of Congress Cataloging-in-Publication Data

Schwartz, Martin D.
    Sexual assault on the college campus: The role of male peer support /
authors Martin D. Schwartz and Walter S. DeKeseredy.
        p.   cm.
    Includes bibliographical references (p.) and index.
    ISBN 0-8039-7026-9 (cloth: acid-free paper).—ISBN 0-8039-7027-7
(pbk.: acid-free paper)
        1. Rape. 2. Acquaintance rape. 3. Sexual harassment in
universities and colleges. 4. Women college students—Crimes
against. 5. Men college students—Psychology. 6. Peer pressure.
I. Schwartz, Martin D. II. DeKeseredy, Walter S., 1959- .
HV6558.S47 1997
362.88'082—dc20   96-35648

            00 01 02 03 10 9 8 7 6 5 4

Acquiring Editor:	C. Terry Hendrix
Editorial Assistant:	Dale Grenfell
Production Editor:	Sherrise M. Purdum
Production Assistant:	Karen Wiley
Typesetter & Designer:	Andrea D. Swanson
Cover Designer:	Candice Harman

Foreword

This book speaks to me on several levels. When I read it the first time, I found myself frequently making notes in the margins: *Get this article, good example, Send to VP of Student Life, longitudinal study needed,* and so on. The loose pages of the manuscript that I have are now well-marked with red ink; some are tea-stained, others are dog-eared. From my experience as a teacher, researcher, editor, and activist, this is usually the sign of a very good book—good not only because it makes an interesting read but, more important, because it is "useful."

As a researcher, I was struck by the book's utility in two ways. First is the authors' attention to methodology. Throughout the book, Schwartz and DeKeseredy highlight the difficulties inherent in researching a topic as sensitive as sexual assault on campus. They discuss such issues as the best ways to word questions to potential or actual victims as well as perpetrators, problems with various sampling strategies, and the effects of using different types of statistical tests on the data. Moreover, they repeatedly remind us of the distinction between causation and correlation. Although such discussions may be especially valuable to newly minted researchers and current students of research methodology, the more experienced among us benefit from them too. We are cautioned about the dangers of making too sweeping claims that extend beyond the strength of our data and our analyses. Thus, we are reminded, for example, of the limitations of the traditional means by which we have conducted studies on sexual assault and woman abuse on campus. It is clear from the discussion in this book that longitudinal research is desperately needed—starting perhaps in the lower levels of elementary school, but certainly following female and male students for a number of years—to try to detect the emergence of attitudes and behaviors supportive of and conducive to violent and abusive behaviors and those factors that contribute to these behaviors.

The second way in which this book appealed to me as a researcher is its contribution to theory building. Schwartz and DeKeseredy capture the complexities involved in trying to explain sexual assault and woman abuse on campus. They emphasize the multidimensional nature of the problem, skillfully addressing both the suggestions of quick-fix administrators (e.g., Ban alcohol on campus, Institute an escort service) and the diatribes of those like Neil Gilbert, Katie Roiphe, and John Fekete who have become media darlings of the anti-feminist backlash. For me, however, the strongest contribution to theory building that Schwartz and DeKeseredy have made here is their test and refinement of the male peer-support model.

Schwartz and DeKeseredy review research showing that when men band together strongly in groups that exclude women, they are more likely to see women as Other. Although women are frequently talked about in these groups, the focal points of the conversations are typically women's sexuality (e.g., stories of sexual exploits with particular women, how to "get" sex from women) and control or domination of women (e.g., tales of how a woman was "put in her place")—both of which, the authors point out, are not unrelated. Schwartz and DeKeseredy concentrate on fraternities as sites for validating and sustaining masculine dominance and female inferiority, but they also make note of other, similar sites, including lodges, locker rooms, and taverns or bars.

Reading the research on male peer support and violence against women called to mind for me a disturbing experience I had while attending a conference in St. Paul, Minnesota, several years ago. The conference hotel was full, so I had to stay at an alternate hotel in Minneapolis. As luck would have it, this particular hotel was also hosting the annual gathering of a liquor dealers' association, the vast majority of whose membership was male. Integral elements of this meeting included several components that Schwartz and DeKeseredy identify as facilitating the degradation of women in all-male groups. One obviously was alcohol. However, closely linked with the alcohol—indeed, the primary means to market it—was the sexual objectification of women. Common were posters advertising various brands of alcohol using seminude models and double entendres. These, of course, are familiar to anyone who has ever seen a beer commercial on television. However, there were also various items that were apparently given out as "favors" to attendees, such as bottles in the shape of nude women, bottle stoppers with "decorative" tops in the shape of nude women, and drink stirrers similarly festooned with the shapes of nude women in various poses.

There was clearly a carnival atmosphere in that hotel lobby the final afternoon of my conference when I passed through to take the elevator to my room. Joining me on the elevator were a young woman and several men. Two of the men were friends who, based on the paraphernalia they were clutching, were attending the liquor dealers' gathering. They loudly exchanged small talk until the elevator made its first stop. The young woman exited alone and as she did, one of these two men said, "So long, baby." She appeared either not to have heard him or to have ignored him, but as the doors closed and the elevator started again, the man looked at his friend and said, "We'll have to come back later and teach her a lesson about friendliness." The two burst into laughter, with the second man adding, "Oh yeah!" I was instantly gripped with fear. I was fearful for the young woman, whom I didn't know and didn't know how to contact; at that point, I couldn't even remember what floor of the hotel she had exited on. I was also afraid for myself. Would I be next? Realizing that I was the only woman left on the elevator fueled my concern. I didn't dare chastise the men for their comments, not trusting any of the other men on that elevator to support me. None of them spoke up either.

Probably less than 30 seconds passed before the elevator stopped again, although to me the time seemed much longer. The two harassers got out then, but I didn't feel much relief. I was left on the elevator with two other men. Were they friends, I wondered? Had the harassers' behavior encouraged them to harass as well? I couldn't even face these men; I stood staring at the elevator doors, my body tense. Mercifully, after a few more seconds, the elevator door opened at my floor. I exited and took a few steps before turning to see if anyone was behind me. Alone, I raced to my room and went inside, finally feeling safe.

Certainly, I recognize that the harassment I witnessed is unfortunately commonplace and the "bonding rituals" of a virtually all-male gathering are not a prerequisite for it. Nevertheless, Schwartz and DeKeseredy's analysis suggests to me that there is an important connection here. The fraternity party camaraderie that the liquor dealers' meeting seemed to generate, as well as the omnipresence of alcohol and the sexual objectification of women, undoubtedly created a social context that was at least conducive to the abuse of women. At the same time, the discussion in this book underlined for me the powerful impact such abuse has on the majority of women. After all, I personally was not harassed on that elevator. Still, simply witnessing the harassment of another woman instilled fear in me—enough fear to silence me. To many readers, this incident probably appears to be minor, but it is precisely because of this that I ask you to consider carefully the effects that a more serious incident of abuse—such as a date or acquaintance rape—most likely has, first and foremost on the victim, but also on others close to her and on women generally. Schwartz and DeKeseredy weave such a consideration throughout this book, but it is to their credit that they also include the voices of Katie, Catherine, and Josh, who speak to us from their experiences about the devastating effects of violence against women.

Schwartz and DeKeseredy raised for me another question about what I have come to call "the elevator incident." I wondered, especially when I read Chapter 5 (Prevention and Policy Implications), what would have happened if the two male observers on the elevator had expressed their disapproval to the harassers? Although Schwartz and DeKeseredy present evidence that indicates that many men (and some women) would likely view incidents like this one as harmless, even humorous, they also suggest ways that pro-feminist men can make significant contributions to dismantling hegemonic masculinity and hence help to stop violence against women. Their logic is appealing in its simplicity: If male peer support promotes or encourages violence against women, then men who confront and openly oppose the sexism of their male peers will likely discourage and perhaps even prevent violence against women. The trick is to get pro-feminist men in the university community to step forward and to take action as a critical mass.

This brings me to another level on which this book speaks to me: as an educator and a member of a university community. As an educator, I am impressed by the accessibility of Schwartz and DeKeseredy's analysis, which makes the book useful as a text in many different courses. It *is* an interesting read; in fact, I predict that most students will report that they liked reading it. At the same time, however, it contains a wealth of information that not only carries the credibility stamp of science but also speaks directly to students' experiences. I would be surprised if many students came away from reading this book without seeing themselves in it somewhere.

It is this aspect of the book that leads me to be optimistic. Although I doubt that many college men who strongly support rape myths and practice hypermasculinity will be changed much by reading this book, I do think that the book will influence others. First, young women who have been victimized may come to understand their experiences better and thus be helped to heal. At the very least, they will know they are not alone. Women who have not been victimized, as I have already noted, are nonetheless affected by the threat of victimization. This book may also help them to understand their feelings as well as the nature of the problem of violence against women on campus. For all women, this book represents an important antidote to victim-blaming books like Katie Roiphe's and may also prove to be a motivator to action against violence on campus.

But Schwartz and DeKeseredy speak to men, too. Some male students may be prompted to reexamine their attitudes and behavior toward women after reading this book. I hope also that men who claim to be pro-feminist will be motivated by what they read to actually act on some of the authors' suggestions for bringing about change. Because the majority of university administrators and faculty are still men, many of whom see themselves as pro-feminist, I would like to put this book in their hands, too. As Schwartz and DeKeseredy point out, despite the greater attention to sexual harassment of students on university campuses, little attention is given to the problems of sexual assault and woman abuse by peers except when an incident occurs. Even then, the primary focus is on damage control. Male students come to believe that they can get away with raping and abusing female students because so often, they do get away with it.

This book is a valuable resource for faculty and administrators willing to scrutinize their personal attitudes and behavior as well as the policies and practices of their institutions. Of course, as Schwartz and DeKeseredy note, many are motivated to do so if only to protect against lawsuits. Indeed, some may soon be forced to reconsider at least their campus judicial systems, given that the first civil suit under the Violence Against Women Act was brought against a university as a result of the way its judicial system and administration handled an acquaintance rape case (Bernstein, 1996b). Nevertheless, I urge readers who are themselves faculty and administrators not only to ask their colleagues to read this book, but to sit down with them afterward to discuss it and to follow up until they act on it.

There is still one more level on which this book spoke to me, a more personal level. I am the mother of two young boys. Although I have long realized that my husband and I are not the sole socializers of our sons, this book made me more fully aware of how soon children begin receiving messages that encourage male hegemony and that degrade women. When reading Chapter 3 in particular (Growing Up in a Rape-Supportive Culture), I was reminded of a day last summer when my 6-year-old came home from camp asking why the boys in his camping group hated girls so much. Having gone to schools that we carefully selected because of their commitment to nonsexist education and having spent most of his classroom time in mixed-sex cooperative learning groups, my son was baffled by the comments and behavior of his new friends. They called the girls names, he told me, and said they're dirty and yucky; they chased them and pulled their hair; and they refused to play with them and made fun of him for wanting to. Needless to say, my son's enrollment in that particular day camp was short lived, and camp counselors and administrators were made well aware of the reason for his withdrawal. Although they said they understood my concerns, they described this sort of behavior as "natural" at this age.

Although I didn't really need to read this book to know that such behavior is not natural at any age, the association that Schwartz and DeKeseredy make between such early socialization experiences and adult sexism that contributes to violence against women jolted me. Taken individually, such events appear minor—like the elevator incident—but taken cumulatively they can have a potent and lasting impact on both males and females. Schwartz and DeKeseredy also made me recognize that my private complaint to those in charge of the camp was not enough; public attention should be drawn to such incidents and the potential consequences discussed. In short, we must make a commitment to what the authors call "news making": reaching out beyond our own circles to get alternative messages heard by as many people as possible.

Finally, one parting comment is in order. When I sat down to write this foreword, I intended to compose a dispassionate academic introduction to what I consider to be a fine piece of scholarship. Instead, I spent a good deal of time staring at a blank computer screen. Every attempt at an objective, impersonal opening seemed disingenuous. The book just evoked too many familiar images in my mind, too many personal connections. And therein lies, I suppose, this book's ultimate value: what we have here is a testament to the fact that the personal *is* political. That old feminist adage has been quoted so often and is on so many bumper stickers that the words sound hollow much of the time. I want to take this opportunity to thank Martin Schwartz and Walter DeKeseredy for reinvigorating it—and me.

Claire M. Renzetti
St. Joseph's University, Philadelphia

Preface

This book weaves together two distinct topics. In the first place, it is the story of sexual assault on the college and university campus. We discuss how often it happens, why it happens, and what can be done about it. Although certainly not every possible topic is discussed, readers will find most of the important facts, figures, and theories covered here. Much of the material is original research, or at least has been previously published by one or both of us, but this is not only a book about our own work—we only bring our own work to bear on the subject where relevant to the topic.

The second goal of this book is to explain why we feel that one of the most important subtopics in this area is the peer support that men get to commit these sexual assaults. This part of the book had its origins 10 years ago in a York University coffee shop, where Walter DeKeseredy overheard a group of six undergraduates provide a group member with "solutions" to his dating problems. The recipient of advice was deeply disturbed because he took a woman out for dinner and she refused to have sex with him at the end of the evening. Some of his peers suggested that he stop seeing her, while others stated that he should have physically forced her to have sex with him.

Interestingly, there turned out to be few attempts in the literature at the time to explain the linkage between male peer support and woman abuse. That discovery, 10 years ago, led to a doctoral dissertation, many articles, and a major research study on the subject. With Martin Schwartz, the theoretical perspective behind this work was vastly expanded and enhanced. That newer perspective forms the theoretical backbone of this book.

Schwartz began working in the field of physical abuse against women in intimate relationships but later began to conduct, with the help of many students, local victimization surveys on sexual abuse on college campuses.

Thus, both authors have had extensive experience in this area, including two doctoral dissertations, several books, and more than 50 articles on woman abuse alone. Both of us have been strongly committed to developing a more adequate sociological understanding of woman abuse in intimate relationships and to participating in the global struggle to end all forms of male-to-female victimization.

Whatever our interest in pro-abuse male peer support, this book would not have been written without the encouragement of Ola Barnett, who not only convinced us to write the book, but to write it for Sage Publications. Terry Hendrix of Sage was very encouraging and helpful, even as this book became impossibly overdue. We are also indebted to Dale Grenfell, who selected excellent reviewers, put up with a variety of pestering requests, and motivated us to finish this project.

Even more central to the completion of this book was the social support provided by our families. We are especially indebted to Carol Blum, Patricia, Andrea, and Steven DeKeseredy, Marie Barger, and Eva Jantz. Without their patience and understanding we would not have been able to muster up enough psychological and physical energy to focus on our work.

Special thanks go to the following people who took time away from their busy schedules to provide us with their comments and criticisms on our research and theory: Desmond Ellis, the late Michael D. Smith, Clifford Jansen, Claire Renzetti, Christine Mattley, Brian D. MacLean, Dawn Currie, Gary Keveles, James Messerschmidt, Linda Davies, Linda MacLeod, Mary Koss, Meda Chesney-Lind, Betsy Stanko, Kersti Yllo, Susan Caringella-MacDonald, Shahid Alvi, Kimberly Cook, Ronald Hinch, Robert Shelly, Ola Barnett, Jurgen Dankwort, John Pollard and his colleagues at York University's Institute for Social Research, the Ottawa Regional Coordinating Committee to End Violence Against Women, and the anonymous reviewers of our manuscript. Because many of these people disagree with one another, we assume full responsibility for what we took from them and what we left behind.

The support of Ohio University and Carleton University is also greatly appreciated. Victoria Pitts, Carol Nogrady, Wendy Taylor, Dana Nurge, and Molly Leggett were all instrumental during their time at Ohio University in working through many issues as part of research projects reported in this book. Several grants by the Honors Tutorial College at Ohio University and by the Institute for Local Government Administration and Rural Development (ILGARD) were important to the completion of these studies. Also at Ohio University, Jennifer Rowe, Kim Varney, Amy Phillips-Gary, and Molly Leggett provided invaluable assistance in gathering or providing research materials, while Arnie Kahn at James Madison University also provided important material.

The pseudonymous Catherine, Josh, and Katie were all students at Ohio University who have given us permission to reprint their writings here. Nona Wilson conducted the interview with Catherine and was extremely generous in providing the transcript for our use.

Financial assistance to gather information was provided at Carleton by the Office of the Dean of Social Sciences and by the Faculty of Graduate Studies and Research, while some of the research and writing was supported by sabbatical leaves provided by Ohio University and Carleton University. One research project reported extensively in this book was supported by a grant from the Family Violence Prevention Division of Health Canada to Walter DeKeseredy and Katharine Kelly. The views expressed in this book are those of the authors and do not necessarily reflect those of Health Canada or Katharine Kelly.

Last but not least, we would like to thank the thousands of the students and many dozens of instructors who participated in the variety of victimization surveys discussed in this book. It is our hope that the results of these studies and this book will help make unsafe learning environments safer.

Small parts of Chapters 2 and 3 include material adapted from Walter S. DeKeseredy, *Woman Abuse in Dating Relationships: The Role of Male Peer Support* (Canadian Scholars' Press, 1988); Walter S. DeKeseredy, "Woman Abuse in Dating Relationships: The Relevance of Social Support Theory," *Journal of Family Violence, 3* (1988), and Walter S. DeKeseredy and Martin D. Schwartz, "Male Peer Support and Woman Abuse: An Expansion of DeKeseredy's Model," *Sociological Spectrum, 13* (1993). A few pages of Chapter 5 were adapted from Walter S. DeKeseredy, "Making an Unsafe Learning Environment

Safer: Some Progressive Policy Proposals to Curb Woman Abuse in University/College Dating Relationships," *Violence: A Collective Responsibility* (edited by Cannie Stark-Adamec, Social Science Federation of Canada, 1996), Walter S. DeKeseredy, "Left Realism and Woman Abuse in Dating," *Crime and Society: Readings in Critical Criminology* (edited by Brian D. MacLean, Copp Clark, 1996), and Martin D. Schwartz and Walter S. DeKeseredy, "The Return of the Battered Husband Syndrome Through the Typification of Women as Violent," *Crime, Law, and Social Change: An International Journal, 20* (1993). Permission to use or reprint this material is gratefully acknowledged.

Martin D. Schwartz
Walter S. DeKeseredy

1

Sexual Assault on
North American College Campuses

There are two purposes for this book. In the first place, it is designed to be an introduction to the topic of sexual assault on college campuses. Throughout this book, we will present both theories and the latest empirical findings on a broad range of issues related to sexual assault. A few of the questions we will discuss include: How often does sexual assault occur? Is alcohol abuse related? What do we know about alcohol abuse today? Are fraternities more likely to be engaged in sexual abuse than other groups? Do education programs have an effect?

At the same time, we will be discussing our own theoretical model of male peer support. In the first place, we think that this model has some important value in tying together a wide range of factors in a way that makes the material in this book more easily understood. Second, we are interested in placing much more than the usual attention on the role of male peer groups. Certainly we fully agree that a broad range of psychological, developmental, and individual characteristics make it easier for some men to commit rape. Furthermore, a central part of our work is the sociological emphasis on social structure: that we live in a society that many have called a "rape culture."

Thus, many men sexually assault women because of the interplay of personality characteristics and the teachings of the society in which they live. Still, a central organizing theme of this book will be that men who abuse women associate with other men who have the same beliefs, and who give them support for thinking in this way. Certainly not all men are in such groups, and some men who are exposed to such pressures either ignore them or condemn them. Still, what we will examine in this book is that many men remain in groups that actively support the emotional and sexual abuse of women. We have, both separately and together, conducted a variety of campus surveys, including one national representative survey, and published dozens of professional articles and several books on this topic. Through this work, we have become convinced that male peer support is an integral underlying factor in campus sexual assault.

As we proceed, we will weave these two themes together. The major goal of this work will be to explain sexual assault on college campuses, but we will use our male peer-support model much of the time to help this process along. In this opening chapter, we will discuss the problem of sexual assault on college campuses; we will begin to discuss the model in the next chapter. Perhaps the first step, however, is to point out that campus crime is neither new nor rare.

Campus Crime

Many people regard North American colleges as centers of higher learning, friendly interpersonal socialization, career training, liberal thought, and athletic achievement. They are "places . . . where the pursuit of truth and the exercise of reason prevail, and where it is assumed our daughters will be safe from 'the lion in the streets' " (Pierson, 1991, p. 10). Even shocking events tend to be forgotten, or at least they do not disturb this overall sunny image of college and university campuses. For example, the December 6, 1989, mass murder of 14 women (13 students and 1 staff member) at the Université de Montréal, École Polytechnique, by a young man who was outraged at feminists generally and at the fact that women were enrolled in engineering schools specifically, was an important event in Canada. It reminded people of the depths to which an anti-feminist backlash might go, and simultaneously the lack of safety for many women on their own campuses. Still, this event never had much impact in the United States and has done little in Canada today to challenge the popular image of universities and colleges as "peaceable kingdoms."

Unfortunately, they are not and rarely have been safe retreats. In fact, college campuses have long been breeding grounds for an endemic level of crime. For example, more than 150 years ago, Harvard University complained that students frequently committed "crimes worthy of the penitentiary" (Shenkman, 1989, p. 135). In the same era, Ohio University and other small rural schools were hiring watchmen because of student crimes such as vandalism. Since then, college students have steadily engaged in theft, violent assault, sexual assault, extraordinary acts of vandalism, and a host of other crimes. With students often targeting other students, Roark (1987) points to a reality that college students typically create a population at risk for criminal victimization.

Why is it that, for so many years, we have rarely heard about crime on college campuses? Why is it that while the rest of North America has been absorbed with a series of "wars" on crime, with crime prevention measures, and with political campaigns that are battles over who is more "macho" on crime, little energy has been devoted to discussing felony crimes at North American colleges? Perhaps it is because the overwhelming bulk of these schools are primarily reserved for middle- and upper-class people, most of whom are white.

We seem to have developed laws and law enforcement policies aimed specifically at disenfranchised people (e.g., the working class, Native American and First Nations peoples, Hispanics, and African Americans) while letting another equally if not more guilty group off more easily. When the college campus is victimized by nonstudent local residents (e.g., stranger rapes, purse snatchings, assaults, muggings, burglaries), the worry about crime has been public. When the criminals are themselves tuition-paying students who engage in acquaintance rapes, thefts, drug sales, gambling, vandalism, and assaults, the rhetoric is much softer.

This is not to say that the hidden nature of campus crime is simply a conspiracy of college administrators to hush up crimes of the middle and upper classes. Although cover-ups may often be the best explanation of what has happened (Sanday, 1990; Warshaw,

1988), a much more important factor is the lack of unanimity among college administrators, faculty, and students on what it means to commit a crime. If a crowd of inner-city youths surrounded a women's dormitory and demanded that each resident turn over a piece of jewelry or a compact disc, the only issue most college administrators would be debating is whether or not to have the local police backed up by the National Guard. However, a similar act, in which crowds of middle-class white men surround a women's dormitory and demand that each resident turn over a piece of intimate apparel, was a tradition in the United States for generations. These "panty raids" were often supplemented by burglary, breaking and entering, and quite a bit of property damage. In cases such as these, the typical campus administrators' response was: "Oh well, boys will be boys."

Panty raids still occur and are not restricted to U.S. campuses. For example, Hornosty (1996) describes a Canadian raid that took place at Wilfred Laurier University in 1989. After the raid, an unidentified group of male students splattered ketchup on the women's underwear, taped the panties to the cafeteria wall, and wrote derogatory captions above each pair. Hornosty suggests that female students at Wilfred Laurier University were rather less likely to define this event as "just a joke" or a "little bit of fun getting out of hand."

There are more serious examples of crimes committed by undergraduate students, and the perpetrators are typically white members of either the middle or upper class. These youths commit a wide variety of offenses throughout their college years, including drug sales, car theft, insurance fraud, massive residence hall vandalism, theft from residence hall rooms, and aggravated assault (Hills, 1984). At some private residential campuses lacking public transportation, students commonly steal cars to drive to local night spots. Furthermore, large bookie rings operate on many college campuses, with vast amounts of money flowing in and out of fraternity houses and dormitories each week. According to *Sports Illustrated* (Layden, 1995), the perpetrators of this crime are virtually immune from police attention.

How can all of this crime occur and not be noticed? One reason is that a large number of people on campus, including administrators, faculty, and students, do not understand the difference between a serious felony crime and a harmless prank committed by exuberant fraternity men or a group of males "cooped up" in a dormitory room. Another, according to *The New York Times*, is that campus judicial systems across the country are designed to hide fraternity crimes at "most" colleges and universities; few of the thousands of criminal cases that enter the system emerge with serious penalties (Bernstein, 1996a).

The Legacy of Ignoring College Crime

It is interesting to speculate on the futures of the men that we are identifying today as acquaintance and date rapists. Is it possible that the lessons they learn today—that one can commit serious felonies and get away with them; that if you belong to elite groups, you are above the law—are lessons that they carry with them as they get older? To what extent can we blame their future crimes on these lessons learned at the expense of women on college campuses?

For example, we have known for decades that many white-collar criminals are identified for the first time long after their college careers are over; they are "first offenders" in their thirties or even their forties. In the 1980s, more than in most decades, Americans were treated to the spectacle of a parade of businessmen and politicians going through our courts and occasionally to prison. There might have been thousands more white-collar first offenders in our courts, thanks to banking scandals involving an extraordinary number of felony crimes by (mostly) men. However, most charges were dropped against bankers accused of serious felonies because local prosecutors did not have the staff to press charges against them (Friedrichs, 1995). "Where did they go wrong?" we lament, noting that virtually all of these middle-class men had spotless criminal records. This is not a new lament; some of criminology's most influential theorizing has focused on why honest and law-abiding citizens suddenly turn for the worse when they become adults (e.g., Cressey, 1953).

In fact, however, many of these criminals have become experienced felons long before college graduation (Hills, 1984). Too often, they had their crimes covered up in college. We will discuss in this book how undergraduate rapists are punished for their crimes only in the rarest cases (Bernstein, 1996c). Furthermore, the youths who are most conservative politically (e.g., the holders of traditional gender attitudes) and monied (e.g., able to gain entry into elite fraternities) may be the ones most likely to commit rapes and often other types of college crimes. Hills (1984) examined elite students who are never charged with their crimes and argued:

Armed with a self-serving rip-off philosophy and a rich vocabulary of justifications of their illicit conduct, many of these students ("tomorrow's leaders") will soon graduate to become elite Wall Street and Boston lawyers, high-salaried executives, and prominent physicians. It seems likely, however, that some of these same students will continue to flout the law as they also become tomorrow's corrupt government officials, tax cheats, toxic waste polluters, defrauders of Medicare, corporate price-fixers, fraudulent advertisers, and other myriad forms of white-collar criminals, whose highly injurious actions are also protected and shrouded in relative immunity from criminal penalties. College life has prepared them well. (p. 69)

College administrators help to provide this immunity. In the area of sexual assault, the problem is particularly acute (Bohmer & Parrot, 1993). As we will discuss later, only 5% of victims report the crime because of the moral ambiguities fostered on campus, and only a small number of these cases go forward. Sanday (1990) argues that a widespread tendency of college administrators to ignore or cover up reports of specific instances is one of the most important social conditions promoting gang rape. Similarly, Warshaw (1988) reports that university proceedings, widely promoted as a less traumatic alternative to criminal court, are perhaps the most likely of all to trivialize the event. Although some schools may have improved the processes since these women were questioned, "not one of the women interviewed for [Warshaw's] book who had taken her case before a university judicial board felt satisfied with the result" (p. 147), as rapists had charges dismissed or were assigned to write a paper on sexual assault. *The New York Times* did not find any improvement in this picture in 1996 (Bernstein, 1996c).

If college men feel that they are above the law when they rape women, it is because they too often are. The lack of a clear-cut policy in this area at most colleges, the lack of enforcement, and the hesitancy of many campuses to work with local police means that "students are given the implicit message that acquaintance rape and sexual assault are tolerated on campuses" (Bohmer & Parrot, 1993, p. 183). Unfortunately, the reality is that these crimes *are* tolerated. One of the most popular criminological theories today, especially among those who are conservative in political outlook, is *rational choice theory*, which generally proposes that criminals are able to rationally weigh the benefits and risks of committing a crime. To the extent that this is true—and presumably it would be more true among our cultural and intellectual elite on college campuses than among our least-educated street criminals—then it should be obvious to most students that the rewards of committing rape far outweigh the costs, which are often minimal.

We will argue throughout this book that North America is a rape-supportive culture where messages are constantly given out that promote the sexual exploitation of women. On college campuses, many faculty and staff maintain attitudes that promote acquaintance and date rape. If they are given the choice, rape will indeed be tolerated on campus. Hornosty (1996, p. 35), for example, describes two cases where students received a strong implied message:

- In a community college in British Columbia, in 1993, a criminology professor gave a class assignment to male students to construct the "perfect rape."
- A professor published an opinion piece in the November 5, 1993, issue of *The Brunswickan*, the University of New Brunswick student newspaper, alleging that "male aggressiveness" and the "male's drive for sex" are part of "human nature" and "therefore the reason and need for the so-called 'date rape.' "

We have decided to limit our attention here to this one type of criminal activity on campus. There has been an increasing amount of data in recent years on the subject, as more and more researchers have turned their attention to what is usually called in the literature "courtship violence." This has produced a variety of studies that empirically document the extent to which physical violence, psychological abuse, sexual assault, or "date rape" takes place on college campuses.[1] It is difficult to wade through all of these studies and to make sense out of them. Simply put, the different methodologies, different questions, and different sampling procedures used in these many studies have rather obviously generated rather different results (Johnson & Ferraro, 1988). Still, it is completely clear that a substantial minority of women on North American college campuses have experienced an event that would fit most states' definitions of felony rape or sexual assault (DeKeseredy & Kelly, 1993a; Koss,

Gidycz, & Wisniewski, 1987). The first step in explaining some of these results on how much sexual assault there is on North American campuses will be to turn our attention to definitions of the term *sexual assault*.

What Is Sexual Assault?

Many definitions of sexual assault are used in the sociological and psychological literature on the subject; all emphasize the notion of nonconsensual sexual conduct (Bohmer & Parrot, 1993; Schwartz & Pitts, 1995). Still, these definitions vary considerably in breadth. For example, some researchers limit their focus to nonconsensual penile-vaginal intercourse and use the term *rape* to describe this example of "not the way to love" (Fitzpatrick & Halliday, 1992). Others use terms such as *unwanted sexual experiences, sexual aggression, sexual abuse,* or *sexual assault* to depict a broader range of behaviors ranging from nonconsensual kissing to nonconsensual anal, oral, and vaginal intercourse.[2]

Feminist scholars and activists often contend that narrow definitions of sexual assault, such as those that focus only on penile-vaginal intercourse, ignore many female subjective experiences of sexual assault or create a hierarchy of sexual victimization based on seriousness (Kelly, 1987). For example, is it really true that completed rape is always more traumatic than attempted rape? One of the difficulties identified by researchers as they interview women who have been through these experiences is that our scales of seriousness may not conform to the subjective experiences of the women who lived through such attacks. Thus, in response to these problems, most researchers now employ broad definitions of sexual assault because they incorporate a more complete range of sexual behaviors that many women regard as major threats to their physical and psychological well-being (Ellis & DeKeseredy, 1996; Schwartz & Pitts, 1995; White & Sorenson, 1992).

Like many researchers, we follow Koss et al. (1987, p. 166) in using a classification similar to their four types of sexual assault:

- *Sexual contact* includes unwanted sex play (fondling, kissing, or petting) arising from menacing verbal pressure, misuse of authority, threats of harm, or actual physical force.

- *Sexual coercion* includes unwanted sexual intercourse arising from the use of menacing verbal pressure or the misuse of authority.
- *Attempted rape* includes attempted unwanted sexual intercourse arising from the use of or threats of force, or the use of drugs or alcohol.
- *Rape* includes unwanted sexual intercourse arising from the use of or threats of force and other unwanted sex acts (anal or oral intercourse or penetration by objects other than the penis) arising from the use of or threat of force, or the use of drugs or alcohol.

The Incidence and Prevalence
of Campus Sexual Assault

For a number of reasons, many people think that there is a sudden epidemic of violent crimes on college campuses. For example, we will later describe the Canadian National Survey (CNS), which measured sexual, physical, and psychological attacks on women in dating contexts. DeKeseredy and Kelly's (1993a) first report of the results of the CNS received unprecedented Canadian media coverage. Immediately, many older Canadians responded by stating that when they went to college, things were completely different. In their opinion, things were quiet and safe, except perhaps on a few campuses where outsiders occasionally came in and made trouble. Now, there are nasty things happening, such as acquaintance rape.

This romantic belief in a golden past is not unlike the common view, especially among white, middle-class North Americans, that life in earlier generations was similar to what was represented on popular television shows such as *Ozzie and Harriet* or *Leave it to Beaver.* Of course, we know that relatively few families (even in the middle class) were like the Nelsons or Cleavers. In the same way, we know that college life in previous generations was not all that simple. On our topic, contrary to common belief, the sexual assault of women on college campuses did not just begin to occur in recent years. For example, approximately 60 years ago, Waller (1937) pointed out that many undergraduate male dating partners were extremely exploitative and competitive. Perhaps more important, about 40 years ago, Kanin (1957) found that more than 20% of the college women he studied had been victimized by rape or attempted rape. Thus, in the generation now nearing retirement, women who are grandparents of today's college-age students might themselves have been victims of sexual assault on the college campus at a rate that rivals the situation on many campuses today.

It says a lot about us, our interests, and our sensibilities that we ignored disturbing research of this type for so many years. There is little doubt that this information was ignored because the protection of women on college campuses has long been a low priority of faculty and administrators, and even of the students themselves. It was only with the development of feminist coalitions, with intensive lobbying and education initiatives, that we began to see university communities begin to take the safety of women more seriously. Someone more cynical might point out that the impetus for some of this change has come from university legal officers, who have convinced university officials of the possibility of losing great amounts of money from lawsuits brought by women who feel that basic institutional frameworks to deal with violent assaults are not in place. Several such lawsuits have been lost by universities, with the result that many campuses quickly scrambled to respond (Bohmer & Parrot, 1993). For whatever reason, the past few years have seen a rapid growth in empirical research, an increase in media attention, attitudinal changes among campus administrators, and a greater university readiness to respond to the needs of female students. The university community now takes sexual assault more seriously than ever before.

It is possible, of course, that the sexual assault problem on campus is getting worse, and that this increase in assault is what is accounting for the increased attention. Kanin himself takes this position (Levine & Kanin, 1987). However, comparing more recent statistics with one study conducted in 1957 does not provide strong support for this argument. Although we cannot determine how the present-day rate of sexual assault compares to previous generations, we can briefly present recent incidence and prevalence survey data to show the current extent of sexual assault on North American campuses. *Incidence* refers here to the percentage of women who stated that they were sexually assaulted and the percentage of men who sexually assaulted women in the past year. *Prevalence* is the percentage of men who reported having engaged in sexual assault and the percentage of women who were victimized over a longer time period, such as the period since leaving high school.

Regardless of whether the rate of sexual assault on campus has increased or decreased over the last three or four decades, the data described in the next two sections of this chapter challenge the popular belief that North American female students' fear of sexual victimization is irrational. On the contrary, their fear is well-founded.

The Extent of Sexual Assault on U.S. College Campuses

The largest and most widely cited survey of higher education students on this subject in the United States was done by Mary Koss and her colleagues (Koss et al., 1987). They administered a self-report questionnaire to 6,159 students (3,187 women and 2,972 men) in 32 institutions of all types of higher education located across the United States. One of the most important elements of this questionnaire was the Sexual Experiences Survey (SES), which (although commonly modified slightly by other researchers) has become the standard instrument in the field. The female version of the survey asks a series of questions about the student's experiences with unwanted sex, whether through coercion or force, while the male version asks almost identical questions, modified slightly to ask the male whether he has ever used coercion or force on an unwilling woman. Just to pick one example of the use of a version of the SES, slightly modified from the original, Table 1.1 shows the questions and findings from DeKeseredy and Kelly's (1993a) work.

Using the SES to measure sexual assault, Koss et al. (1987) found that slightly more than 15% of the women reported that their most serious sexual victimization since the age of 14 (prevalence) had been a completed rape, while another 12.1% reported that their most serious victimization during the same time period was attempted but uncompleted sexual intercourse. These researchers also found that 14.4% of their female respondents experienced sexual contact (defined above as unwanted sex play) and 11.9% reported having been victimized by sexual coercion. When they looked at incidence data, or asked the women to report incidents that had taken place in the past year only, they found 207 women who had experienced a total of 353 rapes. Figures for other forms of sexual assault were: 533 attempted rapes (323 victims), 837 cases of sexual coercion (366 victims), and 2,024 experiences of unwanted sexual contact (886 victims).

Koss et al. (1987) also asked men about their activities. About 25% of the men in this sample reported engaging in some form of coercive sexual activity since the age of 14. Of these offenders:

- 10.2% admitted to having engaged in sexual contact
- 7.2% reported using sexual coercion
- 3.3% stated that they engaged in attempted rape
- 4.4% stated that they raped

When looking just at the past year (incidence), Koss et al. found (1987, p. 167-168):

- There were 36 incidents of nonconsensual intercourse obtained through force involving 20 men.
- Nonconsensual intercourse was obtained through intoxication by 57 men who reported 103 incidents.
- Nonconsensual forcible oral and anal penetration of a woman was reported by 19 men who admitted to 48 incidents.
- Totaled responses to the above individual SES items for the year before the survey yielded 187 rapes perpetrated by 96 different men.
- Incidence rates for the other types of sexual assault were: 167 attempted rapes committed by 105 offenders, 854 unwanted sexual contact incidents committed by 374 men, and 311 episodes of sexual coercion perpetrated by 167 men.

In addition to uncovering incidence and prevalence rates of sexual assault, Koss et al. (1987) elicited many other important data, including detailed information about the women's most serious victimization since the age of 14. For example:

- 95% of the rapes involved one offender
- 84% of the rape victims knew their attacker
- 57% of the rapists were dates (Koss, 1989)

Warshaw (1988) analyzed these findings and, in the context of whether there is a major problem on college campuses today, argued that

[The findings] make acquaintance rape and date rape more common than left-handedness or heart attacks or alcoholism. These rapes are no recent campus fad or the fantasy of a few jilted females. They are real. And they are happening all around us. (p. 11)

Koss and her colleagues are not the only researchers who have uncovered alarmingly high rates of sexual assault on U.S. college campuses and their immediate surroundings. Although different methodologies, definitions, questions, and sampling procedures have produced rather different results,[3] most U.S. research has found incidence and prevalence rates that range between 15% and 25% (Kanin, 1957; Koss, 1985, 1988; Koss & Gidycz, 1985; Koss et al., 1987; Makepeace, 1986; Muehlenhard & Linton, 1987; Rivera & Regoli, 1987). Obviously, sexual assault on campus is a major social problem, even if one bases this argument on the "low" or conservative 15% estimate (Ward, Chapman, Cohen, White, & Williams, 1991).

For those interested in comparative research on sexual assault, an important issue is whether Canadian female students have similarly sexually abusive experiences. It is to this issue that we now turn.

The Extent of Sexual Assault on Canadian College Campuses

There is the possibility, of course, that this phenomenon of sexual assault on college campuses is unique to the United States; that the U.S. violent crime rate (much higher than Canada's) in some way influences the rate of acquaintance and date rape on campus. At least in the studies done in English-speaking countries, there is no reason to believe that the United States is unique in any way. Just to pick one example, in a New Zealand study of 347 undergraduate women, Gavey (1991) found that 51.6% had experienced one of the SES victimizations, and 25.3% had experienced rape or attempted rape.

However, the best comparison to the United States is Canada. First, as we shall see, the data collected in Canada are the best outside the United States. Second, as a country sharing the North American continent with the United States, Canada is similar enough to allow many comparisons. However, it is still a very different culture in many ways than the U.S. culture, which allows for an important comparison also.

One important comparison is that according to the sixth annual United Nations (UN, 1995) *Human Development Report*, Canada is the best country in the world to live. In *overall* human development, measured by a combination of indicators such as life expectancy, education, and income, Canada tops 174 nations for the second straight year (Beauchesne, 1995). Furthermore, many outside observers regard Canada as a "kinder, gentler" nation. There is some empirical support for this perception. For example, Canadians are much less likely to be physically and sexually assaulted in public settings, such as parks, streets, workplaces, and taverns (Ellis & DeKeseredy, 1996). The Canadian rate of homicide is also considerably lower than that of the United States (Silverman & Kennedy, 1993).

However, the U.N. report also states that while Canadians overall do well, Canadian women do not fare as well as men. In fact, Canada is one of four industrial countries that has a "sharply lower" ranking on the gender development index than on the human development index. Canada is also attacked as a nation where many heterosexual women experience a substantial amount of physical and psychological pain in a variety of intimate and domestic relationships. Before we present the sexual assault incidence and prevalence rates generated by the CNS, it is first necessary to describe briefly the methodology used to generate these statistics.[4] We will use data from this study throughout this book, so it is important to first explain the study itself.

The Methodology of the CNS

The Canadian National Survey (CNS) is a national representative sample survey of community college and university students conducted in the autumn of 1992. A research team administered two questionnaires, one for men and another for women, in 95 undergraduate classes across the country, from Atlantic Canada to British Columbia. The questionnaires were administered in both French and English versions. Response rates were high, with less than 1% of the participants refusing to answer.

The sample consisted of 3,142 people, including 1,835 women and 1,307 men. The median age was 20 for women and 21 for men. Although members of a wide variety of ethnic groups participated in the survey, most of the respondents identified themselves as either

English Canadian or French Canadian. The majority (81% of the men and 77.9% of the women) had never married, but for those who had, all respondents were carefully and repeatedly warned that all questions in the survey referred to events that took place in dating (nonmarital) relationships. The sample was composed mainly of first- and second-year students, and a sizable portion of these (42.2% of the women and 26.9% of the men) were enrolled in arts programs. About 3% of the women were or had been members of sororities, and about 6% of the men were or had been members of fraternities.

The incidence (events that took place in the 12 months before the survey) and prevalence (events that took place since leaving high school) of sexual assault were measured using a slightly modified version of Koss et al.'s (1987) SES.

Findings

The responses to each of the items in the SES are presented in Tables 1.1 and 1.2.[5] About 28% of the female participants stated that they had been sexually assaulted in the past year, while 11% of the males reported having victimized a female dating partner in this way during the same time period. As was expected, the prevalence figures were higher, with 45.1% of the women stating that they had been assaulted since leaving high school and 19.5% of the men reporting at least one incident during the same time period. Despite some methodological differences, the findings presented in Tables 1.1 and 1.2 are consistent with U.S. national data produced by Koss et al. (1987).

In sum, although Canadians can take pride in the fact that their streets are safer than those in the United States, they should take careful note of the fact that their country is a nation where, as Currie and MacLean (1993) note, colleges and universities create "a 'chilly climate' for women; that is, Canadian universities exhibit a host of conventional practices which communicate a lack of confidence in women, a lack of recognition for women, or a devaluation of their capabilities and successes" (p. 14).

Other Canadian National Survey findings

Several important conclusions can easily be drawn from the Canadian data presented here. Perhaps most important is that sexual

Table 1.1 The Incidence of Sexual Assault in Canadian College Dating
Relationships

Type of Assault	Men[a] (N = 1,307) %	n	Women (N = 1,835) %	n
1. Have you given in to sex play (fondling, kissing, or petting, but not intercourse) when you didn't want to because you were overwhelmed by a man's continual arguments and pressure?[a]	7.8	95	18.2	318
2. Have you engaged in sex play (fondling, kissing, or petting, but not intercourse) when you didn't want to because a man used his position of authority (boss, supervisor, etc.) to make you?	.9	10	1.3	21
3. Have you had sex play (fondling, kissing, or petting, but not intercourse) when you didn't want to because a man threatened or used some degree of physical force (twisting your arm, holding you down, etc.) to make you?	1.1	13	3.3	54
4. Has a man attempted sexual intercourse (getting on top of you, attempting to insert his penis) when you didn't want to by threatening or using some degree of physical force (twisting your arm, holding you down, etc.), but intercourse did not occur?	.6	7	3.9	67
5. Has a man attempted sexual intercourse (getting on top of you, attempting to insert his penis) when you didn't want to because you were drunk or high, but intercourse did not occur?	2.5	29	6.6	121
6. Have you given in to sexual intercourse when you didn't want to because you were overwhelmed by a man's continual arguments and pressure?	4.8	55	11.9	198
7. Have you had sexual intercourse when you didn't want to because a man used his position of authority (boss, supervisor, etc.) to make you?	.8	9	.5	8
8. Have you had sexual intercourse when you didn't want to because you were drunk or high?	2.2	25	7.6	129
9. Have you had sexual intercourse when you didn't want to because a man threatened or used some degree of physical force (twisting your arm, holding you down, etc.) to make you?	.7	8	2.0	34
10. Have you engaged in sex acts (anal or oral intercourse or penetration by objects other than the penis) when you didn't want to because a man threatened or used some degree of physical force (twisting your arm, holding you down, etc.) to make you?	.3	3	1.8	29

a. The men in this survey were asked not about their own victimization, but about their roles as
victimizers. Thus, the questions were altered slightly to ask whether they *did* any of these
behaviors. The figures in the column labeled Men show the number of men admitting to aggressive
behavior.

Table 1.2 The Prevalence of Sexual Assault in Canadian College Dating
Relationships

Type of Assault	Men[a] (N = 1,307) %	n	Women (N = 1,835) %	n
1. Have you given in to sex play (fondling, kissing, or petting, but not intercourse) when you didn't want to because you were overwhelmed by a man's continual arguments and pressure?[a]	14.9	172	31.8	553
2. Have you engaged in sex play (fondling, kissing, or petting, but not intercourse) when you didn't want to because a man used his position of authority (boss, supervisor, etc.) to make you?	1.8	24	4.0	66
3. Have you had sex play (fondling, kissing, or petting, but not intercourse) when you didn't want to because a man threatened or used some degree of physical force (twisting your arm, holding you down, etc.) to make you?	2.2	25	9.4	154
4. Has a man attempted sexual intercourse (getting on top of you, attempting to insert his penis) when you didn't want to by threatening or using some degree of physical force (twisting your arm, holding you down, etc.), but intercourse did not occur?	1.6	19	8.5	151
5. Has a man attempted sexual intercourse (getting on top of you, attempting to insert his penis) when you didn't want to because you were drunk or high, but intercourse did not occur?	5.5	63	13.6	244
6. Have you given in to sexual intercourse when you didn't want to because you were overwhelmed by a man's continual arguments and pressure?	8.3	96	20.2	349
7. Have you had sexual intercourse when you didn't want to because a man used his position of authority (boss, supervisor, etc.) to make you?	1.4	17	1.5	24
8. Have you had sexual intercourse when you didn't want to because you were drunk or high?	4.7	55	14.6	257
9. Have you had sexual intercourse when you didn't want to because a man threatened or used some degree of physical force (twisting your arm, holding you down, etc.) to make you?	1.5	18	6.6	112
10. Have you engaged in sex acts (anal or oral intercourse or penetration by objects other than the penis) when you didn't want to because a man threatened or used some degree of physical force (twisting your arm, holding you down, etc.) to make you?	1.4	16	3.2	51

a. The men in this survey were asked not about their own victimization, but about their roles as victimizers. Thus, the questions were altered slightly to ask whether they *did* any of these behaviors. The figures in the column labeled Men show the number of men admitting to aggressive behavior.

assault on campus is roughly as common in Canada as in the United States. Thus, it is no surprise that when asked how safe they felt on campus, many female undergraduates reported that they felt unsafe on campus and in the immediate surrounding areas. For example, of the 1,835 women who participated in the CNS (Kelly & DeKeseredy, 1994):

- 36.1% felt unsafe and 25.9% felt very unsafe walking alone after dark.
- 35.7% felt unsafe and 12.9% felt very unsafe riding a bus or streetcar alone after dark.
- 34.8% felt unsafe and 38.7% felt very unsafe riding a subway alone after dark.
- 42.5% felt unsafe and 25.7% felt very unsafe walking alone to a car in a parking lot after dark.
- 41% felt unsafe and 31.2% felt very unsafe waiting for public transportation alone after dark.
- 36.3% felt unsafe and 38.9% felt very unsafe walking past men they didn't know, while alone after dark.

Another finding was large gender differences in reporting the incidence of sexual assault (DeKeseredy & Kelly, 1993a). As with virtually all studies of this nature, women report being assaulted more than men report doing these assaults. What accounts for these discrepancies? One argument popular in conservative men's quarters is that the data here are wrong: "women do often lie about sexual assault, and do so for personal advantage or some other personal reason, which is pretty well why anybody lies" (Fekete, 1994, p. 54). The problem is that such critics almost never have any evidence to offer on this score, other than a deep-seated mistrust of women generally. The debate is similar to earlier ones on marital rape, where large numbers of men without any evidence argued that the law should not allow a husband to be prosecuted for raping his wife, because women are natural liars (Schwartz, 1982). It is similar to the debates over rape law itself, which until fairly recently made it almost impossible to obtain a rape conviction in most jurisdictions because the state had to overcome a presumption written into law that women lie (Schwartz & Clear, 1980; Tong, 1984). In each of these cases, rape law was changed virtually everywhere in North America to remove the presumption that all women are liars. On the college campus, however, and in the backlash literature we will discuss later in this chapter, this presumption continues to exist.

In fact, there is no reason to believe that survey data generated by measures such as the SES exaggerate the extent of sexual assault on college campuses. Rather, it is much more likely that such surveys underestimate the problem. Many survey participants do not report incidents because of embarrassment, fear of reprisal, reluctance to recall traumatic memories, deception, memory error, and many other factors (Kennedy & Dutton, 1989; Smith, 1994; Straus, Gelles, & Steinmetz, 1981). A tremendous number of women report that they have lived for years without telling a single person about their victimization and are revealing the fact for the first time on an anonymous questionnaire. It would be naive not to believe that there are additional women (how many is, of course, unknown) who continue to keep their secret, even when given this questionnaire opportunity.

Thus, it is unlikely that men and women report differently because large numbers of women are lying. Some researchers have argued that a more likely explanation is that social desirability plays a key role in shaping male responses (Arias & Beach, 1987; DeKeseredy & Kelly, 1993a; Dutton & Hemphill, 1992). It is already difficult to obtain honest and complete responses from male perpetrators (Smith, 1987). One worry is that to the extent that we become successful in getting the message out that sexual assault in college settings is illegitimate and illegal, it will become less likely that men will admit to doing it, even when researchers guarantee anonymity and confidentiality.

This has been an ongoing problem of concern to rape researchers, and one where researchers continue to seek innovative methods to minimize underreporting. An entire survey can be discredited if researchers cannot explain whether the women who reported having been sexually assaulted on or near campus are representative of all survivors in the sample. Struggles for effective social support services also are hindered because underreporting at a high level results in lower estimates of sexual assault and ultimately decreases the probability of mobilizing resources to curb this problem (DeKeseredy, 1995; Smith, 1994).

Still, one cannot assume that state agencies and members of the general public will be motivated by accurate statistics derived from large-scale representative sample surveys to devote more resources to the development of prevention and control strategies. For example, even though the Canadian federal government paid hundreds of thousands of dollars to sponsor the CNS, it did not create new legislation or allocate more funds to make female undergraduates' lives safer (DeKeseredy, 1996b; MacIvor, 1995). Backlash authors commonly claim that governments are more and more basing their policies on feminist ideology (e.g., Fekete, 1994), but the Canadian federal government made only the most "feeble and symbolic responses" to the CNS, and other feminist surveys (e.g., Statistics Canada's Violence Against Women survey),[6] despite calls for social transformation (MacIvor, 1995).

Why Aren't Victims of Sexual Assault on Campus Taken Seriously?

How can such a broad spectrum of college students be affected by a serious and injurious event like forced sex, but at the same time this victimization be of so little concern to most students, faculty, and administrators? If 15% of faculty offices were burglarized, certainly the uproar would be deafening. If 25% of college students were the victims of robbery or attempted robbery over the course of their college careers, certainly no campus could avoid massive, high-profile prevention campaigns, from bright lights to increased security patrols, to mandatory robbery victimization training. Yet, at a time when North American crime discussion is dominated by calls for more prisons, more executions, canings, and cries of "what about the victims' rights?" it remains widely popular to belittle crime victims when they are women attacked by people they know. According to Estrich (1987), this is done by claiming that only certain "facts" constitute "real rape" or sexual assault. Stranger rape is seen by many as real rape, she suggests, but acquaintance rape is just dismissed as "boys will be boys," or some sort of exaggeration by the woman, or something she was "asking for."

There are a number of reasons for this, but the more important are gender politics and powerful interest groups. There is an enormous feminist literature on forcible rape that points out the broader social and cultural factors associated with sexual assault in North American society (e.g., Bart & Moran, 1993; Buchwald, Fletcher, &

Roth, 1993). In Chapter 3, we will discuss the idea of patriarchy as an ideology that encourages men to devalue women, to see them as objects to be conquered or used. This interacts powerfully with an American violence ethic, which encourages, at least at the ideological level, a violent reaction to most social ills.

More and more North Americans are upset that criminals are "let off easy" when put in prison for life sentences (Johnson, 1996). Not only are many concerned because prisoners get to watch television, but some because they will not be physically harmed. As an example of something that may be relatively unimportant in the greater scheme of things, but that certainly held the public and media's eye for quite some time, teenager Michael Fay was convicted as a first offender for minor vandalism in the tiny Asian country of Singapore. His sentence included not only a prison term but also a provision that he be flayed until covered with blood and given permanent scars. Public opinion polls showed that a majority of Americans felt that this was a reasonable punishment. If this is a reasonable sentence to most people for first offenders on minor charges, one can only speculate as to what most people would consider an appropriate sentence for a serious offender.

It is not only the criminals who are violent in America. We feel that annoying people "deserve" to be beaten up; that law violators "deserve" physical punishment or at the least, extremely unpleasant surroundings; that flirtatious women "deserve" to be the victims of violent sexual crimes; that the way to deal with countries we don't like is to "bomb them back to the stone age." For the most part, stranger rape in America is reported at a rate equal to most other violent crime: It is relatively higher when all violent crime is high, and relatively lower when all violent crime is low. There may be several reasons why this is true, but the authors believe that this could not be the case unless rapists themselves saw forcible rape as a form of violent crime: as a proper response to women who "deserved" to be raped. For example, according to one man convicted of rape (as quoted in Scully & Marolla, 1985),

> Rape is a man's right. If a woman doesn't want to give it, the man should take it. Women have no right to say no. Women are made to have sex. It's all they are good for. Some women would rather take a beating, but they always give in; it's what they are for. (p. 261)

Attitudes like this reveal a "conquest mentality toward sex," and they are particularly prominent in some male peer groups located on campuses and their immediate surroundings (Curran & Renzetti, 1996, p. 187).

Most of the feminist literature on the violent effect of the devaluation of women, however, deals with stranger rape. What about the forcible rape of dates or people well known to the offender? There are a few important differences between stranger rapists and acquaintance rapists, but only a few (Belknap, 1989). The major one is that the stranger rapist knows that his actions are criminal, and usually goes to some effort to hide his identity. The acquaintance rapist acts, so to speak, in public, with someone he knows and may personally like.

Thus, the feminist analysis of the stranger rape literature becomes even stronger in the case of acquaintance rape. Only a male-dominated society that trains men to use women as objects, and that legitimizes violence as a tool to achieve personal goals with a callous indifference to the feelings of victimized others, could breed a large number of men who openly assault women they know, and, in fact, may even like. It is bad enough to treat complete strangers in this way, but women who are friends? Still, this is not a sufficient explanation for how acquaintance rapists get away with their crimes. If the victims know who the rapists are, why are they not brought to the attention of criminal justice officials? The problem is that women on the whole do not report these crimes, and when they do report them, they are too often not taken seriously by faculty or campus authorities (Bernstein, 1996a).

For example, a number of rape victims have said that their treatment by the criminal justice system amounted to a "second rape" (Madigan & Gamble, 1989), and there is no way of knowing just how many women are deterred from reporting because of this fear. Someone who has just been emotionally traumatized by a victimization will not rush to report the crime if she believes that she will receive treatment just as traumatic from the criminal justice system. Worse, even in the growing number of jurisdictions where the police have learned to respond sensitively to the needs of victimized women, the second rape problem may continue to exist in other arenas: hospital personnel are often attacked as being insensitive, and in court, defense attorneys and trial judges are too often allowed to attack the victim (Fairstein, 1993; Vachss, 1993).

Unfortunately, there is another reason why many women do not report acquaintance rapes. Earlier we discussed women's subjective experiences, commenting that our researcher definitions often do not conform to the reactions of women who live through attacks. However, part of their interpretation process is growing up in the same society as men, receiving most of the same media and societal messages that men do, and suffering all too often from the same problem of negotiating the moral land mines that these socializing institutions plant (Schur, 1984). A telling point: Both Koss et al. (1987) and Schwartz and Pitts (1995) report in two similar but separate studies that only 27% of the women identified as rape victims actually themselves defined their experiences as rape, even though the researchers in each case tightly adhered to the Ohio Penal Code definition of the crime. Only 5% ever sought out victim services, only 5% ever reported the event to the police, and 42% never mentioned what had happened to anyone at all (Koss et al., 1987).

This is not, as some suggest, a simple situation where the women themselves consider what happened to them a minor event ("not rape"). Rather, it is one where the moral lessons taught by society make it difficult for many women to understand when they have been the victims of rape. The problem, it seems, is that college women as well as men are sometimes unsure of the difference between rape and just a horrible thing that happened on a date; when a women can be seen as having deserved to be the victim of violent sexual attacks; and whether women should bear the brunt of blame for being in the wrong place at the wrong time. In the Appendix to this book, Catherine tells her story of being raped by her best friend, a male, when she passed out from drinking too much at a party and he took her home to protect her. She was a student activist and one of the most knowledgeable people on campus about rape (not to mention that both of her sisters had previously been raped), and she was working at the time on a special honors thesis on acquaintance and date rape. Still, it took her 2 full months to register emotionally that she had been raped. She now understands deeply why a great many women never reach the stage she reached: why they never connect what happened to them with rape.

Catherine notes that the most difficult thing she had to deal with were the reactions of her friends, her roommates, her fellow volunteers at the rape crisis center, her boyfriend, parental figures, and more. An event that clearly is a third-degree felony where Catherine lives confused virtually everyone with whom she came into contact: Should they blame her and exonerate the rapist? Do you lose your right to be free of victimization if you voluntarily drink too much wine? Do you deserve what is coming to you if you get so drunk that you lose control of your body? Fenstermaker (1989) points out that people have a great deal of trouble seeing simple facts when their value systems are all confused:

> Acquaintance rape—perhaps even more than spouse abuse or certainly stranger rape—so muddies the normative waters that our very different sense of what is sexually appropriate for women and what is sexually appropriate for men is brought to bear not only on our judgments of differential responsibility for actions, but on our judgments of presumably factual matters like the commission of a crime . . . the only "facts" of acquaintance rape are its ambiguity and the ambivalent ways we respond to it. (p. 265)

Clearly, a great many people are confused on this issue. With this atmosphere of moral ambivalence, it is not uncommon for the victim to be held responsible or at least partially responsible not only by fraternity men or other college men, but also by women students, male and female faculty, and administrators. Worst of all, as we shall see later, victims themselves often feel that they are responsible for male rapists' behavior. Faculty and administrators appointed to oversee student groups commonly see a lot of "boys will be boys" in forcible rape. Even when faculty know that their role is to break it up or prevent it from happening, it is not uncommon for chaperons to be shocked by the idea that multiple sexual intercourse with an unconscious woman could be a serious crime rather than just another rule violation.

A newer literature has recently arisen to argue specifically the point that we *should* blame the victims rather than the rapist when the woman gets drunk. If these women are so confused about what happened to them, perhaps what happened to them wasn't all that bad after all (Gilbert, 1991; Roiphe, 1993). We will discuss some of this literature in the next section.

A study by Pitts and Schwartz (1993) of women who had been raped, which will be described in more detail later in this book, explains that the question of whether women like Catherine understand what happened to them or not may depend on whether or not they have supportive friends to turn to after being victimized. Those with supportive friends who reassured them that they had done nothing wrong defined their victimization as rape. Women whose friends tended to reassure the rape victim that she was the recipient of love, understanding, and support even though she was in some way to blame for the attack (such as being in the wrong place, or allowing the man into her apartment) unanimously said that they were *not* victims of rape.

The facts in these cases were similar; it was only the friends who were different. Is it a surprise that so very many women (73% in the studies here) do not see themselves as having been raped? Many commentators (e.g., Roiphe, 1993) have attacked such studies on the grounds that sociologists and psychologists were stretching the data for ideological reasons, by suggesting that a woman is a rape victim when she does not herself think that she is one. Rather, these studies suggest that it isn't the facts of the case as much as the treatment of the victim that determines how she feels about herself afterward.

The Anti-Feminist Backlash Against Broad Definitions of Sexual Assault

Several years ago, Faludi (1991) popularized the term *backlash* in reference to the attempts throughout the media and popular culture to undermine the minimal gains that had been made by the feminist movement. In the field of campus sexual assault, there has been a massive backlash effort after a period where people were shocked by the results of surveys generally using Koss's SES. For example, Gilbert (1991) sharply attacked Koss for creating a "phantom epidemic of sexual assault" (p. 54). There just is not a tremendous amount of sexual assault on campus, he argued, and any claims that sexual assault is a problem are just the cries of a group of feminist radicals.

Interestingly, Gilbert has received extensive publicity and exposure for this point of view, despite the drawback of having no background or expertise in the area, never having conducted a self-report or victimization survey on sexual assault, and never having revealed any knowledge of this complex field. Nevertheless, he argues that the high rates of sexual victimization uncovered by Koss et al. (1987), among others, are misleading and the products of definitional stretching on the part of radical feminists who are mainly concerned with advancing their political agendas. According to Gilbert (1991), their goal is to "impose new norms governing intimacy between the sexes" (p. 61).

Gilbert (1991) claims that some behaviors included in the four categories of sexual assault addressed in this book are not sexual assaults. He is especially critical of the way the SES operationalizes rape and attempted rape, arguing that these two operational definitions "cast a large, tightly-woven net that snares the minnows with the sharks" (p. 59), and further that they

> imply an understanding of sexual encounters that does not square with human attitudes and experiences. According to this view, a young woman who embraces a man who attracts her must know decisively whether or not she wants to have sexual intercourse at every given moment. Moreover, she must communicate these sentiments explicitly before any physical contact occurs. This perception does not allow for the modesty, emotional confusion, ambivalence, and vacillation that inexperienced young people feel during the initial stages of sexual intimacy. (p. 60)

While these arguments are indeed colorful, they suffer from the problem that the definitions of rape and attempted rape employed by Koss et al. (1987) and virtually all other experienced North American researchers not only do not stretch the boundaries of reasonable definitions, but indeed are consistent with the legal definitions found in most North American jurisdictions (Koss & Cook, 1993). In fact, the definitions used in Koss et al.'s (1987) path-breaking national U.S. survey of sexual assault on campus are based on Ohio's legal definitions of rape and attempted rape.[7]

These attacks achieved some small fame coming from an obscure social work professor such as Gilbert but achieved their greatest fame when they were repeated almost verbatim by self-styled "new generation" feminist Katie Roiphe (1993), a graduate student in literature. Although she could not have had less grounding in social science methods, sexual assault, or any one of the many other topics necessary to adequately critique this study, Roiphe became a media star in New York and Washington newspapers and television because she was willing to publicly attack women. The definitional stretching argument she and Gilbert make is that rates of sexual victimization are artificially inflated by including within the definition behavior that does not coincide with "reasonable" women's attitudes and experiences. For example, they are particularly incensed that researchers include as rape unwanted sexual intercourse that takes place when women are too intoxicated to give consent or to protest effectively. We will later discuss how these are serious felony crimes in most of the United States.

The problem is not that feminist researchers want to expand the definition of sexual assault; rather it is that backlash critics want to set the clock back to earlier times, when rape was limited only to those situations involving what prison slang in many areas calls "tree-hopping," when a greasy guy (preferably of another race) jumps out of a tree or out from behind a bush and forces himself violently upon a modest, hysterical woman.

The strongest attack of the backlash critics is that the questions are broadly phrased, to take into account a wide spectrum of sexual experiences (see Table 1.1). What feminist researchers argue, however, is that any investigation into the sexual assault experiences of women on campus reveals that the women themselves would prefer to have a broad definition used (Hall, 1985). Women are victimized, traumatized, and haunted emotionally by a wide range of victimizations (Muehlenhard, Sympson, Phelps, & Highby, 1994). Reading Catherine's story in the Appendix, a classic example of what the backlash critics insist is not rape, should make it plain that such events can have an enormous effect on women's lives. The letter from Katie in Chapter 4 similarly makes it plain that this woman's acquaintance rape, one of the crimes that backlash critics deny, had an enormous effect on her life. She quit school and moved away from the site of her pain, but certainly has not forgotten it. Indeed, the incidence and prevalence data presented in this book reveals that many North American female undergraduates' lives "rest upon a continuum of unsafety" (Stanko, 1990, p. 85).

Many of the same attacks have been made against DeKeseredy and Kelly's (1993a) CNS, which was described in detail earlier in this chapter. In Canada, the pack has been led by John Fekete (1994), a professor of cultural studies and English literature, who argues that the staggering rates of sexual assault and other forms of woman abuse (e.g., physical and psychological abuse) generated by the CNS are striking examples of "inflationary victimization" and are "contagious instruments" in a project that is a "handmaiden" of a "biofeminist moral panic," whatever that is.

Fekete (1994) views the CNS as an example of a "pseudo-scientific" study guided by feminist stereotypes such as "sex demeans women," "women alone are oppressed," and "women are nurturers and men are abusers" (pp. 332-333). DeKeseredy and other Canadian feminist scholars who have conducted surveys on woman abuse, he argues, are "biopolitical advocates" who have used a "misleading research strategy" to promote this so-called panic.

Of course, Fekete in Canada and Gilbert in the United States both tend to ignore the problem that the findings they dispute typically refer to violations of the Canadian *Criminal Code*, and most state criminal codes in the United States. They may choose to think that boys will be boys, but many of these boys are also felons.

We mentioned earlier that one of the most interesting things about the backlash movement is that in an era when both Americans and Canadians are devoting extensive energy to demanding more prisons and more executions, and decrying the lack of concern for the victim, there remains an enormous market in the media for material that belittles crime victims when they are women attacked by acquaintances, husbands, or dates. This was certainly true in the Canadian media, which had little respect for the findings of the heavily funded and widely acclaimed CNS. Based on their analyses of newspaper and television accounts of the CNS, Currie and MacLean (1993) conclude that the "media response to the findings . . . [was] often similarly unsupportive of a woman-centered approach to dating violence and dismissive of the importance in identifying attitudes which support abusive behaviors toward women" (pp. 14-15).

Summary

A key objective of this chapter was to challenge the popular notion of college campuses as safe havens from crimes such as sexual assault, or as places where female students can invariably find a retreat from the evils and problems of daily life in what they and their professors for some reason insist on calling the "real world." The data presented here show that for many women, campuses are indeed the real world—women are the victims of serious sexual assault that can leave lifetime emotional scars. Many college campuses are centers of sexual assault and other variants of woman abuse.

The most important of these data come from the SES, designed by Koss et al. (1987), and the CNS. Koss's study, North America's most cited survey on campus sexual violence, shows not only that large numbers of women are sexually assaulted on college campuses, but that most do not define what happened to them as a felony rape (even though the activity fits the state definition of this crime). Thus, they do not tend to report it to various police and administrative authorities, and often do not seek counseling help. Koss, then, refers to these victimizations as "hidden rape." The CNS, which generally supported all of the findings of Koss in a Canadian context, will be used throughout this book where relevant, along with numerous other studies done by the authors.

Despite the backlash reviewed in this chapter in both the United States and Canada, which argues that such surveys are invalid, it is the strong contention here that such surveys if anything *underestimate* the amount of sexual abuse on North American college campuses.

Notes

1. See DeKeseredy (1988b), DeKeseredy and Hinch (1991), Ellis and DeKeseredy (1996), and Pirog-Good and Stets (1989) for comprehensive reviews of North American research on various forms of woman abuse in postsecondary school courtship.

2. For example, see DeKeseredy and Kelly (1993a); Elliot, Odynak, and Krahn (1992); Finkelman (1992); Kilpatrick et al. (1989); and Koss et al. (1987).

3. See Ward et al. (1991) for a brief review of the various research techniques used to collect data on sexual assaults against U.S. female university students.

4. See DeKeseredy (1995, 1996b), DeKeseredy and Kelly (1993a, 1993c), and Pollard (1993) for more details on the methodology of the CNS.

5. These tables were previously published by DeKeseredy & Kelly (1993a, 1993c) and include the SES items found in the female questionnaire. Different wording was used in the male questionnaire.

6. See the *Canadian Journal of Criminology* (Vol. 37, No. 3, 1995) for more in-depth information on the Violence Against Women survey and the major results of this project.

7. See Koss and Cook (1993) and Schwartz and DeKeseredy (1994b) for more detailed responses to Gilbert's arguments.

2

Male Peer-Support Theories of Sexual Assault

The statistics described in Chapter 1 show that a large number of women are sexually assaulted on college campuses across North America. Again, for several reasons described earlier (e.g., embarrassment, fear of reprisal), these data reflect only the tip of the iceberg: that which is reported to researchers. The next step for investigators will be to develop new and innovative methods of gathering data that minimize underreporting. However, in order to advance a better understanding of sexual assault on the college campus, and to both prevent and control this problem, more than just accurate data are required. We need to *explain why* men engage in predatory sexual behavior. Thus, in this chapter, we will begin to examine one of the key reasons why these assaults take place.

Of course, it is impossible to simply pick out one "reason" and announce that it covers all cases at all times. Indeed, sexual assault is multidimensional in nature: Women in a broad variety of situations are sexually assaulted in a broad variety of ways by a broad variety of men. As Stanko (1990) points out, "For the most part, women find that they must constantly negotiate their safety with men—those with whom they live, work, and socialize, as well as those they have never met" (p. 85).

One area where there is a growing body of qualitative and quantitative research pointing in one direction is the effect of male peer support.[1] DeKeseredy (1990a) popularized the use of this term, which he defined as having two distinct parts. First, it refers to the *attachments* abusive men have to other abusive men; in other words, the simple fact that these people are friends and have some loyalties to each other. Part of this, as many ethnographers have found, is that men commonly express concern that they maintain their image for other men (e.g., Connell, 1995). The second part of the definition, however, refers to some very concrete issues: the specific *resources* that these abusive male friends provide. These resources (such as verbal and emotional support for engaging in woman abuse) may both encourage and legitimate the abuse of current or former intimate female partners.

Unfortunately, theoretical developments have not kept pace with the burgeoning empirical literature on the relationship between male peer support and sexual assault. In this chapter, we will describe and evaluate four major theoretical perspectives on male peer support that have been proposed: (a) Kanin's (1967, 1984, 1985) reference group theory; (b) Bowker's (1983) standards of gratification perspective; (c) Sanday's (1990) psychoanalytic theory, and (d) two related male peer-support models (DeKeseredy, 1988a; DeKeseredy & Schwartz, 1993).

Kanin's Reference Group Theory

To the best of our knowledge, E. J. Kanin was the first North American sociologist to tackle this important question: How do homosocial (all-male) groups make sexual abuse in courtship legitimate to their members? Furthermore, how do they perpetuate this behavior over time? An important key to Kanin's theory, which we will return to, is distinct from competing explanations. He argues that some men come to college either with a history of sexual aggression or a desire to engage in sexual aggression. These are often men who were highly trained as far back as elementary school to treat women as sexual objects and to use women simply as things to achieve their own desires: "scoring," or engaging in sexual activity.

They do not need further training when they arrive in college. They simply need to locate other similarly minded men to make friends, and to tell each other that they are acting properly.

Kanin interviewed a random sample of 341 unmarried undergraduate male students. Based on these data, he contends that sexually aggressive college men selectively seek out male friends who support and sustain sexually exploitative behavior they learned in high school or earlier. Sometimes we worry about sending our sons away to college, where they will come under bad influences, like older male students. Kanin suggests that momma's perfectly innocent little altar boys don't just happen to come under the influence of aggressive men, who teach the new students a brand new set of college values based on the exploitation of women. Men who are interested in exploiting women tend to seek out (just to pick out one example) fraternities that have a reputation for such behavior.

Kanin (1967) does not suggest that the support of the male friends must be verbal, where the group explicitly and openly encourages the new member to exploit women or to force women physically into sexual acts. More likely, these "erotically oriented" peer groups "stress the value of the erotic goal so that the male will be prone to become physically aggressive at the point when it is apparent that the usual seductive approaches are not going to be productive" (p. 497).

Other theorists have invoked this socialization argument to explain why sometimes rape rates are exactly the opposite of what "logic" suggests. For example, Chappell, Geis, Schafer, and Siegel (1977) suggested that rape rates were higher in California than in Boston because there was more consensual sex on the West Coast. It had often been suggested that rape was a crime of deprivation; that men who were unable to engage in sexual intercourse in any socially legitimate manner would be forced to deviate to an illegitimate behavior (rape) in order to fulfill their biological needs for a sexual outlet. Chappell et al.'s (1977) argument can be read as the exact opposite. In a dating relationship, rape was a crime of relative deprivation. Men in the more sexually conservative Boston were not likely to expect sexual intercourse early in a dating relationship, whereas men in California might become enraged by being denied what they felt they were due. Of course, reporting rates make such theories based on police statistics a bit shaky, but it is interesting to note that date rape does seem to be higher in contexts of sexual freedom than in sexual repression.

It is attractive to think of acquaintance rapists as people who obtain sex by force because it is the only way they can have sex. This is similar to an argument long popular among American academics that rape was caused by population pressures: that where there were too many men to allow everyone to break off into couples, some men had to rape in order to have any sex at all. We have learned this argument has absolutely no basis in fact, and most people studying acquaintance rape would similarly argue that acquaintance rapists are hardly those unfortunate men who have trouble attracting women who voluntarily wish to have sex with them.

So, it is Kanin's argument that there exist on most campuses men who are socialized by their friends or groups into a "hypererotic" subculture that produces extremely high or exaggerated levels of sexual aspiration. They *expect* to engage in a very high level of consensual sexual intercourse, or what is to them sexual conquest. Of course, for most men, these goals are almost impossible to achieve. When they fall short of what they see as their friends' high expectations, and perhaps short of what they believe their friends are actually achieving, some of these men may experience what we might term relative deprivation. This sexual frustration, caused by a "reference-group-anchored sex drive" is what Kanin feels can result in predatory sexual conduct. These men are highly frustrated, not because they are deprived of sex in some objective sense, but because they feel inadequate in engaging in what they have defined as the proper amount of sex.

This last point is important enough to repeat. How much sex does a man need to feel fulfilled? Certainly, as anyone who has looked at voluntary celibacy knows, the answer is none. Throughout world history, a great many men have chosen to have little or no sex at all, without ill effect. Other men decide that if they are not having sexual intercourse once a week, then they are deprived. Still others require three or four acts of sex a week to feel emotionally satisfied. Kanin's argument is that it is the latter group from which date rapists often emerge. These are men who feel sexually frustrated even while they are in actuality engaging in more sex than is typical. Their expectations and goals are so high that they are dissatisfied and feel disappointed and even angry at being deprived by women (sex objects) of even more sex. The date rapists he studied were primarily interested in scoring as often as possible and reported that their friends would approve of forced sex against at least some women.

Kanin believes these friends actually exist—that there is on many college campuses a male "hypererotic" subculture.

A socialization process that generates very high levels of sexual aspiration is endemic to the college hypererotic subculture. Consider the following fraternity member's description of life in a New England state university "frat" house (quoted in Warshaw, 1988):

> I'll say this, at a fraternity, I'd be a liar if I didn't tell you that just the atmosphere of a fraternity or any group of guys in general is they promote how many girls can you have sex with, how many different girls can you have sex with. I hear it every day. At Friday morning breakfast [fraternities on his campus have big parties Thursday night], guys all have stories.
>
> I'd say that 90% of the guys I live with are probably aggressive. . . . You gotta understand that in a fraternity, all the guys are there for common goals, ideals, aspirations. So you get a group of guys who are all thinking the same. Guys will turn on you in a second if you say one thing [to disagree with the group]. After all the things you have to do to get initiated into the house, you better have the same ideals and stuff and the same feelings as the other guys. Because I know in our house, especially, guys are pretty tight. Basically, they're all the same type of guys.
>
> *Questioner*: And one common goal is "scoring?"
>
> Well, yeah, basically. There's individuals for who it's not, but overall, I'd say yeah. (pp. 106-107)

Thus, hypererotic male subcultures socialize men to see sex as an "achievement of a valued commodity: that is gaining possession of a woman" (Warshaw, 1988, p. 93). One of the problems for these men, however, is that the goals they have of extensive sexual conquests are almost impossible to achieve. Some men experience relative deprivation or sexual frustration because they fall short of what they see as their friends' high expectations. The frustration caused by a reference-group-anchored sex drive often results in predatory sexual conduct.

What about college men who are not in homoerotic subcultures? Without pressure from their peers for sexual conquests, Kanin argues, these men are more likely to be satisfied with their sexual accomplishments, or at least less likely to experience dissatisfaction with them, which means that they are less likely to sexually abuse women.

One problem with this formulation is that it is impossible to believe that the men with high sexual expectations who force women into sexual intercourse against their will can somehow justify their behavior as a legitimate "conquest." Particularly when they are using physical force, they must be aware that this behavior will often be defined as deviant or criminal not only by other students, but also by the police, courts, and campus administrators. According to Kanin, this is one more area where male peer-support groups provide a service to their members. These all-male alliances provide what sociologists have often termed a *vocabulary of adjustment*. Those men who might be feeling guilty, conflicted, or stressed learn a vocabulary that defines victims in such a way as to identify them as legitimate objects for abuse. They might be called "pick-ups," or any of a wide number of other general or even more specific and sexually explicit terms. Men who successfully adopt and come to internalize these group-based justifications for the abuse of "deviant" women convince themselves that these women deserved to be treated in this way (Schur, 1984). Thus, the men who committed these acts can convince themselves that they are not criminal. They are able to maintain their own image of themselves as normal, respectable men.

Evaluation

Kanin's theory influenced the development of a few other perspectives, including the male peer-support models constructed by DeKeseredy (1988a) and DeKeseredy and Schwartz (1993). A major strength of his contribution is that hypotheses based on his account can be tested using both quantitative and qualitative data. In fact, empirical support for some of his assertions is provided by several recent studies. For example, we analyzed CNS data and found that men begin patterns of sexual abuse in elementary and high school and bring them to college (see DeKeseredy & Schwartz, 1994; Schwartz & DeKeseredy, 1994a). Our national representative sample survey data do not support the notion that on-campus men's groups, such as fraternities, are the cause of sexual forms of woman abuse in college dating relationships. Rather, many male undergraduates arrive at college fully prepared to abuse women with no additional learning.

One problem with Kanin's work, however, is a lack of specification: For example, he argues that sexually aggressive men seek out friends who share and support the values they learned prior to entering college, but he does not specify the ways in which these individuals locate those who are like-minded. Similarly, Kanin does not really explain the type of pressure male peers place on their friends to have sex.

On the other hand, where he has been more specific, empirical support has sometimes been lacking. For example, Kanin asserts that all-male alliances generally do not *verbally* tell their friends to physically victimize their dating partners. In different studies, both DeKeseredy (1988b) and DeKeseredy and Kelly (1993c) found that one of the most important predictors of which men will become abusive in courtship relationships is whether they have friends who explicitly and verbally tell them to abuse women under certain conditions (e.g., challenges to patriarchal authority and sexual rejections). Thus, Kanin is completely correct in pointing to the extreme importance of indirect pro-abuse peer support: providing vocabularies that give men the ability to convince themselves that they are not deviant. However, direct support for this abuse (being told to do it) must also be taken into account.

This concept of direct support for pro-abuse attitudes shows another problem with Kanin's formulations. His theory neglects the importance of social bonds with sexually aggressive friends and the amount of contact these men have with male peers, regardless of whether they are abusive. Several studies show that men who have sexually aggressive friends are more likely than others to engage in coercive or violent sexual conduct (Alder, 1985; DeKeseredy, 1988b; DeKeseredy & Kelly, 1995; Gwartney-Gibbs & Stockard, 1989; Schwartz & Nogrady, 1996). Furthermore, research suggests that spending a large amount of time with male friends increases the probability of sexual assault (Ageton, 1983), especially in settings where alcohol consumption and patriarchal practices and discourses are routine activities, such as fraternities (Bohmer & Parrot, 1993; Ehrhart & Sandler, 1985; Garrett-Gooding & Senter, 1987; Sanday, 1990). Thus, one factor we will need to take into account in our theory building is the friendship bonds men form with other abusive men.

The Standards of Gratification Thesis

One relevant theory here is actually a theory of wife abuse, which makes it only of tangential value. However, as it is one of the more developed male peer-support theories in sociology, we thought it would be worth a short summary here.

Based on data gathered from the reports of a sample of women, Bowker (1983) found that the more contact there was between wife batterers and their male friends, the more frequent and severe the beatings of their wives would be. He explains this finding by describing a social psychological process in which males develop *standards of gratification* that dictate that they should dominate their wives and children. These standards are developed through childhood exposure to their mothers being dominated by their fathers and by the men themselves being dominated in their family of orientation. In other words, they learn that both women and children are subordinate to the man of the family. When these men find that their patterns of domination are threatened, or even get the impression that there is a challenge to such domination, then they suffer from psychological stress. They react to this stress with a contrived rage, designed to reestablish domination patterns that meet their standards of gratification.

Standards that lead men to wife beating are fully developed in men who are heavily integrated in male peer groups that continually reinforce standards of gratification through dominance. For Bowker (1983), these homosocial networks constitute a patriarchal subculture of violence. The more fully men are integrated into this subculture, the greater the probability that they will beat their wives. The subculture is not restricted to a single class, religion, occupational category, or ethnic group, and it socializes married members to believe in both patriarchal control and the use of violence to maintain their control.

Evaluation

Bowker's perspective has influenced the theoretical and empirical work of several sociologists, and in particular those based in Canada (DeKeseredy, 1988a, 1988b; Smith, 1990b, 1991). Unfortunately, thus far, it remains without empirical support and is therefore speculative. Bowker (1983) admits that his study did not focus directly on a male subculture of violence. In his own words, "one can only guess at its broad outlines" (p. 136). His study only shows that the frequency and severity of wife beating is positively associated with wives' reports of husbands' contacts with their male friends. Because no males were included in the sample, there were no measures of information on husbands' friends' adherence to patriarchal attitudes and beliefs, or the degree to which abuse-facilitating values and norms were actually shared by these men. Bowker is sensitive to these weaknesses and contends that interviews with wife beaters are needed to adequately understand whether or not there is a relationship between wife beating and a male patriarchal subculture of violence.

Another problem with Bowker's perspective is that it views pro-abuse male peer support as a constant rather than a variable. In other words, he regards it as a "universal risk factor" in that all men receive this support regardless of their place on the economic, political, or social ladder of society. Of course, he is correct in arguing that this male patriarchal subculture is not restricted to one specific time, place, or sociodemographic group. But, although many theorists have found it politically useful to see all women as a class, and all men as equally affected by patriarchal capitalism, there is neither theoretical nor empirical evidence to back up this formulation (Schwartz, 1988). Both the amount and types of violence vary by class in most societies, including our own.

Sanday's Psychoanalytic Theory of Gang Rape

Sanday is primarily concerned with gang rape on college campuses, although most of what she has to say is just as relevant to individual acts of sexual coercion. Her concern is that young men, from the time they discover their first G.I. Joe or Star Wars toy, must deal with the problem of separation from their mother as part of the development of a male identity. By the time they enter college, many men are particularly concerned with their teenage sexuality anxieties. That they must work through these anxieties in the new and unfamiliar environment of the college campus could make it worse.

One institution that helps to deal with these anxieties is the social fraternity. Briefly, Sanday's (1990) argument is that fraternity initiation rituals are designed to maximize male bonding and to give young men the confidence to take on this new environment. This is done by forcing young men to raise their sexual identity anxieties as high as possible, and then to resolve this anxiety by defining themselves in opposition to what they consider female traits. Speaking of initiation ceremonies, she argues that "the ritual *produces* the very confusion it supposedly aims to resolve by *forcing* pledges to make the transition from a ritually *constructed* anxiety to a fraternally *defined* sense of self" (p. 175).

Sanday (1990) rejects any psychoanalytic approach that suggests there is a universal male need or process that requires the sexual objectification of women. Rather, she sees fraternity ritual as just one possible way to deal with the need for the male child to break the bond with the mother. Fraternity processes, she suggests, are a mechanism to legitimize male social dominance. They deal with a natural process in a way that requires a sexist answer. Men who feel weak and powerless turn women into objects that men can control as a means of seizing power. Although men must deal with this process of developing an identity, she argues, there is no biological or psychological reason why it must be done in a sexist manner.

Sanday (1990) feels that fraternity brothers' constant concern about engaging in heterosexual sex is a mask for their deep fear and fascination with homosexuality. The deep bond fraternity rituals build could easily lead these men to express these bonds in physical terms. Group sex, she argues, often with an unconscious woman, allows men to satisfy their desires for one another at the victim's expense. The only real role for the woman, Sanday seems to argue, is to allow these men participating in a male group-sex activity to make believe that the object of their desire is not each other:

> The men convince themselves of their heterosexual prowess and delude themselves as to the real object of their lust. If they were to admit the real object, they would give up their position in the male status hierarchy as superior, heterosexual males. The expulsion and degradation of the victim both brings a momentary end to urges that would divide the men and presents a social statement of phallic heterosexual dominance. (p. 13)

Evaluation

Sanday's theory is an ambitious attempt to move beyond mainstream sociological explanations of gang rape. Certainly others agree with her. The best-selling British novelist Len Deighton (1990) has one of his main characters remember without fondness her Oxford days in England, far from the American college fraternity scene:

She recalled the men she'd known and those long evenings in town, watching boorish undergraduates drinking too much and making fools of themselves. Keen always to make the women students feel like inferior beings. Boys with uncertain sexual preferences, truly happy only in male society, arms interlinked, singing together very loudly, and staggering away to piss against the wall. (p. 313)

Unfortunately, Sanday's contribution is as purely speculative as is Deighton's. There really is no tangible empirical support for this theory. No matter how attractive it might be theoretically to relate unconscious homosexual preference or desire as a factor that causes the rape of women, it would be extremely difficult, if not impossible to support or refute it empirically. How would you go about measuring this in a way that can be used in empirical work? It may not be impossible to accurately measure unconscious desire, but it surely is extremely difficult. It may not be much easier to measure such desires on the *conscious* level. Given the widespread North American taboo against homosexual behavior, it is highly unlikely that many victimizers of women will admit (even to themselves) their urges to have sex with other males.

Still, there is some support for Sanday's broader notions that all-male organizations and specifically fraternities are related to the sexual abuse of women. Cross-cultural data suggest that pro-abuse peer relations may be more prevalent in cultures where men band and often sleep together in residences apart from women (Levinson, 1989). It may be that North American college fraternities are examples of these cultures. Members or "brothers" develop quasi-familial bonds with each other, and they live in houses generally off-limits as living quarters to female students.

Sanday (1990) is not alone in her argument that fraternities can also be "fertile breeding grounds" for physical and sexual violence. Unfortunately, research on the ways in which these homosocial networks contribute to woman abuse is in its infancy, and there is little reliable data on the structure and interpersonal dynamics of fraternities that contribute to female victimization.

Furthermore, although Sanday (1990) talks generally about fraternities as an undifferentiated group, she does recognize that just as there is no universal psychological need for men to sexually objectify women, there is no universal need for fraternities to develop rituals that promote rape. Many of them do not. However, some commentators suggest that in those fraternities that do promote rape, the brothers' sexual and physical aggression are strongly related to a narrow conception of masculinity that is closely related to homophobia, conformity, group secrecy, and the sexual objectification of women (Martin & Hummer, 1989).

Of course, it isn't only fraternities that are considered primary locations for woman abuse. The same can be said of some all-male athletic teams and clubs whose members often engage in "compulsive masculine behaviors" (Toby, 1975), such as extreme drunkenness and ridiculing homosexuality in various ways because they are insecure about their male identities (Smith, 1983). An important literature suggests that gang rape and other forms of sexual abuse are also integral components of some male athletes' social activities. We will return to this topic in detail in Chapter 4.

Male Peer-Support Models

DeKeseredy (1988a) and DeKeseredy and Schwartz (1993) label their theories male peer-support models. Both of these perspectives are heavily informed by social support theory, and thus before we describe and evaluate them, it is first necessary to present the basic components of this account.

Social Support Theory

Social support theory is generally used to explain the role of social support in health maintenance and disease prevention. However, researchers interested in violence against women recognize its explanatory value and have reconceptualized it to suit their scientific interests.

Although social support theory is primarily psychological, Ellis (1988) argues that it has sociological roots that can be traced back to the writings of Durkheim (1951) and Mead (1934). Durkheim maintained that high or low levels of social integration are related to suicide. For example, strong group integration may result in altruistic suicide and weak social integration may result in egoistic suicide. Here we are not discussing suicide, but only the fact that the level of a person's social integration may have a strong influence on his or her behavior. For another pioneer sociologist, symbolic interactionist George Herbert Mead, the development of an individual's mind and self is based on social exchanges with various people. An important part of much of sociology is that people are not born with innate personalities that emerge full-blown as the body develops, but rather that mind and self develop uniquely in each person, based on the way in which they interact with other people. Thus, one of the stronger legacies of sociology, based on both Durkheim and Mead, is that social integration and the quality of interactions within social networks have significant individual and social consequences.

Contemporary psychological social support theorists are interested in the relationship between social support, health, and physical and psychological well-being. Many studies show that individuals with friends and family members who furnish psychological and material resources are healthier than people with few or no supportive contacts.[2] Furthermore, research reveals a strong positive association between social support and well-being (House, 1981; Kessler & McLeod, 1985; Turner, 1983; Walston, Alagna, DeVellis, & DeVellis, 1983). Two models explain these phenomena: (1) the main- or direct-effect model and (2) the buffering model.

The main-effect model contends that an increase in social support will produce an increase in well-being regardless of whether people are under stress and regardless of the existing level of support. According to Cohen and Wills (1985), integration into large social networks provides "positive affect, a sense of predictability, and stability in one's life situation" (p. 311). Furthermore, social networks help people avoid negative experiences (e.g., financial or legal problems) that can increase the likelihood of psychological or physical problems. In sum, this model argues that well-being is related to general benefits associated with a person's integration into large social networks.

The buffering model also maintains that social support leads to well-being, but only for persons under stress. Social support "buffers" or protects people from the negative effects of stressful life events. Moreover, social support is most effective when it matches the particular stress being experienced (Cohen & Wills, 1985). For example, for many women, being a teenage mother is stressful because they are likely to encounter problems completing their education and dealing with financial matters. However, material aid (e.g., money and housing) and instrumental support, such as child care

Figure 2.1. Original Male Peer-Support Model

provided by family members, may help adolescent women deal with these concerns (Baldwin & Cain, 1980). Thus, their families protect or buffer them from the negative health consequences resulting from stress.

DeKeseredy's Male Peer-Support Model

Social support in the specific form of male peers is a major component of DeKeseredy's (1988a) model (see Figure 2.1). This model is designed to explain how social interactions (and their nature) with male peers are associated with various forms of female victimization in postsecondary school dating relationships, including sexual assault. Relationship stress is a key component of DeKeseredy's formulation. Figure 2.1 shows that stress factors in dating relationships and social support influence the probability of woman abuse. Dating is associated with stress. It also encourages men to seek social support from their male peers. Social support from these friends influences the probability of woman abuse.

DeKeseredy contends that many men experience various types of stress in intimate heterosexual relationships, ranging from sexual problems to threats to the kinds of authority that a patriarchal culture has led them to expect to be their rights by virtue of being male. Some men try to deal with these problems themselves, while others turn to male friends for advice, guidance, and various other kinds of social support. This is, of course, rather simple, and something that most of us know. If you are a male, and you are confused, angered, or hurt by a female, you may very well bring up the topic with your friends to test out their similar experiences. They may tell you that the woman is right, they may tell you how to drop the issue and get over it, or they may feed your indignation at how poorly you have been treated. Of course, there is no question that many women's friends and groups often serve the identical function for women experiencing stress over dealing with men (Handler, 1995). The key point that DeKeseredy makes is that the resources provided by male colleagues may under certain conditions encourage and justify the physical, psychological, and sexual abuse of women.

One of the things that a male peer group may do is teach or support or suggest to our man here that he should not put up with this behavior by women and should strike back. In DeKeseredy's (1988b) early empirical work, he found that for men with high levels of "dating life events stress," social ties with abusive peers is strongly related to woman abuse. Simply put, among those men suffering from stress caused by their relations with women, the ones who chose to abuse women were friends with other men whom they knew also abused women. Of course, men do not absolutely require a condition of stress in order to justify the abuse of women. Male peer support in particular can also influence men to victimize their current or estranged partners regardless of whether or not they are currently in stress.

The Modified Male Peer-Support Model

Much of this book will be taken up with an extended explanation of the factors involved in this expanded male peer-support model. However, we will introduce it here, in the context of the other male peer-support theories. Because elements of this theory will take two full chapters to explain in detail, we will be returning again and again to Figure 2.2.

The original impetus for the expanded theory came from our own criticism (DeKeseredy & Schwartz, 1993) that the earlier DeKeseredy model seems to be too focused on individual factors. This early model tries to explain woman abuse while using only variables related to stress and male peer support. Given the empirical support that DeKeseredy found for his model, there is no question that he was right in claiming that these variables are related. Yet, what was missing from this model was the recognition that there are quite a number of other related factors that can influence whether a man abuses a woman. Reality, we felt, was much more complex than simply putting a man living in social stress in with friends who supported abuse. Although we made no attempt or claim to explain every single factor that could be related to male peer support and the sexual abuse of women, we did feel that there were four important factors in particular that

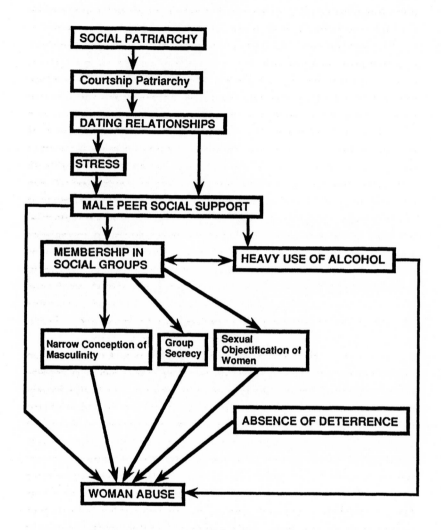

Figure 2.2. Modified Male Peer-Support Model

needed to be added to any model: the ideologies of familial and courtship patriarchy, alcohol consumption, membership in formal social groups (e.g., fraternities), and the absence of deterrence. DeKeseredy and Schwartz developed a new model, which is included in this book as Figure 2.2. As mentioned, much of Chapters 3 and 4 will be concerned with these four factors in the model, but it will be useful to very quickly sketch out an overview of the model here.

The first critique of the earlier model is that it focuses on individual behavior and does not recognize that such behaviors are microsocial expressions of broader societal forces. Men do not grow up in a culture that promises and urges complete equality between men and women. Men who sexually and physically abuse women are not acting in a deviant manner completely opposite to everything they have ever learned about the way to treat women. Although a majority of men perhaps never sexually or physically assault women, certainly all North American men live in a society that can accurately be termed a "rape culture" (Buchwald et al., 1993), where no man can avoid exposure to patriarchal and pro-rape attitudes. For example, rare is the male who has not seen at least mass-market soft-core pornography magazines such as *Playboy, Penthouse,* and *Hustler.* It is also hard to watch Hollywood movies or videos regularly and not be exposed just as frequently to the notion that women are meant to be semi-undressed sex objects, generally treated as inferior to men. In fact, as will be described in greater detail later, our analysis of CNS data shows that pornography plays a major role in the sexual abuse of Canadian college women.

These messages may be relatively subtle, as in the submissive posture or sexual objectification of women in most media presentations such as advertising. The suggestion, for example, that drinking a particular brand of beer is like being with the Swedish bikini team is an obvious attempt to treat women and sex as commodities and objects to be sold, acquired, and shown off. Most beer commercials in the past decade feature young men sexually excited by good-looking women. Many people do not see a harm in such commercials, because they never show men raping or beating these women. Rather, they just leer at them. What these commercials do, however, is teach the viewer that women are legitimate objects of sexual fantasy, existing mainly to create a sexual inequality utopia where "it doesn't get any better than this." Women are not friends, colleagues, or partners.

Such messages may be much more obvious, such as growing up in a home where women are physically assaulted regularly. In homes where violence is the norm, men are more likely to grow up to be violent themselves, even if the violence in the home is directed solely at their mothers and never at themselves (Schwartz, 1989).

Thus, a system where society assumes the dominance of men, and teaches this lesson well, is added to the model. Furthermore, a subsystem we will call courtship patriarchy is added, where such ideals as romanticism are played out differently for dating couples than for married or cohabiting couples.

The original model also did not account for the effects of alcohol. Although few would claim a direct causal relationship, alcohol is related to woman abuse in many ways. It is a common feature of many men's social groups, such as fraternities, and is commonly used as a tool to render women unable to resist sexual aggression. Schwartz and Pitts (1995), for example, found that 17.1% of college women in their sample reported that since coming to college, a man had engaged in sexual intercourse with them when they did not want to but had been unable to resist because of alcohol or drugs. Alcohol is also used in contexts that support patriarchal conversations about women's sexuality and how to control it (Hey, 1986). Whitehead (1976) provides one example of such male peer support, although not from a college scene. She observed sexist male peer-group dynamics in a pub in Great Britain and found that in the context of teasing each other,

> The men acted as if a married man should be able to do just what he liked after marriage. He should be able to come to the pub every day; to stay all evening after "calling in" on the way home from work, and to stay out as long as he liked. He could and must row with his wife, hit her, or lay down the law. Rows and quarrels in which he had the upper hand brought a man esteem, but if his wife rowed with him, locked him out of the house, or refused to cook for him, he lost esteem. If he babysat while his wife went out, he lost face. (p. 193)

As we shall see, many of these same messages are heard by college men who are in fraternities, live in all-male dormitories, have regular friends in the neighborhood saloon, play sports, or have other homosocial networks. They are regularly exposed to messages from other men suggesting that a real man is not under the control of a woman; a real man has sex on demand and does not accept attacks on his masculine authority.

Thus, college men often receive their peer social support within social groups. Here men learn many things, but an important one may be a narrow conception of masculinity. Another, the importance of group secrecy, keeps these men from revealing the deviant behavior of their brothers to outsiders. Group secrecy tells violent men that their actions are not wrong. Finally, they learn to sexually objectify women. Homosocial male groups commonly use women as sexual outlets, as "bait" to bring in new members, as adornments, or as servants at parties. Perhaps the most common method throughout history for people in relatively powerful social positions to make it possible to brutalize powerless persons is by first constructing the powerless as having little personal value. Then, they are worthy of abuse. We find it easy to fight a war against "dirty Huns" or "stinking Nazis," or at least we find it easier than fighting against "our learned colleagues from that long-esteemed and perhaps superior Germanic culture." Similarly, it is much easier to rape sexual objects than it is to force sex on a valued equal or partner.

A final factor missing from DeKeseredy's model is an absence of deterrence. Although social groups may present positive rewards for abusive behavior, a factor that allows these behaviors to continue is a lack of punishment or negative sanction. Harney and Muehlenhard (1991) argue that few in the criminal justice system consider it a crime to forcibly rape an acquaintance under any circumstances. Similarly, it is a difficult task to convince people throughout the university community that it is wrong to rape women; students, parents, teachers, and administrators may all point out that the woman was drunk and therefore shares responsibility.

Interestingly, only a few of these people would suggest that a woman who passes out from alcohol abuse in a bar shares responsibility for having her purse stolen and would therefore argue against prosecuting the thief, even after he was caught using her credit cards. When the topic is sexual relations, people often find the "facts" confusing. Isn't it true that a woman is asking for sexual intercourse if she agrees to allow a man to buy her dinner? Many people would agree with that statement. Still, it isn't only when the "facts" seem ambiguous that men have immunity from punishment; there will be no serious punishment on many campuses (although there are strong signs of change) even in fairly serious cases such as gang rape (McMillen, 1990; Schwartz, 1991).

Evaluation

The expanded male peer-support model's greatest drawback, of course, is that although each of the individual elements has been tested empirically, there has not yet been an empirical test of the entire model. In fact, given its complexity it very well may be that it has more value as a heuristic or teaching model than as a predictive model. In other words, its greatest value may lie in summarizing the complex literature (a teaching model), rather than to isolate and predict which specific men on college campuses are most likely to sexually assault women (a predictive model). Here in this book it will be used to accomplish that summary. It will provide the backbone for the discussions in the next two chapters, as we attempt to describe some of the reasons why men rape and why male peer-support models are important.

It should be noted, however, that several hypotheses derived from this model have been tested. For example, Ageton (1983) found that over 40% of the perpetrators of adolescent sexual assaults reported that their friends knew about their behavior and that virtually all approved of it or at least expressed indifference. Similarly, data generated by the CNS show that there is a relationship between sexual abuse in college courtship and two key variants of male peer support: (1) attachments to male peers who physically, sexually, and psychologically abuse their dating partners and (2) friends who verbally encourage the physical, sexual, and psychological abuse of dates or girlfriends in certain situations, such as challenges to patriarchal authority (DeKeseredy & Kelly, 1995). Furthermore, males who report physically, sexually, and psychologically abusing their dating partners are more likely to agree with the ideology of familial patriarchy (described in Chapter 3) than those who do not report abusive behavior (DeKeseredy & Kelly, 1993c).

Some people have felt that there are some data that seem to argue an opposite position to the one outlined above. For example, Heilbrun and Loftus (1986) found that college men who view sadistic sexual practices as erotic were loners—unlikely to be the creations of peer pressure. Although this may be true, in acquaintance rape we are rarely dealing with sexual sadism. The problem in acquaintance rape is rarely a young man who finds sexual pleasure specifically in the pain he inflicts on a young woman. Rather, we are most often dealing with a man who is concerned with sexual force and domination. In acquaintance rape, the male's object most often is conquest: to obtain sexual intercourse. These are men who have learned that women's feelings do not count. They have learned that what counts, in the popular sports term invariably adopted here, is that they "score." To make this distinction clear, a sadist would gain sexual pleasure directly from the pain he was causing. The acquaintance rapist most typically ignores the pain he causes; he sees the woman as an object for his pleasure or his conquest.

However, the same criticism that has been made of other theories also applies here: this model does not account for the ways in which social networks develop that promote the abuse of women. Rather, it starts with the proposition that these groups already exist and discusses their role in woman abuse. For example, one empirical question that remains is whether those college fraternity chapters that are pro-abuse shape and mold pledges to learn these new behaviors, or whether they attract pro-abuse men who need nothing more than a new sweatshirt with Greek letters sewn on. It is a central element of Sanday's (1990) theory that fraternity rituals mold this behavior, at least in pro-abuse fraternities. She argues that although this does not define all abuse, in many cases, the young man comes to college and then goes through ceremonies that involve the "transformation of consciousness": "By yielding himself to the group in this way, the pledge gains a new self" (p. 135). Warshaw (1988), on the other hand, suggests that men with sexist ideologies seek out fraternities to join so that they will receive support for their attitudes and behaviors.

Because, as we have suggested, this modified model will form the backbone of this book, we shall return to it in the next chapter.

Suggestions for Further
Theoretical and Empirical Work

This chapter began with the proposition that empirical work in the field of male peer support has outstripped theoretical developments. As has been made clear, there remain some important problems in the field that future empirical and theoretical work will need to cover. We hope to make a start by suggesting several. Among the areas to deal with are the related fields of personality and motivation.

Motivation and Routine Activities Theory

We have mentioned several times in this chapter that one of the problems of all male peer-support theories is that although they have been helpful in discussing how these groups operate, there has not been adequate theoretical or empirical work on how these male pro-abuse subcultures or social groups emerge or begin. As we have seen, Sanday presumes that such behavior is learned on the college campus, whereas Warshaw, Kanin, and others presume that it is learned much earlier. In our own work (DeKeseredy & Schwartz, 1994), we have found significant evidence that men who admit to sexual victimization of women on college campuses are more likely than other students to have a background of similar acts in elementary and high school. Still, this only accounts for a portion (about one third) of the admitted sexual victimizers, which leaves a great deal to explain.

Psychologists in particular have taken on the task of attempting to locate personality and motivation factors that could help us to explain which men are more likely to sexually victimize women on college campuses. This does not mean that they have discovered a particular mental illness or psychopathy that explains sexual assault. Quite the opposite is true: Virtually all studies support the view that men who commit sexual assault are not seriously mentally ill. Psychologists have found quite a broad number of terms to categorize sexual aggressors based on various tests: difficulty with expressing anger (Crossman, 1994); egocentric, less integrated, and more external in their orientation (Lichtenberg, 1993); hostile attitudes and personality resulting in coerciveness (Malamuth, Sockloskie, Koss, & Tanaka, 1991); more impulsive (Calhoun, Selby, & Warring, 1986), and so on. It is important to note, however, that although aggressors may have these personality factors, researchers typically cannot find any reason to believe that psychologically disturbed men are more likely to commit acts of sexual aggression against women than are other men (Koss, Leonard, Beezley, & Oros, 1985). Even some imaginative tests based on such measures as sexual arousal to audiotapes of consensual versus nonconsensual sexual activities did not uncover differences (Eccles, Marshall, & Barbaree, 1994).

The literature in psychology may disagree on many things, but one point of agreement has been that men who have been identified as sexual aggressors on college campuses have been generally those men who are immature and irresponsible and have less respect than others for society's rules. They not only have callous sexual attitudes toward women, but also see violence and danger as masculine and exciting. Berkowitz, Burkhart, and Bourg (1994) argue that the combination of these traits in these young men means that they can affirm their masculinity by being sexually aggressive toward young women on college campuses. This argument fits in perfectly with the discussion in Chapter 3 on the study of masculinities: in language we will introduce later, these men are "doing masculinity" by acting sexually aggressive around women.

There is another way to deal with this problem of locating just exactly what the psychological motivation might be of the men who are sexually aggressive. One of the most popular theories today in criminology and criminal justice is Cohen and Felson's (1979) routine activities theory. They suggest that the entire issue of motivation can be eliminated by making it nonproblematic; by just making the assumption in their theory that certain areas have "motivated offenders" who will commit crimes under the right conditions. In other words, they recommend just dropping the discussion of why men rape and centering criminological discussion on the times and situations under which rape occurs (Clarke & Felson, 1993).

Schwartz and Pitts (1995) have taken strong exception to this suggestion, arguing that (as this book will make clear) the study of why men are motivated to commit sexual assaults against women is an essential topic. Routine activities theory suggests that the amount and location of crime are affected by three factors: the presence of likely offenders, the absence of capable guardians, and the availability of suitable targets (Cohen & Felson, 1979). We will spend much of Chapter 3 making their routine activities argument in the case of campus rape (although this is a topic Cohen and Felson, or their followers, have never discussed). We argue that North America is a "rape-supportive culture," where values and beliefs that support and encourage the sexual victimization of women are widely available to all men (Cross, 1993). This culture may not only encourage aggression but may make it easier to get away with it by failing to provide any informal or formal deterrence. Although Cohen and Felson suggest that it would be easier to just ignore the issue and assume that there are a number of men willing to commit rape, Schwartz and Pitts take the position that feminist theory is particularly useful in helping us to understand just why it is that so many men develop such attitudes, and how male peer-support groups function to maintain such attitudes.

Either way, whether one centers on psychological conditions that promote the use of sexual aggression or on the sociological explanation of the values that society promotes that encourage rape, we still have the empirical problem that one of the most important elements in predicting sexual assault is membership in a male peer-support group (Berkowitz et al., 1994). A key argument here, which will underlie much of the rest of this book, is that some explanation of male peer-support groups is needed. Although holding rape-supportive beliefs may be a necessary precondition to committing sexual assault on campus, it is not a complete and sufficient explanation. Simply put, large numbers of American men have attitudes that are rape-supportive, but they do not commit physical or sexual assaults. A male peer social support group is also necessary to "reinforce these beliefs and help keep them accessible so that the rapist is cognitively ready to act" (Shotland, 1992, p. 139). The problem for further research, as we have made clear in this chapter, is the need to discover how these groups tend to come together and maintain themselves. Even if those who attack fraternities are correct in pointing their finger at such groupings, it still does not answer the question of whether fraternity ritual changes men's attitudes and makes them into sexual assaulters, or whether men more prone to committing sexual assault are more likely to join fraternities.

Other Areas in Need of Research

Class differences. Few of the works on college campus sexual assault have taken into consideration economic or class factors. For example, are working-class men more likely to belong to pro-abuse collectives than middle-class men? Given the consistently high rates of sexual assault at middle-class college campuses over the past 40 years, there is no question that many middle-class college men are heavily engaged in sexual assault. We also know that working-class men are heavily engaged in a discourse of domination of women (Hey, 1986). However, are there any class differences? As Schwartz (1988) has pointed out, it would be more surprising to find *no* differences at all between socioeconomic levels in terms of interpersonal one-to-one violence than it would be to find such differences. Both mainstream and socialist theories, he argues, would predict such differences. Still, we continue to study mainly white middle-class college men, for the obvious reason that they are the easiest and cheapest ones to study. There has been little study of men who do not go to college, or, for example, men who attend technical schools.

Nonuniversity groups. Male peer-support theory has centered on a few groups, mostly because researchers have had access to college campuses, where fraternities, athletic teams, and other such groups can be more easily located. In addition to the suggestions above—that working-class men's groups need to be studied—groups in other male middle- and upper-class contexts away from the university campus need study. This is essential to deal with the question of whether the college campus is something particularly special, where men act in a certain way. Another possibility is that what we are studying is only the age- and class-specific form of doing masculinity and woman abuse, and that it is repeated, although in different form, in other age groups and in other surroundings.

Most of the work thus far on male peer support has been organized to explain university-level sexual assault, and in some cases, the studies have been limited to sensational cases such as gang rape. What are the differences in homosocial groups that operate in corporate and upper-middle-class environments? To what extent are the same purposes served by all-male country club environments; more informal but regular homosocial lunch or drinking groups; other all-male athletic ventures such as hunting, golfing, or fishing; or other occasions when men in middle-class or corporate worlds get together? Do they provide some of the same functions for reinforcing lessons about the proper role of men within relationships?

Of course, the same can be done in studies of working-class men. One might be studying a tavern or the American Legion hall rather than a yuppie bar or the country club, but the questions are identical to the ones in the above paragraph. Do men's hunting trips, evenings out, or afternoons together after work provide some of the same male peer-support functions for reinforcing men in their attitudes toward women? This would deal with the question of whether we are talking about something that is common to North American men in general, rather than to college and university students only.

Growing out of it? Perhaps the opposite is true. Is it possible that there is a maturation effect, where men are less likely than boys to be influenced by their pro-abuse peers? Is male peer support a young man's need? Teenagers are notorious for their need to be accepted by certain of their peers, and their willingness to engage in behavior that others of us might term nonrational, in order to gain respect, status, or admiration of their male peers. Perhaps one working hypothesis, for which there is extensive anecdotal support, is that as many men grow older, they become more sure of themselves, more willing to act according to their own inner views (whatever they might be), and less willing just to go along with the gang (Connell, 1995). This is, of course, one of the advantages of longitudinal research. College men could be followed over a period of years to discover their major influences.

One might refer to this process as maturation, although it may turn out to be more learning than gaining in maturity. The possibility exists that in college these men live in "pluralistic ignorance," where everyone claims to believe in something like the inferiority of women, even though most do not in fact share the vocalized belief. In other words, many of these men may not have had a particularly strong psychological investment in the attitudes and behaviors they acted out in college, and the change of scenery afterward may give them the opportunity to stop this behavior with no important attitudinal changes.

Similarly, Matza (1964) suggested that many boys grow up in an atmosphere where they engage in constant talking about masculine values, constantly probe each other for weaknesses, and constantly need to assert an extremely strong adherence to hypermasculine values, all in order to deflect verbal attacks on their masculinity. In other words, anyone not loudly proclaiming their hypermasculinity at all times is immediately attacked by the male peer group as a sissy or much worse. This can, Matza argues, all lead to a "mutual misconception culminating in a system of shared misunderstanding" (p. 54). Simply put, that means that perhaps few or none of the boys actually believe in these attitudes, but they all believe that they are the only ones who do not, and they all believe that they must constantly vocalize these attitudes in order to avoid status attacks by their male peers.

If these ideas are true, they could account for some of the mixed results of researchers: that studies like Sanday's find fraternity rituals extremely important to male attitudes, but at the same time other researchers (Boeringer, Shehan, & Akers, 1991; Koss & Gaines, 1993; Schwartz & Nogrady, 1996) are finding that membership in these groups does not empirically differentiate sexual aggressors from nonaggressors very well. Perhaps being in some fraternities requires young men to proclaim beliefs and attitudes they do not necessarily hold.

Summary

The goal of this chapter was to introduce the idea of male peer-support theories, and in particular the literature that in the past has supported some of the development of this work. Some of this work has been very influential in the development of this book and has been described in some depth here: Kanin's reference group theory, Bowker's standards of gratification thesis, and Sanday's psychoanalytic theory of gang rape. Furthermore, the work on male peer support by the authors of this book was introduced, including DeKeseredy's original male peer-support model based on social support theory, and the DeKeseredy and Schwartz expanded male peer-support model. The latter will provide the backbone behind the discussions in Chapters 3 and 4.

Furthermore, we outlined some of the problems in the state of male peer-support theory, and the research that needs to be done in the future. Chief among these problems is the question of how male peer-support groups form or come together: whether they are the result of influences on the college campus, or whether they are just examples of like-minded men finding each other and working together. There has been very little work done on men outside the mostly white, mostly middle-class confines of large university campuses—for example, on working-class men of the same age—to see if their experiences are similar. Just as important, there has been no research in the work world, to see if male groupings in this arena provide the same support for violence against women as can be provided in the university and college environment. Finally, there was a recommendation that older men be studied, to see if the male peer support group is as influential as men get older as it is in the college years.

Notes

1. See DeKeseredy (1990a), DeKeseredy and Kelly (1993c), DeKeseredy and Schwartz (1993), and Koss and Gaines (1993), for reviews of the empirical literature of the relationship between male peer-group dynamics and the abuse of women.
2. See, for example, Caplan (1974), Cassel (1976), Cohen and Wills (1985), and Sarason and Sarason (1985).

3

Growing Up in a
Rape-Supportive Culture

In the previous chapter, we introduced the original male peer-support model on how certain factors can lead men to sexually assault women. Because DeKeseredy was able to find empirical support for his theory, this model was an important step forward in our understanding of how male peer-support groups can make it easier for many men to commit violence against females in college settings.

However, we also outlined some of the factors we feel were missing from the model, and in Figure 2.2, we suggested a modified model, which is the basis for much of this book. In this chapter, we will begin expanding upon that discussion, using the model as an outline to discuss some of the most important factors that influence the sexual victimization of women on college campuses in North America.

We will, in this chapter, center our attention on some of the social structural factors that influence men. These include larger patriarchal structures in society that affect the socialization patterns of men and the ways they learn to do masculinity. Many men learn that there is nothing wrong with forcing a woman to have sex with them; this sometimes flows naturally from the objectification of women, the holding of rape myths, and the lessons learned from pornography.

A Male-Dominated Society

We said that the problem with the original male peer-support model is that it is focused on individual behavior. Although that focus is certainly important, the behaviors of men who sexually abuse women do not operate in a vacuum. Men learn a substantial number of actions, values, and beliefs from growing up in and being part of a larger culture: North American society, in this case. The values and beliefs they express are microsocial expressions of broader social forces, which in North America are too often patriarchal forces.

But what does it mean to say that our society is marked by patriarchal forces? It would be convenient if there were a single definition of patriarchy that we could present here. Unfortunately, there is not, as that term has been the subject of considerable debate. If, for convenience, we were to choose a simple definition of patriarchy, it might be good to follow Eisenstein (1980): "a sexual system of power in which the male possesses superior power and economic privilege" (p. 16). Over the years, exploring patriarchal structures has been an extremely helpful tool in uncovering layers of male domination that unfold throughout our culture in many different arenas, layers that might not be immediately visible to many people. The biggest attack on the concept, however, is that it presumes that there is something solid, firm, and unyielding about patriarchy. It presumes that it is a fixed system of relationships whereby men maintain power over women, who have no power to resist. In fact, even in systems where men have maintained power over long periods of time, the patriarchal systems can change dramatically over these periods, as they adapt to differing needs, cultures, technologies, politics, and to the resistance of women to male domination. Often the use of a term like patriarchy hides the fact that although men are dominant overall, women have carved out various pockets of power and influence. Worse yet, many women have felt that overarching concepts like patriarchy hide the fact that they are suffering from domination from other sources, related to their class position and

their race. Although they may feel like the victims of gender domination, they may feel *more* victimized in other arenas (Messner &
Sabo, 1990).

Still, the argument here is that building a new model of male peer
support requires that the model take account of the fact that North
American culture is a patriarchal culture. As we shall see, our model
does note that there are various types of patriarchal structures, but
it is important as a first step to recognize the influence of male-
dominated structures. Our use of the term patriarchy is broad and
overarching, recognizing that there will be many variations affecting
women and men differently, based on their race, sex, class, and sexual
orientation.

Within the area of our concern here, male sexual assault on
college women, there is a definite attraction to using the simple and
clear Eisenstein definition of patriarchy. Even here, however, it can
be argued that there is more than one type of male power system.
Specifically, one argument is that there are two basic forms of male
power systems in operation in North America. The first, a *societal
patriarchal system,* refers to the broader overall forces within North
American society that maintain or hold in place male domination
patterns (recognizing, of course, that this system changes and flows,
sometimes rather rapidly). *Familial patriarchy* is somewhat different
and refers to systems that maintain male control in specifically domestic settings (Barrett, 1985; Ursel, 1984). Students of campus violence have found this division of patriarchy helpful in showing how
such violence can be different from violence in other arenas. Still, we
can argue, this is not enough. Even though we now have two variants
of patriarchy, Smith (1990a) argues, neither can be understood without reference to the other.

Furthermore, this new dichotomy does not end all of the debates.
There is ample room for discussion on whether it is truly *familial*
patriarchy we are concerned with on college campuses. Certainly
familial patriarchy is commonly used to explain college violence.
According to this way of thinking, college students engaged in dating
relationships are learning the most important lessons about adult
heterosexual relationships. Therefore, their dating relationships are
essentially mirroring patriarchal marriages in which the male partner
has superior power and privilege (Lamanna & Riedmann, 1985;
Laner & Thompson, 1982; Mercer, 1988).

Courtship Patriarchy

There is an alternative explanation, however. Lloyd (1991) argues that courtship is much more than merely a mirror of the family. Rather, it is a patriarchal system in and of itself, where the rules and customs of male dominance are played out differently. For example, the ideal of romanticism may be more important in courtship than in marriage. This romanticism is not necessarily the model portrayed in comic books and movies: images of the coy and flirtatious woman out to snare the innocent male, who is much more interested in golf, poker, hunting, and fishing. Handler (1995) portrays a male-dominated culture of romanticism as a form of considerable stress for women. She suggests that sororities are one collective response to help women walk through this minefield, although sororities never challenge this male dominance but only help women cope with it.

The very nature of dating and courtship has changed dramatically in the 20th century, From a 19th-century, small-town system where parents closely monitored courtship based on (at least in the middle class) the front parlor, walks, and the front porch swing, the development of automobiles, the city, and public transportation allowed couples to move to an unmonitored system that few recognized had the potential to be exploitative (Sanday, 1996b). Lloyd (1991) argues that courtship evolved and began to center around a series of ideals that don't exist in other types of relationships: love at first sight, love is blind, love conquers all (including his violence), love is passionate, and love entails both pain and ecstasy. This romanticism, she says, explains why people tend to forgive or dismiss violence or bad behavior even more in courtship than in marriages. Before marriage, it is much easier to explain away violence as being due to outside factors and to feel that with enough love (and a marriage), such behavior will disappear over time.

The problem here, as it relates to this book, is that people often feel that under the rules of what we will call *courtship patriarchy*, the male under many circumstances is entitled to sex provided by the female. If she does not fulfill her part of the bargain, the argument goes, the male is entitled to use force to gain what he wants. One way in which this can be easily seen is that people usually feel rather uncomfortable about giving approval for a male to force a female into sexual acts on a first date: in other words, before he has a right to assume patriarchal control over her sexuality. However, if they begin to date steadily or regularly, his "right to sex" steadily grows. For example, Shelton-Keller, Lloyd-McGarvey, West, and Canterbury (1994) found in their survey of over 2,000 college students that in reading several scenarios of rapes, men rated the identical behavior of the men (rapists) as being more excusable when they were portrayed as dating the victim steadily than when they were portrayed as just friends with the victim. This kind of belief does not begin in college. In one survey of high school students, 43% of the boys and 32% of the girls said they felt it was acceptable for a man to use force to make a woman engage in sex if they have been dating for a long time (Giarrusso, Johnson, Goodchilds, & Zellman, 1979, as cited in Allison and Wrightsman, 1993). As Allison and Wrightsman (1993) point out, this form of excusing the behavior of rapists is accomplished by blaming the victim, by suggesting that she was not correct in her behavior of refusing sex. The presumption under courtship patriarchy is that the longer a relationship lasts, the more power men are given to decide when and where sex will take place and to enforce that power through the use of physical force.

Another variation of courtship patriarchy is that many men and some women feel there are rules relating to economic and sexual trades: men provide services and money, while women provide sex. For example, if a man asks a woman out on a date, provides the transportation, and pays for all of the expenses, he often expects to be rewarded for his efforts with sex. Some men find this expectation strong enough to be sexually forceful and aggressive with women who do not agree (Muehlenhard & Linton, 1987). Although some argue that men here just feel that they are "owed" sex for their efforts, another explanation might be that these factors increase the patriarchal assumption that it is a man's role to decide what happens on a date (Berkowitz et al., 1994).

Whatever the correct model, researchers tend to argue that the more couples agree on the right of control by men, and the greater the dependency of women on men, the greater the potential for violence and exploitation. Furthermore, most of the research on pro-abuse male peer groups has found a social support discourse that reflects the ideology of courtship or familial rather than social patriarchy.

Part of Smith's (1990a) definition of familial patriarchal ideology informs the definition offered here: a discourse that supports the abuse of dating partners who violate the ideals of courtship patriarchy. According to Smith, relevant themes of this ideology are an insistence upon women's obedience, respect, loyalty, dependency, sexual access, and sexual fidelity. That some women do not conform to these "norms" is stressful for many men. Such women are also considered appropriate targets for abuse by some of the male friends of these men. They tell the men dating these women to sexually, physically, and psychologically mistreat dating partners who challenge their authority and/or who refuse to provide them with sexual gratification. Several studies have described social networks that approve of sexual assaults on certain dating partners, such as *teasers*, *economic exploiters*, *bar pick-ups*, and *loose women* who do not want to engage in sexual intercourse (Kanin, 1985). As we have noted elsewhere, these male homosocial cohorts often provide sexually aggressive members with a *vocabulary of adjustment* so that their violent actions do not alter their conceptions of themselves as normal, respectable men (Kanin, 1967).

Growing Up Male in North America

In Chapter 2, we made it plain that there is some debate in this field as to whether men come to college campuses primed to commit physical and sexual assaults against women, or whether they learn lessons in such events as fraternity rituals that allow them to commit such assaults. No matter which side you take in this debate, one source of agreement is that men do not grow up in a society that is completely neutral on the question. North American culture provides powerful lessons for both men and women that, to state it in the most conservative manner, make it easier for men who are predisposed to assault to go ahead and commit such crimes. Our modified model takes account of the fact that social patriarchy and courtship patriarchy are systems of beliefs that influence dating relationships. How does this happen? How do people learn what it means to be a boy or a girl, and to internalize the belief that male dominance is natural?

Let's start at the beginning. Most introductory sociology and psychology classes cover some basic materials on how boys and girls are brought up differently in North American society. There are almost as many theories as there are writers on how men and women grow up in the way that they do. Still, there are some broad themes within these theories.

Biological Explanations

Some writers argue that there are important biological differences between males and females, beyond the obvious ones such as the reproductive organs. For example, some psychologists argue that there are innate differences between boys and girls, based on the fact that researchers have been unable to locate an environmental cause for the consistent finding that males score higher on math tests. If there are no environmental causes, they argue, that leaves the presumption that the cause is biological. Others have found consistent sex differences in activity and passivity (Henslin, 1994). In a merging of biological and sociological theories, sociobiologists have argued that male dominance is an evolutionary trait, where men's sexual control over women is a process that has maximized the propagation of the genes of aggressive men (Layng, 1995). Less aggressive men have fewer opportunities to have offspring in many cultures. Thus, more and more men are aggressive as time goes by. Some anthropologists have just argued that in a rough life with particular physical needs, someone has to "act like a man" and run around killing people. While poking fun at the idea that we can all be "Peter Pans," anthropologist David Gilmore (1990) suggests that "So long as there are battles to be fought, wars to be won, heights to be scaled, hard work to be done, some of us will have to 'act like men.' " (p. 231). Harris (1989) even suggests that male warfare has had the value of serving as some sort of retroactive birth control, preventing starvation from overpopulation. Of course, these authors never suggest why men have to be the ones to fight these wars, scale the heights, or do the hard work, except possibly the assumption that the average and typical man is stronger than the average and typical woman. One problem is that there are many cultures where it is the women who do the hard physical labor, presumably thus fulfilling Gilmore's notion that the women just have to "act like men" to get the work done, whatever that means. If it is women who do the hard work, why isn't it "acting like women" to do the hard labor?

Other, more directly biological and physical theories and arguments have been proposed by biologists in Europe and North America. Generally, these arguments are related to physical differences in brain structure, which are claimed to cause differences in sex roles. However, few scientists accept that the small biological differences represented in these theories (the relative thickness of one tiny piece of the brain, for example), even if they eventually can be proven to exist, could cause the major differences between men and women that we often see in today's world. As Schreiber (1995) complains a bit sarcastically, the unproven theory that men and women are born with differing abilities to read maps and find missing socks "rests upon the unproven theory of different brain structures, which rests upon a string of unproven theories about how these structures function" (p. 62).

Cultural Explanations

Cultural differences are probably significantly more important in teaching men and women to behave in different ways. Although there are some biological differences, the lessons people learn in their own culture and/or subculture generally are powerful enough to become the most important factors in determining how men and women act. At the same time, however, "people of every society . . . wear cultural blinders that mask the workings of their own culture. Each considers the characteristics implanted into their males and females to be overwhelming evidence of the 'natural' differences between the sexes" (Henslin, 1994, p. 331).

How do these natural differences get implanted by various cultures, or at least by our culture? Once again, there are many suggestions. Some argue for a sociological process of socialization. Richmond-Abbott (1983), for example, argues that children are taught (socialized) the proper behaviors for their sex. Knowing nothing else but a series of powerful messages, they tend to learn these lessons and conform to what is expected of them. From the time they are newborn infants, they learn these socialization messages from their parents, toys, games, and clothing. Later, language, the media, and schools become important. Boys are taught to avoid "sissy stuff" and to repress emotions (Rabinowitz & Cochran, 1994). Some of the lessons they learn are delivered in a fairly obvious way; for example, children are scolded by adults for acting outside of traditional sex roles (boys playing with dolls, girls playing rough sports). Some of the lessons they learn can be fairly subtle although powerful: for example, children soon learn that the important figures to look up to are all male. They might notice that virtually all of the characters in children's books who have a paid profession are male; until recently, all of the adult characters on Sesame Street were male (Eitzen & Baca

Zinn, 1994). When they grow up, theorists of socialization argue, "men's sexuality and their relationships with women provide a sphere for the enactment and confirmation of these traditional gender-role expectations, which assign men the role of aggressor and women the role of gatekeeper in sexual intimacy" (Berkowitz et al., 1994, p. 7).

Psychologists have often described the same phenomena, although they might be more prone to describe learning environments such as classical conditioning (see, e.g., Wesley & Wesley, 1977). Others feature discussions that are a bit more complex and discuss individual mechanisms of psychological development and individuation. Chodorow (1978), for example, suggests a process by which a male child must learn to break away from his connection to his mother. He must begin to emulate his father while going through the frightening process of renouncing his close attachment to his mother. Kaufman (1995) argues that the general arguments explained above—that boys are socialized into a particular male social role—are not enough to explain what ultimately happens:

> Rather, through his psychological development, he embraces and takes into himself a set of gender-based social relations: the person that is created through the process of maturation becomes the personal embodiment of those relations. By the time the child is 5 or 6 years old, the basis for lifelong masculinity has already been established. (p. 16)

One of the problems with this approach is that in many people's minds, all of these explanations have become altogether too simplified. Students too often leave Sociology 101 and Psychology 101 with a simple message: I got the blue nursery as an infant, I had a baseball bat and a cap pistol when I was a toddler, so therefore I am an adult male with all of these macho, woman-hating attitudes. Unsurprisingly, many scholars find this approach rather limited. First, many of these theories present the entire process as a rather simple process of learning to conform to norms. There is often little room within these theories to understand the tremendous anxiety, angst, fear, and pain of people going through these processes, fighting against them, and creating their own spaces within the broader overall themes. Second, the overwhelming bulk of these studies have been done on white college students, and the childhood studies have been done on white, middle-class families (Richardson, 1988). The lack of information on potential ethnic, racial, and class differences leaves out the experiences of a wide group of Americans who may experience gender in a very different way, although the learning processes may be similar. What emerges all too often is the feeling that one is either masculine or not masculine, feminine or not feminine, sort of like looking at a thermometer to see if the temperature outside is above or below freezing.

In fact, this is what has literally been done in many cases. In hundreds of studies, including some of our own, surveys of individual perceptions of sex-role orientation such as the ones developed by Bem (1974) or Spence, Helmreich, and Stapp (1974) are used to classify people as feminine or masculine. Based on how much you feel that you match a set of gender characteristics thought to be typically male or typically female in American society, you might be classified by researchers as one or the other. Much like your red blood count or your cholesterol score, you can find out if you are high masculine or low masculine. As Schwartz (1996) said in relation to growing up male, this simplistic thinking suggests that everyone exposed to the same set of beliefs comes out the same way. Men are men, and this is how they think. As a result of a typical male upbringing,

> I have this set of built-in beliefs, and act accordingly. If I turn out well, I will be constantly dreaming of a new power tool or hunting implement, won't be able to boil an egg, and will think that co-parenting means coaching the Little League team, where I teach boys that not being a star means that you are girl-like. If I am not a nice guy, I'll become a dictator in my own home and maybe a batterer. (p. 3)

The Study of Masculinities

Thus far, we have seen that traditional sociology explains that young men who might become sexual predators have grown up in a patriarchal society with anti-female attitudes, which they activate and act out on the college campus. As men's rights groups have correctly pointed out, it has become commonplace to attack all men for their socialization: for being unable to find socks or make a dental appointment, for being consumed by sports, unable to feel emotions except lust and anger, and unable to relate to their own children. Recently, for example, one major chain of greeting card shops began selling an entire line of "humorous" cards bashing men for just these faults.

Lately, however, many researchers have been arguing that this form of study can hide as much as it reveals. They have stopped using the terms *sex roles* and *gender roles* and have taken to using the word *masculinities* rather than *masculinity*. Using the term in the plural tries to make it plain that there is not just one masculinity. There are, in fact, many masculinities. Becoming masculine is something that must be constantly negotiated, constantly accomplished throughout the life span. Furthermore, it may need to be accomplished differently in different settings within the same time period. Interestingly, this study has been heavily influenced by feminism, which began the process of what is often called "problematizing" men by suggesting that gender has traditionally been *assumed* but rarely explicitly made a central focus of studies. The study of masculinities is the gendered study of men (Morgan, 1992).

Connell (1995) has developed the basic vocabulary that many of the writers in this field are now using. He talks about the fact that in most areas, there is one *hegemonic* masculinity, which is the dominant form. In the United States, that masculinity is often best exemplified by movie actors such as Charles Bronson, Sylvester Stallone, or Clint Eastwood. Most men are brought up to aspire to be just like John Wayne or Arnold Schwarzenegger: They rescue the woman or girl from the Indians or the Mafia, they never cry even when surrounded by Navajo or Germans or mobsters or evil robots, all of whom are shooting at them. Why is this a problem? As Allison (1995), points out, "Two or three things I know for sure, and one of them is that no one is as hard as my uncles had to pretend to be" (p. 32).

Levant (1994) lays out the basic components of hegemonic masculinity. Men are supposed to (a) avoid all things feminine; (b) restrict their emotions severely; (c) show toughness and aggression; (d) exhibit self-reliance; (e) strive for achievement and status; (f) exhibit nonrelational attitudes toward sexuality; and, (g) actively engage in homophobia.

Who can *really* be as hard as all this? A few of us, sure. But most of us have to make choices, based on the fact that we are supposed to be like Clint Eastwood and we are not. We can, in Connell's (1995) term, develop an *oppositional* masculinity. Here we can set an alternative definition of what masculinity really is all about, and just live with the consequences of being outside the mainstream of society. The first scholars to bring this option to our attention were those who studied gay communities. Often gay men had not rejected the notion of masculinity, these scholars discovered. What they were rejecting was hegemonic masculinity. They were still very concerned with what it meant to be a man, and how to achieve masculinity. Many other groups in North America have developed their own oppositional masculinities. McCandless (1994), for example, has argued that there is significantly less sex role differentiation in the African American community than there is in white communities.

As Jefferson (1994) points out, there are some other alternatives to hegemonic masculinity, none of which are particularly attractive to most men. We can fake it, knowing that we are not really the man our hegemonic masculinity says we should be, and spend our entire lives looking over our shoulders, afraid that someone will find out and expose us. In other words, we walk the walk and talk the talk, but deep down we really don't believe in it. As we shall see later on, there is some serious worry about the extent to which this kind of faking it may account for such behavior as fraternity participation in gang rapes, where each man in the house may be afraid to be the only one willing to speak up and draw the derision of others for failing to sexually attack and ridicule women. Another possibility is that we can spend the rest of our lives in conflict or "quiet desperation." We just don't know what we are supposed to do. Do we give big hugs to our sons when they need it, or teach them not to show their emotions? Do we ask for those hugs ourselves when we need them? Individual men are drawn in different directions, pulled apart, often living in much pain and angst.

These works on masculinities have important implications for the studies in this book. First, they point out that men are concerned on many different levels, at many different times, with "doing" masculinity. Messerschmidt (1993) looked at a wide variety of what he called *gendered actions* and developed an influential argument that a wide variety of men "do masculinity" in a wide variety of ways, depending upon their resources. Inner-city gang boys and law firm junior clerks were all interested in doing masculinity, but their different resources meant they were able to accomplish what they felt provided their masculine identity in very different ways. The relevance to this book is that, as we saw in Chapter 2, many men on campus have come to see the sexual conquest of women as a form of doing masculinity. The hypererotic notion that they can achieve status (or security in their gender identity) only by "working a yes out" of a woman, even if she is unconscious or struggling physically, is an important reason why college men devote so much attention to "scoring" (Sanday, 1996a).

Another point of relevance is that much of American society is devoted to convincing men that they can only achieve masculinity by putting down and ridiculing everything that is female or feminine. Fine (1987), for example, studied Little League baseball in great depth, and found that it served quite a number of functions that were detrimental to boys who wanted to develop normal relations with a female. Boys are taught that failure is feminine, that sex and aggression are major themes for their lives, and that to avoid group ridicule one must avoid being too friendly with girls. In fact, they must present themselves as sexually aggressive, secure in the knowledge that females truly favor sexually aggressive males. This message is repeated in the media, the military, other sports avenues, male peer-support groups, and perhaps even at home, where boys are told that crying after an injury, showing emotion, or failing to excel at sports all mark the boy as girl-like or a sissy. It cannot be a wonder if many boys come to college convinced that to gain the admiration of their friends, they must continue to be sexually aggressive and to constantly put down women and everything they perceive as feminine. If they join with other young men who feel the same way, thus providing a male support group that reinforces these attitudes consistently, then this all turns into a self-fulfilling prophecy: they *will* gain the respect and admiration of their support group for ridiculing women, treating them like objects, and being sexually aggressive with them.

Schwartz and Pitts (1995) deal with the issue of how the popular routine activities crime theory simply assumes that there are "motivated offenders" on campus ready to commit crimes if there are suitable targets available and an absence of guardians. The theory, as discussed earlier, purposely fails to discuss why offenders commit crimes; instead, it suggests that offenders and potential offenders exist in the world and can be "assumed." What we have been discussing tries to do the opposite: deal with some of the issues around what it means to have motivated offenders, rather than to just assume that they exist. There are large numbers of men on every college campus who are concerned with doing masculinity; developing their self-worth and self-esteem by doing acts that will win them the approval of their peers. Unfortunately, many of them have been taught since they were barely out of diapers that an appropriate form of doing masculinity is to ridicule women, to deny everything they think is feminine, to treat women as sexual objects who exist for men's pleasure rather than as human beings, to refuse to see women as people with real feelings who might be hurt by men's actions or even as people with the same rights as men (such as the right not to be forced into sexual acts). When these men then belong to a male peer-support group that maintains and reinforces these attitudes on a constant basis, this is a powerful combination: a male motivated to prove masculinity by scoring by any means necessary, who has no empathy for his sexual partner/victim, and who is sure that he has the right to do so.

One of the most important lessons that the study of masculinities has taught us is that we should give up the romantic notion that all men feel they are winners of the patriarchical game. From the classroom to books and magazines to men's rights groups, men proclaim themselves victimized by women, whom they feel are the real winners in the game of life. Accusations of rape are commonly seen as some sort of plot to attack innocent men. Simply put, as one bestselling author said, women lie (Fekete, 1994). This has bothered women and feminist theory for some time. How can we see these men as confused, hurt, anxious, uncertain, and upset? There has just been an accusation of a rape in a fraternity house and many residents are really upset. They really believe that there is some sort of conspiracy, maybe led by those dreaded radical feminists, to attack fraternities when they did nothing wrong. It isn't that they are covering up; they *did nothing wrong* as far as they can see.

Of course, to the extent that we can objectively measure these things, men *are* the winners in much of life—around the world they have most of the income, the jobs, the wealth, the land, the power tools, and the TV remote controls. We do live in a society that is dominated by men on every front. Americans have fewer women in their legislatures than virtually any other industrialized country; the gap between women's wages and men's is still maintained in most quarters; and certainly it is not the typical scenario that women have an equal voice in the family in how the money is to be spent. Feminist writers have for some time been confused and angered by the fact that violent, irresponsible, misogynist, privileged men can whimper on a level hardly imaginable that they are victims, that women are pushing them around, that women have all of the power, that no one listens to men any more, that they are afraid. Afraid? You have taken part in four gang rapes this year in your fraternity house, and you sent your girlfriend to the emergency room the last time you punched her, and you are the real victim? Are you serious?

They are serious. Believing in hegemonic masculinity can be more dangerous than is often realized. These men are often not being completely disingenuous. They truly feel hurt and slighted, as amazing as that sounds. Baker (1992) argues, "Men are constantly reminded of their power and dominance, but they *feel* ceaselessly under threat from women. They do not feel powerful and, moreover, they feel as if women have power over them" (p. 132). What men too often feel is the pain that comes with the knowledge that they cannot live up to the impossible standards set by hegemonic masculinity.

An Example of Objectification

We have made the argument several times that one of the features of our rape-supportive culture is the objectification of women, but we have not given extensive examples of how this is done. One example of the treating of women as objects that exist for the use of men is the use of talk and vocabularies that support a rape culture.

The explanation best covered thus far in the literature has been the notion of motive sharing—that many or most men use language justifying rape, which is available for some men to adopt and use to support their violent behavior. In other words, although only a minority of men sexually assault or physically harm women, a much higher percentage of men provide an atmosphere that violent men translate into an endorsement of sexual abuse. This is why, in Chapter 5, we will argue that it is important for men who oppose sexual assault to make attempts to stop the use of language that sexually objectifies women.

Scully's (1990) work provides an interesting example of how rapists often use widely shared vocabularies either to deny that the acts they commit are rape (by blaming the victim) or to deny responsibility for the crime. Using the types of excuses that we will discuss later in this chapter as rape myths, they are often able to convince themselves that what happened isn't really rape, because the victim really wanted it (he could tell that she loved "rough sex"), or that she only called the police because she didn't have the nerve to tell her husband that she was cheating on him, or whatever. Scully wasn't dealing with acquaintance rapists here—she was in prison interviewing men who violently broke into people's houses and raped them by violent force, such as holding a knife to their throat. If men can convince themselves that these women, struggling, screaming and begging, all wanted rough sex, and in fact loved it, imagine how much easier it is to engage in self-delusion when the woman has passed out or lost her ability to struggle because she is drunk.

Many of Scully's other rapists offered another excuse that is relevant here. They admitted they had committed an act that on the surface seemed to be rape, but said that they were drunk or high, and therefore not completely in control of their actions. It is not unusual to argue that many men drink heavily on campus before a date rape not to loosen their inhibitions, but to give themselves the excuse that they were not in control of their actions.

All in all, it is remarkable to see from reading the stories of men on campus who engage in forced sex, and reading the stories of men who are in prison for forcible rape, the extent to which their stories and excuses overlap. The language and vocabulary of rape justification is available to men in many different parts of society. As Sanday (1996a) points out, another lesson that men learn comes from the fact that even in the rare case where a prosecutor takes on an acquaintance rape case, such cases have an extremely high acquittal rate, which suggests that the criminal justice system does not see these rapes as crimes either.

Although there have been several studies of vocabularies, it is less common to study other aspects of this culture. One, which we would like to quickly point out here, is the role of artifacts (often common physical objects) in American popular culture that help to create and maintain exclusive identities among men in male peer groups, while at the same time reinforcing the ideology of what we have called social patriarchy by presenting women as objects to be conquered and consumed. Of course, a great many cultures have embraced art works that were based on sexual objects. Simpson (1994), for example, has devoted an entire book to a collection of traditional folk erotica, mostly carvings and drawings by American folk artists with a sexual theme, and sometimes with an extremely explicit sexual theme. Still, it is a unique contribution of modern capitalism to expand the manufacture, distribution, and sale of the commodities that sexually objectify women so that they come to virtually symbolize male culture. As Schur (1988) points out,

> [The] social subordination and sexual objectification of women are central to much of the depersonalized, commercialized, and coercive sexuality found in modern American society. At the present time, it is primarily female sexuality that is objectified, commoditized, and coercively violated. (pp. 12-13)

How can this be done? Miller and Schwartz (1992) point to a number of objects common on college campuses that carry this message. American culture supports a number of artifacts used on ritual occasions when men gather to affirm their relationships with other men, especially through "drinking with the boys." Here one might use trays that produce ice cubes in the shape of nude women, drink stirrers in the shape of nude women, glasses with cartoons on them featuring exaggerated sex, or glasses with pictures of sexy women whose clothes disappear when the glass gets wet.

It is common in these artifacts for women to be reduced to depersonalized body parts: a breast, a torso, armless, headless. For example, Figure 3.1 is the "Big Sipper" mug. "Woman" in this instance is a large white breast with an overly stylized nipple. The handle to this mug is a female figure, bent backwards and attached at the hair and the feet. In order to consume liquid from this mug the user must "sip" it through the nipple. When used in a group setting, this action can reinforce the collective identity of the group as a whole. Members can interact with each other by sharing an artifact, such as passing the "boob" mug around so that everyone drinks from the nipple.

It is important to note that this mug is not meant to be erotic or physically arousing, but rather to be humorous. Still, humor used in this manner can be an important aid in attitude formation. It can lead to desensitization about the seriousness of sexual assault, for example. Topics that might be otherwise inappropriate (such as blatantly sexist attacks on women) can be allowed if they are couched in a context of humor. These kinds of sexist jokes "are 'nonserious' acts that have serious consequences" (Seckman & Couch, 1989, p. 342). Lyman (1987), who analyzed in detail a specific fraternity's degrading sexist ritual on one campus, explained that these men "argued that the

Figure 3.1. The "boob mug" is a common form of reducing women to their body parts, not for erotic arousal but rather as a form of "humor"

special male bond created by sexist humor is a unique form of intimacy that justified the inconvenience caused the women" (p. 87).

One of the implications of this discussion, and indeed most of this chapter thus far, has been that a patriarchal society provides many messages for men that encourage, promote, or at least allow sexually exploitative behaviors. As we shall see in the next section, these messages affect people long before they set foot on a college campus.

Sexual Abuse Before Coming to College

In Chapter 2, we discussed Kanin's idea that many people come to college with attitudes that support the sexual abuse of women and compared this to other theories suggesting that men learn these attitudes after they arrive on campus. It is difficult to study this particular problem and to attempt to figure out which theory is correct.

Logically, there should be a significant amount of sexual abuse in North American high schools, and anecdotally, we have had significant proof that this is the case. In fact, as many readers of our work who have young children have pointed out to us, the predatory behavior of young males starts before high school, in elementary and middle school, perhaps even before boys and girls start dating. As Mercer (1988) has argued,

> Adolescence is clearly not a period when young people reject the traditional gender roles for which they have been groomed. It is characteristically a time when they act them out—sometimes to their worst extremes. The alarming revelations about this process testify to the grave personal implications that male power has for females long before they become adults. (p. 16)

For example, Davis, Peck, and Storment (1993) found that 60% of surveyed high school students approved of forcing sexual activities upon a girl at least in some circumstances. Unfortunately, there is little in the literature to discover whether those who hold such attitudes actually act them out.

Of course, the proper way to study this would be to simply ask elementary, middle, and high school students if they have ever been victimized by sexual assault in a dating relationship, or whether they have ever committed such an assault. Unfortunately, this is almost impossible to do. In the United States, human subjects research boards housed at the researchers' universities typically would require that academic researchers obtain written permission from the parents of each student under 18 years old before the questionnaire could be administered. Typically, Canadian school boards would act similarly. As one might guess, when a questionnaire about sexual experiences is on the table, even if it is to be filled out anonymously, asking permission is a strategy is designed for failure. A great many parents would refuse, no doubt so many as to raise serious questions about the quality of the sample of respondents that remained. For this reason, researchers in this field have never asked those under 18 years old direct questions about sexual victimization. Those researchers who have not abandoned the topic instead ask questions that are difficult to interpret, or difficult to compare to surveys being done with college students. For example, rather than ask high school students in London, Ontario, to report abusive acts committed by or against them, Jaffe, Sudermann, Reitzel, and Killip (1992) and Sudermann and Jaffe (1993) asked them if had they "experienced" abuse in teen dating relationships. This leaves us wondering if they had done the acts or received the acts.

We attempted to look at this question in a way that has some value, although to be sure our work is still far from satisfactory. As part of the Canadian National Survey (CNS), male college students from across Canada were asked whether in high school or elementary school they had, with a female dating partner and/or girlfriend, ever "used physical force in an attempt to make her engage in sexual activities, whether this attempt was successful or not?" Unsurprisingly, many fewer men responded to this question than women who said that they had been victimized in this way (DeKeseredy & Schwartz, 1994).

Our concern, however, was whether this behavior starts in high school and continues on into college. Needless to say, the most satisfactory way to conduct this research is not to ask college men to "remember" whether they committed similar acts years ago in elementary or high school. First of all, all researchers in this area like to keep the time frame being investigated fairly short, to eliminate possible memory problems. Second, this method does not tell us much about the extent of victimization in elementary and high school, because the only people who get a chance to fill out the questionnaire are college students. The males who do *not* go on to college are not given the opportunity to respond. Still, the method of inquiry does fit the needs of what we are asking here: do the men in college who are sexually predatory have a history of committing the same acts before they came to college?

Of course, all surveys of this nature are also handicapped by the fact that few men are willing to admit to committing serious offenses, perhaps even felonies, even on an anonymous questionnaire. It is widely presumed that if women underreport their victimization, then men *drastically* underreport their victimizing behavior. Still, 25 men reported that they physically forced a woman into sexual behavior in elementary school or high school. Although most were still in their first or second year of college, fully 32% (8) of them reported that they had already repeated this behavior in college. This can be looked at in reverse also. A total of 23 men admitted to forced sexual behavior in college, and eight of them (34.8%) said that they had also used force in this manner in high school or elementary school.

Thus, we did develop a partial answer to our question. Although the numbers are small, among that group of men who have admitted using physical force to engage in sexual behavior with an unwilling woman, at least one third of them are continuing a pattern of behavior that began before college. Whatever blame we place in the rest of this book on the college campus and its institutions, some of the blame must be placed in other places. One of these other influences, rape myths, is just as strong in elementary school and high school as it is later on in college.

The Influence of Rape Myths

An important argument to support the claim that North Americans live in a rape-supportive culture is that large numbers of people are part of belief systems that support and promote rape (Orcutt & Faison, 1988; Ward, 1995). These belief systems, part of what we have termed the patriarchal system in North America, are taught as part of the socialization patterns commonly available to both men and women. One of the most important parts of these belief systems are rape myths, defined by Burt (1980) as "prejudicial, stereotyped, or false beliefs about rape, rape victims, and rapists" (p. 217). To pick just one example, Abbey and Harnish (1995) gave undergraduates vignettes to read about men and women who were out together drinking alcoholic or nonalcoholic beverages. Men who scored high on a scale measuring rape myths believed more than other students that the women were acting sexually. They evidently believed that women who go out for a drink with men are appropriate targets for sexual aggression, including forced sex. Still, this is just one minor example. As Ward (1995) points out, North American psychiatry, sociology, and legal practices have traditionally been highly influenced by such beliefs.

Typically, a person who believes in rape myths feels able to differentiate between "real rape" and other events (Estrich, 1987). What does this mean? Interestingly, the holder of rape myths does not typically believe that all women are fair game, or that all rapes are allowed in society. He or she may, in fact, strongly argue that rape is a bad thing and should be punished severely (Scully, 1990). The trick is to answer the question "what is rape?" The holders of rape myths may have a very narrow definition of rape. Typically, they don't believe that one should rape Mother Teresa or their own mother or some other women who are beyond reproach by the person's own private definitions. However, those women who do not meet these stringent definitions of behavior can't (to the holder of rape myths) be considered the victims of a crime. After all, they argue typically, women can't really be forced to engage in sexual intercourse against their will, women secretly wish to be raped (they all want it), and women who call the police are doing so to hide something else, such as their guilt, or to keep their behavior secret from their mothers or boyfriends (Allison & Wrightsman, 1993). Other rape myths suggest that all women are liars, so we can discount their accusations; that no harm has been done when sexually active or experienced women are raped; that women not only secretly want sex, but they fantasize about rough sex; and that rape can only be committed by strangers (Nogrady, 1992). So only women who fulfill the behavioral expectations of rape myth holders in every way, usually including being violently raped by strangers, are in fact real rape victims (Estrich, 1987). The others, such as college women raped by their dates, are not really rape victims. What all of this accomplishes is to define rape as the violent act of a few very deviant men (the ones who rape nuns or my mother). The implied definition is that normal men don't rape. They may act out their natural sexual impulses with women who really want it, or deserve it, or are asking for it, or they may work a "yes" out, but they don't commit real rape.

As Weis and Borges (1973) have pointed out, such beliefs allow men to "engage in otherwise forbidden behavior and to rationalize and justify it after the event" (p. 11). This is not a situation where men know that they are committing rape and make up a pack of lies afterward to hide the fact. Rather, the argument by theorists in this field is that these men develop psychological devices to convince themselves that they are normal men acting out normal impulses. They don't feel guilty because they do not think that they have done anything wrong. For example, related to this book, Sanday (1990) argues that on college campuses, fraternity men learn that forced sex with a drunken woman is not wrong. Thus, why should they feel guilty when they force sex? They don't believe it is wrong.

Rape myths are not simply a device whereby some men do not have the guilt that they should. Rather, the effects are much more serious. For one thing, people who may not be rapists often hold the same attitudes. By agreeing with the rapist that such behavior is correct, because the victim was not a "true" victim, they provide the emotional support that has allowed many people to term North America a rape-supportive culture. For example, in one recent case, the judge decided that a woman cannot be considered a rape victim unless she has offered physical resistance to the rapist (Schafran, 1995). Although, in fact, perhaps a majority of rape victims do not offer resistance after being presented with superior strength or weaponry, this judge decided to describe such a scenario as "nonsense." This message, of course, is a public announcement to men that they can legitimately rape any woman they can scare, and it is a humiliating attack on all women who fear for their lives during a violent criminal act.

Pollard's (1992) massive literature review on the reaction of college students to vignettes or short stories shows that rape may indeed by condoned by broad segments of the population, or at least the college population. Most directly, men seem to be on the lookout for any behavior by women that the men found unacceptable or incautious, even though this behavior would be perfectly legitimate for men. If this behavior is found, then they generally will blame the female for any victimization that follows.

These messages are heard not only by men but by women. Women grow up in the same society as men, are exposed to many of the same influences, and often hold some of the same beliefs. Almost before they are old enough to completely understand the meaning of what rape is, American youth have begun to adhere strongly to rape myths. Although Boxley, Lawrance, and Gruchow (1995) found that more eighth grade boys than girls accepted rape myths, they found that both sexes by this age already believed in some myths. Certainly there is no doubt that high school students often have strong rape myth beliefs. Cassidy (1995) presented a vignette about a date rape to male and female high school students and asked them to indicate whether the rape victim was responsible for the rapist's behavior. Those students who were shown a picture of the victim in "provocative" clothing were more likely to blame the victim than those who were not shown a photograph at all, or those who were shown a photograph of the victim dressed in conservative clothing. It is important to note that the vignette stayed the same—the rapist did exactly the same thing in all three cases, but the students were more likely to blame the woman for her own victimization if they felt that she was improperly dressed.

It is these types of beliefs that make women who are victimized worry about whether they were wearing provocative clothing and caused their own victimization. Did they give off secret flirtatious signals that led the man to believe they were acquiescing to sex? It leads women to skip the question why did this man choose to victimize an innocent woman and instead ask what did I do to bring this upon myself. If women with these beliefs acted in a manner that they feel might throw doubt upon whether they are "perfect" blameless victims (perhaps they were wearing provocative clothing), then they may not define what happened to themselves as rape and may not seek help for their needs. For example, Leggett and Schwartz (1996) asked a group of rape victims to report who they blamed for the rape taking place. Of those women who were raped by physical force, 22.7% said they blamed only themselves, and 27.3% said that they blamed both themselves and the man. Thus, exactly 50% of the women took all or some of the blame for a physical rape upon themselves. It is unlikely that they could do this unless they believed that they were doing something wrong, like being in the wrong place at the wrong time, and therefore "deserved," at least partially, to be raped.

Such rape myths cause intense problems for the victim. Often the myths tell the victim that she is not valued enough to even be considered a victim (Miller & Schwartz, 1995). When rape is seen as just seduction, or just having worked a yes out, the emotional distress of the women involved is amplified. For example, Gilbert (1992), Roiphe (1993), and other backlash theorists suggest (albeit without evidence) that most acquaintance rape can be seen as something unpleasant, but generally not anything that would emotionally harm the victim. They strongly accuse researchers of claiming serious victimization when the women involved do not see themselves as particularly harmed.

To specifically look at this allegation, Leggett and Schwartz (1996) asked 65 rape victims the extent to which they thought that they were affected by their experiences. Unsurprisingly, the victims of physical force reported that they were affected by their experience, but those women who reported that they were the victims of sexual intercourse accomplished when they were too drunk to protest also reported strong reactions. Virtually all of the latter reported being affected emotionally and psychologically on some level, with 31.4% reporting being *affected* (not as trusting, depressed, unhappy, or some other reaction) and 11.4% being *deeply affected* (it caused emotional pain). These figures are only for the women who were raped while they were too drunk or high to resist. These figures are, as one might imagine, higher for those women who were raped by physical force.

Rape Myth Scales

So, we have now discovered that some people hold rape myths. Several rape myth scales have been designed in an attempt to measure the extent to which an individual holds such rape myths. All have been used to show that there is a high acceptance of such myths in our society, and that these myths are closely connected to narrow definitions of rape (Burt & Albin, 1981; Feltey, Ainslie, & Geib, 1991; Giacopassi & Dull, 1986). In an attempt to link such beliefs to behavior, Koss et al. (1985) found that males who admitted to engaging in nonconsensual sexual intercourse with women acquaintances differed from nonaggressive men by scoring higher on Burt's scales.

However, several researchers have found Burt's scales problematic (Ward, 1995) and have developed their own. In particular, Gilmartin-Zena (1987) has argued that Burt's Rape Myth Acceptance Scale has an interpersonal orientation that discounts the importance of the structural causes of rape. She designed her own Acceptance of Rape Myth Scale (ARM) to include such items and has shown that it is reliable and valid (Gilmartin-Zena, 1988, 1989).

Throughout the literature, one of the common suggestions is that one of the groups most likely to hold a different view of women than other college men is the member of the social fraternity (Martin & Hummer, 1989; Sanday, 1990). In particular, it is often claimed that these men hold the particular set of attitudes we have termed rape myths. These myths make it easier for them to become sexual aggressors. However, the only study that supports this finding was done by Schaeffer and Nelson (1993); they argued that although fraternity house residents were relatively accepting of rape myths, this acceptance was shared by other residents of single-sex housing. Meanwhile, coeducational residence hall residents were much less accepting of rape myths.

Gilmartin-Zena's Acceptance of Rape Myth Scale was given out by Schwartz and Nogrady (1996) to a group of men at a large campus with an active fraternity system. The authors were not able to test whether some fraternities were more accepting of rape myths than others, but overall they did not find that fraternity men as a group were much more accepting of rape myths than other men. In a test where lower scores meant more rape myth acceptance, the differences between fraternity men (mean = 88.08) and nonfraternity men (mean = 89.22) were not statistically significant on a t-test for the differences in the group means ($t = .75$, $df = 117$, $p = .454$). In other words, there is no significant difference between the fraternity men and the other men on this rape myths test.

Of course, there are some great differences between women and men. Using Schwartz and Nogrady's data, men score a mean of 89, whereas women score a mean of 98.3, a statistically significant difference ($p = .000$). Interestingly, Kalof (1993) has found that compared to other women, sorority women believe more in rape myths. This finding can also be found in Schwartz and Nogrady's data set, where sorority members were also significantly more likely than other women to believe in rape myths. There were no differences between whether or not men or women lived in residence halls, and although there were fairly few African Americans in the sample, there were no race differences in rape myth scores.

Much more interesting comparisons are found between those who admitted being sexual aggressors and those who did not make such admissions. For these men, there were some differences (nonaggressors had fewer rape myths), but these differences were not statistically significant. On the other hand, the differences between those women who had not been victimized and those women who had were fairly distinct, and statistically significant: the women who had been victimized were less likely to hold rape myths. One can only presume that whereas the process of being a victimizer teaches men little, the process of being victimized can change women's minds about sexual assault.

Pornography and Sexual Assault

One of the strongest arguments made both in mainstream rape theory (e.g., Baron & Straus, 1989) and in certain parts of feminist theory has been that pornographic media provide strong support for the sexual victimization of women. There are many different forms of this argument, but an interesting one has been made by Longino (1995). She argues, and it is impossible to be fair to her complex argument in a few sentences, that sexual content is not the problem with pornography. Rather, it is that by its very nature, pornography lies about women. By portraying women as subordinate to men socially and sexually, by showing that women's only important pleasure lies in pleasing men, and that women are sexual objects that can be used at the whim of men, "pornography lies explicitly about women's sexuality, and through such lies fosters more lies about our humanity, our dignity, and our personhood" (p. 39).

The argument, then, is that one of the lessons that men learn in a patriarchal society comes from pornography. That lesson is that women exist to serve and service men. Perhaps to some men, that means that women are "fair game" to rape or sexually abuse. MacKinnon (1993) makes some of the most famous arguments on the subject, contending that pornography silences women and creates a hostile environment that attacks women in a broad variety of ways that might be seemingly unrelated to pornography (e.g., jobs, housing, education). Baker (1992) lays out the argument concisely:

> Pornography expresses more than the view that women are mere sex objects. It tells men that women enjoy sex and are always available for it, even when they deny it. It tells men that women secretly enjoy rape. . . . The constant repetition of false information is a key part in the maintenance of any oppression: the more it is repeated, the larger the number of people (even in the oppressed group itself) who are likely to come to believe that it is true. (pp. 140-141)

On the college campus, several theorists argue that pornography is related to the sexual abuse of women in dating relationships. Often this has further been related to male peer-support groups. For example, if some men learn to sexually objectify women through their exposure to pornographic media (Jensen, 1995), then they often learn these lessons in groups, for example, watching pornographic films together at fraternity houses. Sanday (1996b) argues that "in my research on gang rape in college fraternities, the pornography connection was very clear" (p. 202). Although these are not college studies, some research (e.g., Harmon & Check, 1988; Itzin & Sweet, 1992; Russell, 1992) demonstrates at least some link between the victimization of currently or formerly married or cohabiting women and the consumption of pornography. Generally speaking, more of these women than would be expected by chance report that the men they live with use pornography in a way that the women find degrading.

Here, however, we are interested in the sexual abuse of women on the college or university campus. Although this is an area where quite a number of people have suggested a relationship, it is not one where there has been much empirical investigation. In fact, to the best of our knowledge, there have been no empirical attempts to study this question on the college campus: is exposure to pornography related to the sexual or physical abuse of women in dating relationships?

One place to study this question is with the data in the CNS. As we have discussed before, there are two types of rape commonly discussed in the acquaintance rape literature. First, are the rapes accomplished by physical force, which is the standard definition of rape in all contexts. Second, are the rapes accomplished when the woman is too drunk or high to resist the male. It is clear to us that the latter acts are crimes of sexual assault (see, e.g., Schwartz & Pitts, 1995). However, we chose to limit the analysis on pornography to cases where the question clearly asks the woman whether she was forced into sexual acts against her will through the use of physical force.

To measure whether women were upset by the use of pornography, we used a slightly modified version of a question developed by Russell (1992). Female respondents were asked to answer yes or no: "Thinking about your entire university and/or college career, have you ever been upset by dating partners and/or boyfriends trying to get you to do what they had seen in pornographic pictures, movies, or books?" Of the 1,638 women in our sample who both said that they dated men and who answered this question, 137 (8.4%) stated that they had been upset by their dating partners trying to get them to do what they had seen in pornographic media. This is similar to the 10% figure that Russell (1992) reports for her similar question, although it should be pointed out that for the most part, Russell interviewed women significantly older than the women here. What may be most important to this study is that there is a statistically significant relationship between sexual victimization and being upset by men's attempts to imitate pornographic scenes. Of those who had been forced into sexual acts since leaving high school, 22.3% had also been upset by attempts to get them to imitate pornographic scenarios (see Table 3.1). Only 5.8% of the women who were not victimized reported being upset by pornography. These figures compare well to Itzin and

Table 3.1 Comparing Postsecondary Forced Sexual Abuse to Being Made Upset by Being Asked to Act out Pornographic Scenes

	Have you been made upset by being asked to act out pornography?		
	Yes	*No*	
Have you been forced into acts since high school?			
Yes	57	199	256
	22.3%	77.7%	100.0%
	41.6%	13.3%	
No	80	1,302	1,382
	5.8%	94.2%	100.0%
	58.4%	86.7%	
	137	1,501	1,638

NOTE: Chi Square = 76.51
$df = 1$
$S = .0000$
Phi = .216

Sweet's (1992) report of the British Cosmopolitan survey, although their crude methodology and cruder style of reporting the results make any real comparison impossible. Tables based only on unmarried women, or women who were never married but living with a male partner, look virtually identical to the full table.

Interestingly, fully 6.8% of the men in this survey admitted on a similar question phrased for men that they had upset dating partners by trying to get them to imitate pornography. The men also were more likely to also admit being forcible sexual victimizers if they admitted upsetting a women in this way. Almost four times as many upsetters (9.3%) as nonupsetters (2.4%) admitted to forcible sexual victimization after high school. This relationship is statistically significant ($p = .000$), although weak (phi = .104). We will discuss fraternities more in the next chapter, but it is worth noting here that there is no difference between fraternity men and other men on campus in the rates at which they admit to upsetting a woman by trying to get her to imitate pornography.

This is, of course, hardly strong proof that a causal relationship exists. However, it does suggest strongly that there is some relationship between sexual victimization and the use of pornography. In fact, there is good reason to believe that a methodology such as this one is fundamentally conservative and can be expected to *underreport* the true extent of the problem. For example, what these women are reporting are those cases where the man explicitly points out in some manner that his disturbing behavior is based on his viewing of pornography. Some unknown number of women have been disturbed by identical male behavior but are completely unaware that the viewing of pornography is behind the man's behavior (Harmon & Check, 1988). Finally, a more comprehensive study might investigate the differing and changing nature of messages in pornography and the effect that this might have (Brosius, Weaver, & Staab, 1993; Cowan & Dunn, 1994).

Thus, we can conclude, at least in Canada, that pornography plays a major role in the sexual abuse of women in college relationships. Of course, much as sexual abuse questions only ask about unwanted sex, the pornography question only asks about attempts to imitate pornography that caused distress. If the woman was receptive to the suggestions, or at least was not upset by them, then she would not be located in our findings.

Does pornography cause woman abuse? Certainly that question cannot be answered from correlational data. On the one hand, the data certainly make it look like this is the case, and it very well may be true. However, the problem is that it equally well may be true that the same factors that cause a man to abuse women also cause him to purchase pornography. So, for example, if there is a factor such as an identified group of men with exceptionally anti-female attitudes on campus, it is possible that these anti-female attitudes cause them to attack women, and the same anti-female attitudes cause them to purchase pornographic materials. Statisticians are very familiar with this problem, which suggests that if the *true* relationship is that anti-female attitudes (remember, this is just an example) are causing *both* assault and purchasing porn, then getting rid of all pornography would not change anything at all. The anti-female attitudes would still cause the sexual assault of women.

The Rape Supportive Society
and Hidden Victims

Part of the problem in assessing the harm that comes to women from sexual assaults is that we really do not know just how many women are assaulted on college campuses each year. What we do know is that a very small number of women report their assaults to official agencies, so any counts we have are extraordinarily low. Just to pick one example, one of the authors here, Martin Schwartz, has for several years conducted local victimization surveys of women on his campus. Although there has not been a single reported rape on this campus in some years, each year dozens of women report to him on anonymous survey forms that they have been raped. These women—who have been raped and are not included in official statistics—are often called hidden rape victims. They do not report their victimization, so we do not know much about them.

Why don't victims report? There are many answers to this question, but one we want to focus on here is self-blame. One of the legacies of the rape-supportive culture is that it teaches both men and women that women are responsible for preventing sexual assault. In the extreme case, men are not blamed, no matter what their behavior, and virtually anything can be used to convince women that they are to blame for assaults on them. Various surveys have located rates of 20% and more: Ward et al. (1991) found that 20% of their sample had experienced unwanted sexual intercourse; Koss (1985) found that 27% of her sample had experienced rape or attempted rape; and Russell (1984) found that 24% had experienced forceful attempts at sexual intercourse by dates. Yet, only 8% of the students in the Koss (1988) survey reported to the police, whereas 4% of the Ward et al. respondents talked to a counselor.

Pitts and Schwartz (1993) attempted to study some of the perceptions of rape survivors to try to understand why some women report that they have been raped and some do not. They asked women who were the victims of completed rapes whom they talked to, who was the most helpful person they talked to, and what that person said to them that was so helpful. In an exact replication of Koss (1985), they found that only 27% of the women said they had been raped, even though they *all* described a victimization experience that completely fulfilled the state law for rape. An important question, then, is just why it is that so many women are raped but do not define their own experiences as rape.

The question we were most interested in was that of attribution. Of the 45 survivors who said that someone was helpful to them, 16 specifically mentioned that this help had something to do with blame, twice as many responses as the next most common item.

Thirteen of the 16 were survivors of completed rape (the other three were survivors of attempted rape), and we turned our attention to them. The key point is that some "most helpful" people explicitly told the survivor that the experience was not her fault, it was the fault of a man who was looking for a victim, or it could have happened to anyone. In other cases, the "most helpful" people did not explicitly tell the survivor that she was free from blame. Rather, they allocated some or all of the blame to the victim, but then understood, or forgave the victim for her behavior. So, for example, they might point out that it was stupid to try to walk home alone late at night, but then assure the victim that there was absolutely nothing she could do to lose the love and support of her family.

The key to understanding what happened came from another question at the end of the survey, which asked each woman whether or not she had been raped. Recall that every single woman listed in Table 3.2 had been raped. In *every single instance* in which the "most helpful" person the survivor told either blamed her or encouraged her own self-blame, the victim *did not* define her experience as rape. She reported to us that she had never been raped. The tentative conclusion to reach here is that women who are blamed by confidants, who thus accept self-blame, do not accept that they have been raped. Rather, the self-blame helps them to accept responsibility for "mistakes" they made, rather than placing the responsibility onto a rapist. This conclusion is strengthened substantially by looking at the four instances in which the survivor was explicitly told that she was not responsible for what had happened to her. In *each* of these cases, the woman *did* define her experience as rape. The women who were not encouraged to blame themselves for the behavior of men were all able to define their experiences as rape; they were able to blame a rapist for what happened rather than themselves.

In a more recent but similar survey, Leggett and Schwartz (1996) obtained similar results. Here, of the 21 women who had been raped by physical force, only five (23.8%) agreed that they had been raped. More important, of those women who had been raped because they were too intoxicated to stop the man, only one (3.3%) out of 30 said that she had been raped. These women have heard this message loud and clear all their lives: when women get drunk and are victimized by men, it is the women's fault for getting drunk, not men's fault for committing rape.

It is important to note that the women here do not differ in terms of their psychological reaction to the rape. As noted earlier in this

Table 3.2 Most Helpful Response To Women Who Were Raped, And Whether They Recognize Their Experience as Rape

Response	Have You Ever Been Raped
1. Told that it "wasn't her fault"	
Told me that I wasn't to blame—it's not my fault	Yes
They did not judge me . . . did not blame me	Yes
I was not blamed for anything	Yes
Helped me see that I wasn't at fault for what happened	Yes
2. Not told that it "wasn't her fault"	
Unconditional love	No
The person it happened with was a friend because I was drunk and I wasn't thinking clearly	No
Helped me learn from my mistake	No
I don't know—I was drunk—really stupid move on my part	No
They understood that it was a mistake	No
Blamed me partially	No
They encouraged me to learn from it. Knowing that she loved me unconditionally and didn't judge me made me let go	No
He's my current boyfriend and he doesn't pass judgements (sic) on mistakes or situations I may have gotten into in the past	No

chapter, almost all rape survivors report that they were affected by the experience. In fact, Leggett and Schwartz (1996) found that 42.8% of the women who were raped by a man taking advantage of the fact that they were too drunk to resist said that they were deeply affected or affected emotionally or psychologically. Another 51.4% of these women said that they were somewhat affected emotionally or psychologically. There is no reason to argue that women who are raped while drunk are not psychologically harmed by the experience.

Thus, what is clear is that rape survivors are hearing loud and clear the voice of a rape-supportive culture telling them that they are at fault for engaging in unwanted, nonconsensual sexual intercourse. Although most rape survivors have some difficulty in this society dealing with issues of self-blame, the problem of the hidden victim is particularly strong, in that she must first deal with the issue of whether she is in fact a victim at all. If women are told that they are to blame (they shouldn't have let him in, gone walking alone at night, asked to borrow his class notes), then they will not report the crime to the police, and they will not seek help from the rape crisis center or various other support services for their emotional and psychological reactions to victimization. Worst of all is that there is a literature in the field suggesting to rape crisis counselors that it is healthy to allow women to feel self-blame for their behavior, as long as they are given emotional support otherwise (Janoff-Bulman, 1979, 1982; Karuza & Carey, 1984).

Sometimes people do not understand just why it is that some rape prevention workers attack pamphlets and other advice suggesting that women avoid rape by not engaging in behavior that the pamphlet writer feels might be dangerous. The problem is that many rape prevention pamphlets turn around what survivors need to hear and offer exactly the wrong advice: if you do get raped while coming home from the library at night, it is *your* fault for being out alone at night. Pitts and Schwartz (1993) have pointed out that blaming women for such behavior

> ignores the fact that women have a right to walk alone at night, the right to go on dates, the right to go to a bar, or to drink alcohol. Women have to restrict their lives not because their behavior is wrong or illegal but because men take advantage of the vulnerability of women. In the short run, restriction may be the best advice for women who wish to avoid rape, but blaming survivors for the degrading and violent behavior of men not only legitimizes a society in which women are forced to restrict their lives out of fear of rape, but it even takes away their right to be angry about it. (p. 396)

Of course, it is not only women who are affected by rape. Josh tells his story here about how affected he was by the rape of his girlfriend.

Woman Abuse Affects Men Also: Josh's Story

The following was written by Josh, a college senior. It clearly shows that men's violence against women also has a strong effect upon men. Josh, it should be noted, is a very muscular body builder who was a star lineman on his high school football team.

> I met Jennifer about two years ago. She was at the time 21 years old. She had been married right out of high school and was divorced a year later. When she went through this

divorce, she met a man named Zach. With nowhere else to turn, she lived with Zach in a trailer about 20 minutes out of town. He had seriously abused her but I as many others could only ask one question: "Why didn't you just leave?"

When we became involved, she finally felt safe from him. We started living together and became personally involved romantically. However, I felt her constant paranoia about my physical strength. When we would have a disagreement resulting in yelling, she would run away as if I was going to chase her down and beat her. That is when I finally got her to open up about the physical abuse that Zach had done to her.

Zach was a person I had known from the time I was 12 and had entered middle school. It was a shock to me to think that someone I had known for years would be capable of such abusive violence. What she saw as her victimization was that he had beaten her and forced sexual acts upon her. But I began to see the emotional scars that he had left upon her as well. She had a constant disbelief in her own self-worth. She had no self-confidence in anything. I saw this as the result of Zach's abuse over a couple of years.

Shortly after I had established this relationship, Zach came back onto the scene. He was scared of me, so he would do nothing in my presence, but there were a number of incidents including Zach hiring a man to assault me. I turned to the police, but they could not prove the connection. The police officer, a high school football teammate of mine, told me that Zach was in constant trouble in town but that the judge would not do anything about it.

These were all minor incidents up to the point when Jennifer informed me that she was pregnant. This was around Christmas. The next March I was activated for duty at a prison riot as a member of the state National Guard. My activation was in the local paper. Upon reading that I was out of town, Zach went to our apartment, broke in, and kicked out Jennifer's friends. Then he proceeded to rape and beat her. When I returned home some days later, I found an empty person.

Jennifer was destroyed physically and emotionally. She had gone to the hospital and was checked for rape. The medical report showed forcible entry, and I had photographed the bruises on her body. She had belt marks all along her back, and her ribs were badly bruised. I told her that to call and press charges was her decision. I would not force her to go through the process of being labeled a rape victim by society. I was sure that the first thing that people would say is that the minute I left, she moved him in.

Two days later, Jennifer began experiencing health problems. She went to the hospital, and they informed her that when she was beaten, the placenta had been ripped and the child would have minimal chances for survival. If my boy did survive, he would likely be malformed due to the loss of vital fluids. The doctor advised Jennifer to receive an abortion due to these complications.

After this, we both decided to press charges. When she went to the police, they made her make an appointment with the County Prosecutor. She went, and the prosecutor said that he would not prosecute due to her previous relationship with Zach. He said that this situation was too unbelievable, and he would not be able to successfully prosecute.

So, Zach to this day runs free. He raped and beat Jennifer and was responsible for the death of our child. I repeatedly called law enforcement officials when he would stalk us. He would repeatedly do "donuts" with his car in front of our apartment. He also harassed us on the telephone. After reporting all of this, nothing would happen. The police said they would have to catch him in the act or they could not do anything.

Not until the system of law enforcement caters to the safety of women in general of all races and economic backgrounds will they be safe from domestic violence. I grew up watching my mother being abused and I was the victim of abuse myself. I thought that when I left my house and childhood behind, it would no longer be a problem. I realize now that through the death of my son and Jennifer's suffering that domestic violence is a problem for all society.

Summary

In this chapter, we have summarized a variety of material on how men and women grow up in a rape-supportive culture such as the one in North America, and how it can affect their attitudes and behavior. It is important to note that while only a minority of men actually commit sexual assault or battery, the vocabularies and attitudes that give support, permission or approval for such actions are held by a wide variety of people.

In beginning to flesh out the modified male peer-support model, we described how it is not only the social structure of a patriarchal society, but the more narrowly defined and specific familial and courtship patriarchies that help to instill various rape supportive attitudes in men and women. We argued that the socialization patterns in America suggest that men are brought up differently than women and that the study of masculinities makes it particularly plain that this is a complex phenomenon. There are many masculinities and always some men trying to redefine what it means to be a man. Some of these men, unfortunately, choose to define their masculinity in terms of sexual assault on women, whom they objectify sexually, so that women become the road to scoring, not equal partners in society. We discussed how other men, rape myths, pornography, and other factors all come together to convince both men and women to blame the victim rather than the rapist. When this happens, often the victim herself will take on self-blame, and refuse either to seek help or to report the incident to the police. Even those whom the rape victims feel are particularly helpful to them are influential in convincing the victim that she was to blame for the attack, and that therefore what happened could not be rape. These women become hidden rape victims.

4

Factors Associated With Male Peer Support for Sexual Assault on the College Campus

In Chapter 3, we set up some of the broader societal factors that influence college students. We concentrated on the top part of the modified peer support model in Figure 2.2. In this chapter, we will head downward, covering those factors more and more specific to the college campus. In particular, we will focus of the role of alcohol, the role of such male membership social groups as college fraternities, and the similar role of athletics and, in particular, sports teams. These membership groups are not themselves as much a problem as are the associated issues of group secrecy, a narrow conception of masculinity, and the sexual objectification of women. Finally, we will discuss the absence of deterrence on some college campuses today.

Alcohol Consumption

If there is one "fact" that college and university students, faculty, and administrators can agree on across North America, it is that heavy drinking is exceedingly common on campuses (Levine & Kanin, 1986; Margolis, 1992). Whereas drug use is stable, alcohol use and abuse is going steadily up (Gallagher, Harmon, & Lingenfelter, 1994). Not only do the overwhelming majority of students drink (despite the fact that most of them are under-age and therefore engaging in illegal activity), but more than 40% reported to the Center on Addiction and Substance Abuse (1994) that they had engaged in binge drinking in the past 2 weeks. Actually, to tell the truth, few students see *themselves* as heavy drinkers. They agree that their friends are heavy drinkers but tend to see themselves as being in control of their own social drinking (Burrell, 1992).

Of course, that does not mean that all students are heavy drinkers, or, for that matter, alcohol drinkers at all. Within different groups, there are important variations in the amount of alcohol consumption on college campuses. Race, to pick one obvious area, has been looked at in studies of alcohol abuse on campus only relatively rarely. However, those infrequent studies have found whites to be much more likely to drink. For example, Engs and Hanson (1985) found that 41.8% of African American students did not drink at all, and only a very small number were heavy drinkers. On the other hand, 22.3% of the white students were classified as heavy drinkers, and only 14.6% abstained. Gonzales (1990) had similar findings in comparing both white and African American men and women. Furthermore, he also found that white women had significantly higher scores on a test of frequency and quantity of drinking than Hispanic women. However, there was no difference between white and Hispanic men. Although Reese and Friend (1994) did not measure actual drinking behavior, they did find that white students had much more positive alcohol expectancies, which they felt partially accounted for the difference in drinking between different ethnic groups. All of this information is interesting, of course, because it is quite the opposite of various stereotypes: when people are asked to close their eyes and to imagine a picture of an abuser, the picture that comes into almost everyone's mind is that of an African American or other minority (Burston, Jones, & Roberson-Saunders, 1995), students who are often among the least-frequent abusers on campus.

Although not a perfect measure of social class, Crawford (1995) found that there was a significant association between family income and drinking behavior. Higher income students were more likely to drink than lower income students. Of course, one difficulty with this analysis is that only the students in the lowest income category had rates much different than other students, and even in that group, the overwhelming majority of students engaged in drinking: 62% of those from families with less than $25,000 annual income. Generally, what is being compared is *very high* rates of drinking with *extremely high* rates of drinking, rather than high versus low rates. Overall, 85.2% of the 845 students in her sample reported that they had consumed alcohol in the prior 2 months.

It is generally accepted that there has been substantial change in drinking among women: Drinking heavily is on the rise (Chomak & Collins, 1987; Sherry & Stolber, 1987). This makes it even more difficult to make simple comparisons between the rates of heavy drinking by men and women, although most authorities argue that men are still heavier drinkers than women.

However, one of the most important differences, and one that has an essential importance here, is the *reason* that men and women drink heavily. Of course, there are some similarities. Various psychological tests measuring a desire for social facilitation and sensation seeking do not find much in the way of gender differences. Women in particular seem to drink as a way of making friends and cementing relationships (Gleason, 1993). On the other hand, Beck, Thombs, Mahoney, and Fingar (1995) found that men's drinking is often bound up in a context of sex seeking. Women are much less likely to make the connection between alcohol and sex. Women who do drink heavily are more likely to drink in a context where they are seeking relief from emotional pain. Both of these findings were statistically significant.

It isn't only race and sex that provide us with differences in the amount of alcohol consumed on college campuses. We also know that alcohol abuse is more prominent in social networks such as fraternities and sororities (Martin & Hummer, 1989). Klein (1992a), for example, found that fraternity and sorority members, and especially men living in fraternity houses, were much more likely to have attitudes that showed a tolerance for alcohol abuse. Furthermore, he found that such attitudes were a good predictor of how much people actually drank. In other words, people who were tolerant of alcohol abuse were more likely to abuse alcohol themselves. Baer, Kivlahan, and Marlatt (1995) agreed that this does in fact happen; following students from high school into college, they found specifically that frequency of drinking alcohol was strongly associated with living in a fraternity or sorority residence.

Some notes of caution are in order, however. For example, Lichtenfeld and Kayson (1994) found in their statistical analysis of drinking behavior that all fraternity and sorority members were not alike; the younger members of the Greek letter organizations were much more likely to be the alcohol abusers. Similarly, Baer (1994) found that fraternity members agreed that drinking itself, and the pressure to drink, was greater in fraternity houses. However, much like Kanin's argument that some men come to college primed to sexually assault women, Baer found that these men tended to believe *before* they came to college that fraternities were heavy drinking establishments. That could be why men who want to drink heavily join fraternities. Baer found it possible that support for heavy drinking may decrease as students get older.

What worries many researchers in this field is that two things often happen at campus and off-campus parties organized by men. Not only are these sites the location of some of the highest levels of alcohol consumption on many campuses, but they are also too frequently the social context of various forms of woman abuse (Ehrhart & Sandler, 1985; Sanday, 1990). The problem is that researchers in this area have not often been clear about how the relationship between alcohol and sexual abuse works. Some have just been content to argue that something must be amiss, because the two take place at the same time.

Others have tried to find an *indirect* link between alcohol abuse and sexual aggression. As a start, several studies have found that men who were sexually aggressive were also typically heavy drinkers (Lisak & Roth, 1988; Schwartz & Nogrady, 1996). This would be a *direct* link if the researchers were arguing that drinking alcohol makes men into rapists. Few actually make such an argument, although some follow the lead of Boumil, Friedman, and Taylor (1993) in suggesting that "the extensive use of alcohol and drugs on campuses contributes to the reduction of inhibitors, the relaxation of behavioral controls and the impairment of sound judgment" (p. 122), which in turn contributes to a higher rate of coercive sexual activity. Another indirect link argument is that women who are drunk are seen by men as less deserving of respect and of a lower character, and therefore more available for sexual acts (Richardson & Campbell, 1988). Women who are drinking are commonly seen by college men as "more sexual" than the same men view men who are drinking, and "more sexually available" than nondrinking women. These men further perceive drinking women as more likely to "enjoy being seduced" (George, Gournic, & McAfee, 1988).

In another area of research, we have discovered that men's alcohol consumption is strongly associated with sexist conversations about women's social status and their sexuality. For example, some men gather at bars or pubs to drink, have fun, and to avoid women (LeMasters, 1975). Women are not allowed to join them because female exclusion serves to validate and sustain masculine superiority, solidarity, and dominance (Farr, 1988). Men often use tavern events, especially "nights out with the boys," to prove to each other that they are not "under their girlfriends' thumbs." Nonetheless, women remain focal points of conversation. In fact, according to Hey (1986), "their 'presence' dominates the discourse, in that the main topic of conversation in the pub is women's sexuality and the effective control of it" (p. 66). Moreover, these discussions often emphasize violence as a means of maintaining control (Whitehead, 1976) and may even encourage some men to become sexually aggressive toward specific women.

Seduction or Rape?

Of course, not all of these discussions are initially aimed at violence or sexual aggression. One of the most common male discussions about women, particularly in the context of groups such as fraternities, focuses on how to "work a yes out." The idea here is to take a woman who is saying no to consensual sexual acts and to somehow convince her to say yes. This can be through verbal persuasion, or more often, with alcohol (Sanday, 1990). Quite simply, men "learn" through conversations with their friends that sexually reluctant women are more likely to "put out" if they are drunk. Thus, the man's goal for the evening is to get the woman to drink as much as possible, and to use that alcohol as a tool that can turn a "no" into a "yes."

This is a difficult area to discuss. To some, this is yet another example of how men are sexual predators who victimize women. Many people find it repugnant that men would actively plot to get women to engage in sex for which they originally had no interest. On the other hand, many men and women view this as the great art of seduction. For generations in Western culture, a romantic attitude, candlelight, a bottle of wine, and perhaps a moonlight stroll by the lake, have all been considered by both men and women to be legitimate methods by which to convince a reluctant woman to engage in sexual intercourse.

Where is the problem? Certainly Sanday and others who agree with her are not against romantic interludes, where we are discussing some wine with dinner. One problem is when alcohol is part of an active strategy by men to work out a yes by getting a woman so drunk that she cannot resist his advances. Few of us have been taught to understand the difference between seduction and rape, despite the fact that the law is fairly clear in most cases. Generally, the difference is simple. No matter how morally reprehensible it might be, getting a woman to voluntarily say yes to sexual intercourse by lies, persuasion, voluntarily taken drugs or alcohol, or other verbal strategies is legal. When it begins to cross over the line, in most states, is when women are not given the chance to voluntarily take the alcohol or drugs, or else to voluntarily say yes or no to sex.

For example, one strategy that is illegal in many states, but is virtually never enforced anywhere, is for men to work out a yes by feeding an under-age date at a fraternity party drink after drink of a sweet punch made with grain alcohol (so that she is unaware of the high potency of her drinks). To many men, after they have learned that this is a standard and legitimate method of seduction, it is an easy move to the next step: they fail to see a problem in sexual intercourse with this same woman after she passes out.

Typically, not only will students fail to see this as a problem, but many others in positions of authority will feel similarly. For example, as we shall see below, in Ohio it is a serious felony to have sexual intercourse with a woman after she passes out from alcohol or drug use. Yet, *The New York Times* discovered that even in a college town there is no reason to expect the prosecutor to take action on acquaintance rape cases in which the woman was drinking, no matter what the facts. As an explanation, one Ohio prosecutor with a large Division 1 university in his jurisdiction said that if an intoxicated woman was in a man's place late at night "most people would ask themselves, 'Well, what did she think was going to happen?' " (Bernstein, 1996c, p. 16). We can see, then, that part of the problem is just plain victim blaming. Women in our culture are expected to be responsible for sexuality: Men seek sex, women guard the gates. We tend to feel that if sexual intercourse takes place, it is either violent forcible rape, or else the woman consented at some level. As Roiphe (1993) notes in her best-selling book attacking feminism, "if we assume that women are not all helpless and naive, then shouldn't they be responsible for their choice to drink or take drugs?" (p. 15). This is not just the word of one author. In a survey of college students generally, Norris and Cubbins (1992) discovered that college women who have been raped after drinking with their dates may not be taken as seriously as women who are raped under other circumstances. Other surveys have had similar results (George et al., 1988; Richardson & Campbell, 1988).

Interestingly, although a great many people seem to think that a drunken woman is fair game to be forced into sexual acts, they don't seem to apply that same logic to other situations. For example, what if the man "worked out" her car keys and drove off while she was still too befuddled by drink to know that her car had been stolen. Is he a car thief? Should women be forced to take responsibility for the fact that they might become victims of theft if they take drugs or drink? Do all criminals automatically get immunity from prosecution if they only prey on people who are drunk? For some reason, many people think that the man should be prosecuted for car theft, but not for felony rape.

Although many people are somewhat hazy on what is right and wrong, the law is fairly clear in most jurisdictions. Although it is not practical here to quote from 50 different state laws and the Canadian law on the subject, it might be worthwhile to quote just one law. Ohio law is useful to examine, because it has been the basis behind many of the important U.S. surveys in the field, including the highly cited study by Koss (1988). The Ohio Revised Code (§2907.02, 1993) provides that the usual requirement in rape prosecutions of showing a lack of consent by the victim to the sexual conduct is not required if a person (the offender) provides drugs or alcohol for the express purpose of rendering consent meaningless. Now, this requires some agency on the part of the offender: that he or she in fact provided the alcohol in a purposeful attempt to allow unwanted sexual intercourse to take place without a struggle. What about those situations where the woman got blindingly drunk all by herself? This is exactly the situation posed in the Appendix by Catherine. Ohio law, which is not at all uncommon, provides that it is still a major felony crime (although a lesser crime than first-degree rape) when "the offender knows that the other person's ability to appraise the nature of or control his or her own conduct is substantially impaired" (§2907.03).

In other words, if a woman gets herself voluntarily into a condition where she is unable to consent to sexual intercourse, and a man "forces his affections upon her," he is guilty of a crime that could land him in the penitentiary for many years.

Interestingly, this is not some bright new idea of a recent political feminist movement, as claimed by many conservatives. It has become popular, as we pointed out earlier, to argue that there has been a feminist revolution to change the definition of rape, when there really has been no change for the worse in men's behavior at all (Carlin, 1994). In fact, this principle has been upheld in Ohio since the first controlling case in 1861. In the current controlling case, from 1924, Chief Justice Marshall ruled that "the crime of rape . . . is complete even though no resistance be offered, if the female is in law incapable of consenting. This is true if she is . . . intoxicated" (State v. Schwab, 143 NE 29). One standard national reference work, found in pretty much every law library in the United States (75 *Corpus Juris Secundum* §29) holds that in forcible rape, the fact that the woman got herself seriously drunk does not excuse the rapist: "the offense may be committed although the female voluntarily imbibes intoxicating liquor." What about the man? Can't we just as easily claim that he was drunk too and really didn't know what he was doing or wasn't able to control his actions? Sensible as that may sound to some of us, the law couldn't possibly be clearer on this subject. As another standard reference work available in most every law library puts it: "it is a generally recognized rule of jurisprudence that voluntary intoxication is no defense to a criminal act" such as rape (65 *American Jurisprudence 2d* §36). Really, the law could not operate in any other way. If we drop the charges against all offenders who claim that they are under the influence of drugs or alcohol, there will be few offenders left to bring to trial.

Thus, we have a difficult situation. Many men and women are often unaware that to have sex with a woman who has passed out, or lost the ability to meaningfully consent, is in most jurisdictions in the United States and Canada a serious form of rape. In fact, in many social groups such as fraternities men are taught that having sex with a woman who has passed out is a legitimate form of seduction because physical force was not used (Sanday, 1990). Since they do not see it as, in Estrich's (1987) words, "real rape," there is no reason for the men to feel guilty or to think that they are anything except law-abiding, upstanding citizens. If there is one consistent finding about both acquaintance rapists and stranger rapists, it is that a great many men define their actions in such a way as to actually believe that the victims of their assaults wanted to engage in sex with them (Scully, 1990). It may be hard for some of us to believe that a woman wanted to be stripped and forcibly entered by several men while crying and protesting, but it is obvious to researchers that some of these men do believe just that. Given these beliefs, these aggressors contend, their behavior was appropriate (Ward et al., 1991).

It is not a hypothetical argument that fraternities teach this behavior. We will argue in this book that researchers have not been able to uncover a direct link between fraternities and acquaintance rape. Many groups of men on campus are able to provide the male peer support for such actions. However, there is some clear evidence that fraternity men are more likely than other men on campus to use actions short of force in order to engage in sexual behavior. This includes all forms of legal sexual coercion (lies, threats to break off a relationship, etc.) and the use of alcohol and drugs to get her too intoxicated to consent (Boeringer, 1996).

This does not mean, of course, that no men use physical force or violence in campus situations. Some men turn to the use of violence because they are unable to work a yes out of a drunken woman. Although this may not be the typical situation, this behavior can be the consequence of a "hypererotic" peer group socialization that tells members it is appropriate to force a drunken woman to have sexual intercourse because she is designated as a *legitimate sexual target* (Kanin, 1985). These definitions are also part of what sociologists often call a *vocabulary of motive*, where men convince each other that they excuse and justify violence against women (Berkowitz, 1992; Franks, 1985).

Is Alcohol the Link to Sexual Assault?

Some researchers have tried to find a direct link between alcohol and sexual aggression. Kanin (1984), to pick just one example, argues that alcohol was a factor for 66% of the date rapists in his study. More specifically, others argue that the physiological effects of alcohol increase the likelihood that men will commit a sexually aggressive act (Bohmer & Parrott, 1993). This view has not been well-accepted in the field. Abbey (1991), for example, argues that the link is not real but more of an illusion. Men have a strong expectation of alcohol's effects, she argues, which fuels their misperceptions of women's sexual intentions and may serve as a justification for men's sexual violence. The real physiological effect may not be very important.

Still, if there are few in the field willing to accept a strong causal link (Brain, 1986; Murdoch, Pihl, & Ross, 1990), most researchers feel that alcohol certainly plays some important role. They feel that a number of other factors must be taken into account in any explanations. In fact, Ward et al.'s (1991) summary of their research is helpful in summarizing the entire field:

> While this is not sufficient evidence of a causal connection between alcohol use and sexual aggression, it shows, at a minimum, that alcohol is an important part of the student lifestyle and that unwanted sexual experiences are a product of that lifestyle. (p. 68)

Whatever the reason, although the relationship may not be causal, alcohol abuse is strongly related to abuse of women. Barnes, Greenwood, and Sommer (1991), in fact, argue that in their sample of male college students, alcohol was the strongest predictor they found of courtship violence, when combined with an extroverted personality. Similarly, Lisak and Roth (1988) found that sexually aggressive men were more likely to have a high use of alcohol. In our own work, we have had similar results. For example, in one study of 119 male college students, Schwartz and Nogrady (1996) found a significant difference between admitted sexual aggressors and nonaggressors based on the number of drinks they consumed each time they went out drinking.

However, the last two studies have a much more important finding, at least in the context of the overall argument being made in this book. They both used fairly complex statistical analyses. Lisak and Roth (1988) used factor analysis to find that the heavy use of alcohol loaded highly (was strongly associated) with a question on whether the man discussed sexual experiences with his friends. One possible explanation here is that men who drink heavily, and who discuss sexual experiences with their friends, are reinforced in definitions of exploitation of women that allow them to become sexually aggressive. Schwartz and Nogrady (1996) used some different questions to come to similar findings. As noted above, in a discriminant function analysis, they found that the quantity of drinking differentiated between admitted aggressors and nonaggressors. Even more powerful differentiators, however, were whether the men think that their friends would approve of getting a woman drunk in order to have sex with her and whether they reported actually having friends who have gotten a woman drunk or high on drugs in order to have sex with her. Men who reported that they are part of a social network that approves of using alcohol as a weapon to get women to engage in sexual intercourse they do not want were more likely to actually engage in agressive behavior.

Of course, as with all of social science, nothing is ever that easy. The problem is that there are other possible explanations of the same findings. On the one hand, men may be sexual aggressors in the first place and may therefore drink heavily to relieve guilt. They may join groups of similarly minded men, who spend time convincing each other that they are right in sexually objectifying women and using alcohol heavily. On the other hand, the same data would support an explanation that men come to college and fall in with groups, such as certain fraternities, where they learn that such behaviors are in fact legitimate. At that point, they begin to act in this manner. We really cannot tell at this point which is more true.

In sum, alcohol abuse plays a major role in peer group processes related to woman abuse in university dating relationships, although most likely it has the most effect when it is combined with the effects of male peer-support groups. In the next section, we will explore some aspects of these support groups. When alcohol is used directly and specifically to gain a goal, such as sexual intercourse, this may be called the instrumental use of alcohol. Such a use may be especially evident in formal social groups such as fraternities. As discussed below, privileged social groups often have members who sexually and physically attack women.

Male Support-Group Membership

This book does not argue that male peer support for the abuse of women occurs only in certain places. One can find such support virtually anywhere geographically and within any social class or religious group. It is found in all occupations, all racial groups, and all ethnic groups (Bowker, 1983). However, there is an argument to make that when men band together strongly, the chances are increased that they will see women as the Other, a weaker sex that can deservedly be abused. We noted earlier that in a study of virtually all cultures for which we have data, Levinson (1989) found that woman abuse is most likely to be absent in those cultures where men and women sleep together, rather than in men's and women's group residence houses. Spain (1992), another anthropologist who studied nonindustrial societies, also found that men's power seemed to be enhanced by sex segregation. She found that where there is a ceremonial men's hut, there seems to be more male solidarity and more men's power. She speculates that this might be applicable to men's college fraternity houses. Such huts help to set up a situation where women's friendships are more intimate and involve fewer people, whereas men's friendships tend to be more impersonal but involve larger groups of people.

As any cultural anthropologist can explain in detail, moving from small preindustrial societies to large capitalist societies with these sorts of generalizations is something that, at the least, must be done with the most extreme care. (Many would argue that it should not be done at all.) Still, one can only wonder whether university fraternities are examples of those cultures that maintain men's houses. Members or "brothers" develop quasi-familial bonds with each other. Much like the men's houses of the cultures Levinson reports on, fraternity residences are generally off-limits as residences to female students.

More important, fraternities are also fertile breeding grounds for woman abuse, especially sexual assault. In general, a number of studies have found that fraternity and sorority members report that their peers are more likely to support a permissive atmosphere toward sexual activity (e.g., Lottes & Kuriloff, 1994). More specifically, fraternities have been the setting for most known acquaintance gang rapes on American college campuses (Ehrhardt & Sandler, 1985; Sanday, 1990). There are few campuses with an active Greek social organization life where the campus grapevine is not aware of at least one recent example of an episode at a fraternity house where students engaged in "pulling train," or a "gang bang" (Warshaw, 1988). As we saw earlier, part of the reason why this behavior can continue is that the victim is held to be responsible, or at least partially responsible, not only by the fraternity members and other college men, but also by women students, male and female faculty, and administrators.

Several researchers have tried to move beyond the anecdotal evidence cited above into some type of empirical examination of the question: Are fraternities really closely associated with the sexual coercion of women? There are different ways to look at this question. One way is to ask the men themselves. For example, Garrett-Gooding and Senter (1987) used a campuswide sampling procedure to investigate through surveys men's level of participation in sexually coercive activities. One of their important findings was that there was a statistically significant relationship between two variables: (a) how often the man engaged in sexually coercive relationships, and (b) how involved these same men were in certain campus activities. When we slightly reorganized their data to compare fraternity men against all other men, we found that fraternity men were much more likely than other men to sexually abuse women (Schwartz, 1995).

Another way to look at the same question is to talk to women. In one random sample of 925 undergraduate women, students were asked to describe the most sexually stressful thing that had happened to them since enrolling in the university. When the authors looked at those men accused by these women of causing a stressful event, they found that members of fraternities were greatly overrepresented (Frintner & Rubinson, 1993). Using a different sampling procedure, Copenhaver and Grauerholz (1991) looked at sorority women only, on the grounds that they spend a lot of time with fraternity men. They found that a high percentage of these women had been the victims of sexual aggression; more than 40% since enrolling in college. Of the reported acts, 57% either took place during a fraternity function or were done by a fraternity member. In virtually every case, the women and the men had been drinking or taking drugs.

Why is it that fraternities have come to be associated with violence against women? Certainly that is not the main reason for the existence of fraternities, as most such organizations are the home of a great deal of innocent fun, friendship, and "good works" for the campus and the community. For this reason, it is common for critics to claim that it is unfair for books like this one to concentrate on the problems of fraternities without spending equal time discussing the good side of fraternity life. Merton (1985), for one, dismisses this argument: He asks "whether journalists writing about Charles Manson had an obligation to note that on most days of his life, he did not kill anyone" (p. 122). Here, the widespread popularity of social fraternities makes it obvious that a great many people are aware of the good things that these organizations have to offer.

Still, over the years, a number of studies have shown that "fraternities may provide a subculture which insulates their members from the ongoing campus climate" (Bohrnstedt, 1969, p. 36). Fraternities promote conformity (Hughes & Winston, 1987), and seem to produce members who have less moral concern about social injustice (Miller, 1973). Morris (1991) argues that those who live in Greek housing are more accepting of racial segregation, prejudice, and the rise of hate crimes. Of course, it is always possible that much of this effect comes from self-selection; that men who think alike band together. Muir (1991), for example, argues that southern white Greek organizations recruit "relatively prejudiced students, who are then reinforced by in-house cultures approving discrimination at levels significantly higher than the general campus" (p. 98). However, the most widely cited works on fraternities argue that the highly masculinist, racist, homophobic views promoted by fraternities; the preoccupation with loyalty; the use of alcohol and physical force as weapons; the obsession with competition, physical force, superiority, and dominance, all encourage social and sexual violence against women (Martin & Hummer, 1989).

Worst of all, some researchers think that fraternity rituals that are central to these groups also promote rape. Sanday (1990), for example, finds that fraternity rituals provide an important mechanism for breaking feelings of dependency upon women. In some houses, this involves the provision of a new ready-made self that includes sexist and homophobic attitudes, designed to show virility and dominance to cope with feelings of powerlessness.

These attitudes do not even need to be kept a secret. On many campuses, women hold Take Back the Night marches to demand a rape-free environment. It is not uncommon for some fraternities to chant pro-rape slogans at marchers as a planned event. At Queens University in Ontario, an anti-rape campaign with the slogan "No Means No" was countered with large banners reading "No Means Now," and "No Means Kick Her In the Teeth" (Thorne-Finch, 1992). Of course, one cannot always judge an organization by its public posture. For example, on some campuses the fraternities (under advice from their national office) who support Take Back the Night marches most strongly are often rumored in the sorority grapevine to have the most actively sexually coercive individual members.

Research on Fraternities and Sororities

Still, one cannot talk long about fraternities without returning to the topic of alcohol. In the section above, we discussed the problem of alcohol abuse, and the contentions of some theorists that fraternity

Box 4.1

Are Fraternity Newsletters Sexist?
A Report From One University

The following posting on the main computer of a southern state university contains a fraternity newsletter piece and a response to it by some other students. Much of the fraternity piece contains very offensive slang, so please skip to the student response about halfway through if this will offend you. The first section contains a section from the fraternity newsletter, with all names removed and replaced with either the word *male* or *female.* We will call the fraternity *ABC.* The passage is filled with bad spelling, bad grammar, jargon such as b/c for because, and unusual use of such words as *meat.* The point of printing this excerpt and response is not to argue that this fraternity or university is unique, except perhaps for the public eloquence of the students who chose to make this public. Depressingly, the fraternity and university are hardly unique.

Meats

(Male) and some chick from Randolph Macon got busy and somewhat bloody the other night. He was all scratched up and shit, and she was all screamin' or something and (male) all heard her and shit then fuckin' (male) hooked up at AST and disappeared. (Male)'s little poetry readin' nits fucked some girl named (female) but about halfway thru, Alex, Mallory, Jennifer, and Mr. Keaton walked in all cryin' about how (male) had just destroyed their family and they won't be together for "a million more years." Anyway, (male) jumps out of bed and starts swingin' a baseball bat around cuz he thought they were all hittin' on his girl. But let's just meat (male)'s dick b/c "he's probably been spankin' it so hard since he hadn't been getting any" (male). Okay, this the best part. Fuckin' smegette (female) who has been getting down w/ (male) and (male) started talkin' shit about how she knew all this stuff about Apocalypse but she won't tell who told her and she's about the dumbest bitch I've ever met almost. So she ends up telling (male) that (male) told her and now everyone's all pissed off at least I am. But anyway, I say we blackball all of these guys and just start over next semester b/c I hate these guys w/ a passion. But (male) and (male) met this girl at Hampden Sydney and (male) was all hangin out w/ her all night getting her all wasted until she passes out on top of him and he's all askin' people for cigs and beers. Right on. So this Lambda Chi guy grabs her and takes her up to his room so (male) and (male) run around the house b/c they want her for themselves and some guy tells (male) that he looks like a girl when he walks in the bathroom and everybody's just so excited about the Homecoming game that (male) and (male) decide to give this girl what she needs and just throw her in the middle of the party room and everyone got laid. Hence the movie w/ Jodie Foster getting raped on a pinball table in a bar. How about that? So I met Gibb Dross on Friday night and he is a damn nice guy. He said that he'd come hang out at ABC when they come back to [this university]. Oh yeah, back to smeg faces saying, "I don't want a relationship, I just want to hook up." She even stood up on (male)'s couch and started kissing him while he was asleep. What a freak. And smeg (male) is never here cuz he's too busy getting hummers, so he says, at Shorts. This guy is all about wearing the hat Mr. Studboy. Anyway, fuck all these guys and Thurs night we can share warm beverages in the attic to get to know each other a little better. God bless you all.

Student letter in response:

Attention

The enclosed document has been circulating amongst a number of [this university's] students. We, the undersigned, are very concerned about the content of this piece of writing, and subsequently have decided to bring it to your attention through this letter. We are confident that the enclosed is part of an ABC fraternity circular intended to reach the brothers of that fraternity. While we would normally avoid getting involved in the private business of a group of fellow students, no matter how distasteful we perceive it to be, we think you would agree that the content of this newsletter excerpt is too frightening to ignore.

In blatantly misogynistic terms, the author implies one rape incident and openly describes another. In the first case, a rape is implied in the sentence "(male) and some chick from Randolph Macon got busy and somewhat bloody the other night. He was all scratched up and shit and she was all screamin' or something and (male) all heard her and shit . . ." In the second case, a gang rape is described, ". . . (male) and (male) decide to give this girl what she needs and just throw her in the middle of the party room and everyone got laid. Hence the movie w/ Jodie Foster getting raped on a pinball table in a bar. How about that?" (Although the gang rape incident is described as occurring at another university, it is supposedly initiated by two [of our university's] ABCs).

Despite what the author of the newsletter may profess, we are certainly NOT accusing the ABC brothers of rape. We also realize that ABC is not the only fraternity that produces newsletters of this type. Instead, our main concern is with the reckless attitudes about rape that are portrayed by the author and subsequently propagated throughout the fraternity through distribution of the letter to other fraternity members.

In a recent article in [a campus newspaper], a spokesperson for the Greek housing system, Robert . . . , said: "We're always in a process of self-evaluation . . . our goal is to make the Greek system as good as it can be." Certainly, callous attitudes about rape do not reflect positively on either the author of the ABC newsletter, ABC, fraternities, or the Greek system. Even if the content and language found in the ABC newsletter excerpt is supposed to be an inside joke, there is a great danger in allowing such misogynistic sentiment to exist. The joke, then, is at the expense of women who come

in contact with men who may be desensitized to sexual
violence against women.

We hope that by exposing this particular incident, awareness will be raised about the ignorance that still runs rampant
on the [this university] campus. It is the potential consequences of this ignorance that we fear the most. If rape can
be treated with such a dangerously casual and cold attitude,
then how far off is dangerous behavior? We anxiously await
immediate action by the recipients of this information, so
that steps can be taken toward raising awareness about the
serious issue of rape.

members were particularly likely to learn to use alcohol or drugs to
commit acts which are legally rape. One important study that lends
strong support to this argument is reported by Boeringer et al. (1991).
They found that fraternity members were no more likely than nonmem-
bers to use physical force to commit rape. However, fraternity members
were significantly more likely to use drugs, alcohol, or various forms of
nonphysical force (such as threats to end a relationship or making false
promises) to obtain sex. Of course, every study has its problems. One of
the important questions in this study was whether the man had ever
"been in a situation where you became so sexually aroused that you
could not stop yourself even though the woman didn't want to have
sex." If a man says yes to this, is it a violent act of rape? Or a nonviolent
and nonphysical act of coercion? Here, the researchers counted it as
nonphysical. You may or may not agree.

Generally, however, research on whether fraternities contribute
to woman abuse is in its infancy. This is especially surprising when
compared to the amount of data on other factors that are statistically
related to female victimization in the university context (see, for
example, Sugarman & Hotaling, 1989). Whether one is discussing
quantitative (statistical) studies or qualitative (theoretical or case)
studies, there is very little information on the structure and interpersonal dynamics of fraternities that contribute to abuse.

There have been theorists who have suggested exactly which
factors should be strongly related to victimization by fraternity mem-

bers. These include a narrow conception of masculinity, which is closely related to homophobia; strong pressures toward conformity within the group; a strong value for group secrecy; and the sexual objectification of women (Hughes & Winston, 1987; Martin & Hummer, 1989; Sanday, 1990). Of course, there is no reason to believe that these factors are something peculiar to fraternities, or that they are only found on college and university campuses. A number of pro-abuse elements are also evident in nonuniversity, all-male groups (Bowker, 1983; Schwartz, 1995). Although certainly most groups have not been studied, it is common to find that all-male social groups are based on elements that promote violence against women. For example, 100 years ago, Clawson (1989) argues, U.S. male fraternal orders were extremely popular in virtually every community. Adult men gathered together for secret meetings based on secret rituals, and, of course, a good deal of male companionship. These groups, however, she argues, were based on rituals designed to celebrate male separation from and domination over women. One can find similar group dynamics in various all-male occupational groups. For one example, men who have worked in policing have seen that occupation as a fraternity-like domain where they could assert their masculinity in a context that often denigrated women (Martin, 1980).

Thus, it cannot be said that college and university fraternities are completely unique in their ability to provide the peer pressure and social support to enable their members to victimize women. Any group of men gathered together can serve that particular purpose. Furthermore, it would be a mistake to argue that all fraternities are designed to promote the sexual victimization of women. Even in those fraternities that do provide such supports, it would be a mistake to assume that all members of the fraternity are similarly influenced to begin to act in this manner.

For example, on some campuses, fraternities can be very large. Let us presume that there are 150 members of the ABC fraternity, which has all of the elements we will discuss below that promote the objectification and denigration of women and which further strongly provides social support for its members for the sexual victimization of women. It would be hard to imagine that all 150 members are similarly affected by this ideology. Some men become closely identified with their fraternity, including its values. Others are only interested in a marginal attachment, perhaps to get invited to the parties and play on the intramural sports teams. Let's further assume that on the campus we are discussing, some fraternities are very sexually aggressive, and some are quite active in opposing acquaintance rape. When a researcher comes in to study this campus, asking "are you a member of a fraternity," what will emerge is a hodgepodge: Some victimizers, some nonvictimizers, some members of victimizing fraternities who do not themselves victimize, some members of nonvictimizing fraternities who do themselves victimize.

What can then happen is that two findings emerge at exactly the same time. First, that some fraternities actively promote sexual victimization of women and have many members who do exactly that. Second, that in a campuswide survey, there is no difference between fraternity members and nonfraternity members in the percentage of men who sexually victimize women.

Indeed, although more simple statistical procedures often show that there is a relationship between fraternities and sexual victimization, when researchers use more complex and sophisticated statistical techniques, this relationship may disappear. This is not because the sexual victimizers disappear: more likely this happens because what is *really* causing the problem can be found outside fraternities as well as inside fraternities. For example, when Boeringer et al. (1991) entered a number of social learning variables into a multivariate (several variables at the same time) analysis of their data, fraternity membership was no longer statistically significant. Rather, the most significant variables in predicting sexual abusers were how many (self-reported) friends the men had who had gotten women high on drugs or drunk in order to have sex with them and how many (self-reported) friends the men had who forced women (or tried to force them) to have sex with them after the women refused.

Similar findings were reported by Schwartz and Nogrady (1996). Here, in a multivariate analysis, the most important variables differentiating sexual victimizers (self-reported) and nonvictimizers were whether the men's friends would approve of getting a woman drunk in order to have sex with her (self-reported) and whether these same friends have actually acted on this belief—whether these friends have actually gotten a women drunk or high on drugs in order to have sex with her (self-reported). There was a third valuable factor in this study: how many drinks the man reported he had each time he went out drinking (sexual victimizers had higher levels of alcohol use). However, fraternity membership as a variable was of no value in this analysis.

Finally, Koss and Gaines (1993) did a study of sexual aggression on a western U.S. campus and found that although fraternity membership and sexual aggression were statistically related (correlated) at a significant level, in a statistical analysis where several variables were entered at once into the analysis, this correlation disappeared. Just as in the above studies, the more important issue seems to be the drinking behavior of the man. Koss and Gaines speculated that the reason fraternity membership was so highly related to sexual aggression was that fraternity members engaged in such an enormous amount of heavy drinking. In other words, any finding of a relationship between fraternity members and sexual aggression may actually be a finding of a relationship between heavy drinking and sexual aggression.

Fraternities and Alcohol

We have devoted some energy to discussing the relationship between alcohol abuse and the sexual victimization of women. If we are concerned about this linkage, then the next step is to look carefully at just where this alcohol abuse (and victimization) is going on. At that point, it is hard to step onto almost any campus and not notice that fraternity houses are the geographic site of a good deal of the alcohol abuse. It does not require a particularly trained observer's eye to figure this out. Most surveys of college students themselves suggest that this is true (Malaney, 1990), and it has been the finding of most researchers who have studied the question (e.g., Hunnicutt, Davis, & Fletcher, 1991). Of course, this does not mean that all fraternity and sorority students drink heavily, or at least drink more than the average college student. As you might expect, there is great variation within all fraternities and sororities on how much members drink and how much these members approve of heavy drinking (Goodwin, 1989).

That said, it still remains true that on the average, fraternity and sorority members drink significantly more than nonaffiliated students. Furthermore, the perceptions of these Greek organization members of the risks involved in heavy drinking are significantly lower than the rest of the student population (Tampke, 1990). We have discussed this point before in the context of whether such abuse is connected with sexual abuse, but we did not look particularly deeply at the connection between fraternities and alcohol.

Klein, for example, has found such connections. He found that in general, college students supported statements promoting responsible drinking behavior, but those most likely to endorse less than responsible behavior were fraternity and sorority members (Klein, 1992a). When drinkers were asked why they engaged in drinking, negative or disintegrative attitudes were mainly given by fraternity and sorority members (Klein, 1992b). Interestingly, although theirs was not a study of victimization, Tyler and Kyes (1992) found that not only were senior members of Greek organizations more likely to report drinking more frequently than other seniors on campus, but they were more likely to report that they consumed alcohol before engaging in sexual intercourse.

Some have suggested a slightly stronger alcohol connection with the fraternity and sorority houses. Globetti, Stern, Marasco, and Hoeppner (1988) found that actual residence in Greek housing (rather than just membership in the organizations) was strongly associated with alcohol abuse. Men in Greek housing did not drink more frequently, but they did drink much more. Women in sorority houses both drank more and more frequently.

The Particular Elements of
Male Peer-Support Groups

The conclusion to draw from the above discussion is that there is no reason to presume that the home of all sexual victimization is the college fraternity, nor that all fraternities or all fraternity members are sexual victimizers. As we shall see below, however, this does not necessarily get fraternities off the hook. However, it should draw our attention to the fact that other groups on campus, such as athletic teams, may provide the same male support as fraternities. Other male groups that might provide this support could be a dormitory floor unit or a group of men who live together off campus. It might be worth noting that just as we cannot automatically assume that all fraternities are the source of increased sexual assaultive behavior, we cannot automatically assume that all-male living arrangements in general, such as dorms, provide more rapists than other types of living arrangements (Boeringer, 1996). Still, although fraternities may not be a unique source of social support for the victimization of women, they certainly are a strong and common source.

If fraternities are not automatically to be presumed as the source of sexual victimization of women on campus, why spend so much time discussing them? The reason is simple. Particularly on residential college campuses, fraternities provide an important part of the campus social life. They provide bonding, friendship, role models, and an opportunity to work together toward a common group goal (Schuh, Triponey, Heim, & Nishimura, 1992). Furthermore, there is no question that many fraternities are sexually predatory, and there are many aspects of fraternities that promote such behavior on the part of at least some of their members. In the sections below, we will discuss what factors promote and make easier this victimization. Still, what we say should be carefully weighed in terms of our two warnings: first, that not every fraternity will be accurately described below, and second, that many other all-male groupings will fit these descriptions.

A Narrow Conception of Masculinity

In the revised model we presented earlier, one of the factors that we felt was related to sexual assault, and that was promoted by such male peer-support groups as the fraternity, is the narrow conception of masculinity. As noted earlier, the ideas involved in doing masculinity are partially the product of sociocultural and psychological shaping, patterning, and evaluating of male behavior (Schur, 1984). In other words, masculinity is socially constructed (Kimmel, 1987) within a complex interaction of systems developed out of race/ethnicity and class relations, along with sexual orientation. Just as with any other ideology or group value, everyone in the social community does not have equal access to the means of socially constructing meaning. Some factions or members have a greater power than others to define what is "appropriate" masculinity, or what we have termed earlier hegemonic masculinity.

There is quite a bit of evidence that fraternity members do not represent a cross-section of North American youth, or even a cross-section of college and university students. Earlier studies found fraternity members more conservative politically and personally than independents (Miller, 1973; Wilder, Hoyt, Doran, Hauck, & Zettle, 1978). More recently, Kalof and Cargill (1991) found both independent women and independent men rejecting ideas of male dominance, sorority women much less rejecting, and fraternity men quite accepting of ideas of traditional male dominant/female submissive attitudes. Of course, just having traditional attitudes toward women does not mean that a person will become sexually coercive (Rapaport & Burkhart, 1984). He might, for example, become chivalrous and condescending, but not sexually coercive. Although they are dealing with the similar problem of physical abuse of women rather than with sexual abuse, Worth, Matthews, and Coleman (1990) were surprised to find that 50% of their abusive students, but only 8% of nonabusive students, were in Greek organizations. They speculated that technically it is not membership in such groups that causes the mathematical effect, but rather the different sex-role orientation of fraternity men, compared to other men on campus. However, it isn't just narrow questions of male dominance that are involved in these studies of Greek life. Other studies have found fraternities much more likely than others to promote both subtle and fairly blatant sexism and racism (Goettsch & Hayes, 1990; Muir, 1991).

Fraternity men, then, may have a narrow notion of masculinity that is the product of peer pressure and various other social exchanges. "Brothers" commonly learn from their friends that they are supposed to have stereotypical masculine attributes, such as a clean-cut, handsome appearance, athletic skills, wealth, a high tolerance for alcohol, and sexual success with women. In addition, they learn that they should not have effeminate physical and personality traits or take courses in disciplines regarded as the domains of women and homosexuals. Examples of these classes are nursing, social work, art, and music (Martin & Hummer, 1989). Thus, in fraternities, masculinity is also defined according to what it is *not* feminine or homosexual (Herek, 1987). Worse, one of the effects of the male bonding and peer relations in fraternities is that it may be more difficult to break out of this social learning to express one's own feelings. Greek men, particularly in the first 2 years of college, often feel compelled to adopt without challenge the various norms espoused by their fraternity. At the same time that other college students are facing new challenges, practicing introspection, learning, and growing morally, fraternities breed in their members a form of dependency that protects members from challenging the beliefs they have been given. Kilgannon and Erwin (1992), for example, found the moral development over time of fraternity men to be significantly below that of other students on campus.

Fraternities use a variety of procedures to ensure that members adhere to their standards and expectations of masculinity. The initiation ritual is, however, one of the most successful methods of ensuring conformity to gender-appropriate norms. It is also a bonding mechanism that attempts to ensure life-long loyalty to the fraternity. As Sanday (1990) points out, the initiation ritual produces

> a transformation of consciousness so that group identity and attitudes become personalized. The process includes a symbolic sacrifice of the self (or some part of the self) to a superior body that represents the communal identity of the house. The sacrifice acts to seal a covenant between the individual pledge and the fraternal organization. Reinforced by a vow of secrecy, the covenant promises masculinity and superior power. By yielding himself to the group in this way, the pledge gains a new self, complete with a set of goals, concerns, visions, and ready-made discourses that are designed to help him negotiate the academic, social, and sexual contexts of undergraduate life from a position of power and status. (p. 135)

As stated previously, group secrecy is a fundamental component of fraternity discourse (Roark, 1987). It is also a support function that contributes to woman abuse.

Group Secrecy

One of the more difficult topics to discuss about groups such as fraternities is the development of a pact of group secrecy. Silence is one of the most common ways in which fraternities perpetuate and legitimate individual and gang rapes. Whether it is a college fraternity, a street gang, or a tightly knit group of police officers engaged in graft, "brothers" do not reveal their peers' deviant or abusive behaviors to "outsiders." This is true even if these actions are investigated by campus authorities and criminal justice personnel (Martin & Hummer, 1989). Although it no doubt happens often enough, the usual case is not a conspiratorial plot. Fraternity members do not sit around tables, like some terrible made-for-TV movie about the Mafia, discussing group secrecy and the penalties for those who violate "the code," although certainly we have evidence that this has happened many times. Still, the codes of silence and the demand for group loyalty mean that few crimes committed in fraternity houses are punished (Bernstein, 1996a).

For the most part, members do remain silent. Why would this be the case? Why would one member of such a group cover up for another member, who might not even be a friend, when to do so might mean engaging in serious felony behavior? Given the size of many fraternities and the diversity of opinion within them, it cannot only be because members are afraid of reprisal. The source of the problem goes deeper than that.

One reason is the development of a new self in the fraternity. Sanday (1990), as quoted above, has pointed to the fraternity ritual as a source of this new identity. She is not alone in her arguments. Smith (1964) agrees with Sanday that the degradation ceremonies in initiation rites are designed to transform the new members into people who identify with the group. His basic argument is that the real change comes when this group loyalty stops being based on instrumental goals (e.g., win the softball tournament, get "best fraternity" honors) and turns to expressive group loyalty.

> Pledging of commitment to the group cannot be simply a matter of oaths and signatures but must involve transition through a period of instrumental degradation which compels the group of recruits to develop a sense of solidarity regardless of whether they have at the time developed friendships with one another. The solidarity which they develop during this period persists when the instrumental cause has disappeared. (p. 32)

Thus, it is these "bonds of brotherhood," created through initiation rituals and other social interactions, that encourage members to protect their friends from public stigmatization and punishment, even if they must lie to investigators in order to achieve this end. What is most important about this is not the end result in any particular case. Of course, it is important that in any one specific and particular case, one or more men evade punishment for rape because of an implicit code of silence. However, the message that this delivers to all of the other men on campus is much more important. From that time on, when a brother victimizes a woman, he knows that his peers will not attempt to stop him or cooperate with "agents of social control," such as advisers, Greek Affairs counselors, the police, or student judiciary officers. Certainly Merton (1985) is quite right when he argues that acts of public silence teach men that "no matter how sleazy your actions, there is always the fraternity to hide behind" (p. 64). What is so important in all of this discussion is that group secrecy tells all violent men that their actions are not wrong. It is a lesson that a great many have learned very well, and put into action.

Perhaps this lesson would not be easy to learn if many violent men were being punished, either formally or else at least by the disapproval of most of the college community. Unfortunately, this silence is linked to another important variable to be discussed later: the absence of deterrence.

The Sexual Objectification of Women

In addition to learning to hide their peers' deviant activities, fraternity members are often taught to sexually objectify women. Rather than regarding them as complete people, brothers often conceptualize women as subordinate "things" to be used as sexual outlets, as servants at parties, or as "bait" to attract new members (Stombler, 1994). There are a number of methods by which this can be done. Language is an important method of dehumanization. We have mentioned before that Scully (1990) has shown that imprisoned rapists often use shared vocabularies to either deny that the acts they have committed are rape (she wanted it, she deserved it) or to deny responsibility for the rape (I was drunk and therefore not responsible). In another example, Miller and Schwartz (1992) argued that the widespread use of sexual objects ranging from inflatable dolls to nutcrackers made in the shape of nude women are important props in the maintenance of an ideology of objectification. The key point, as Schur (1984) points out, is that in these groups women tend to be seen through a lens in which the only thing of importance is their femaleness, not their accomplishments, status, intelligence, or position. This narrow focus makes it possible to be treated only as a member of a category, devalued and objectified. It is possible to see individual accomplishments as secondary; to see all women as alike, as subordinate, as something that things can be "done to."

Some "brothers" are first exposed to this type of sexual objectification when they join a fraternity. Others, however, devalued women before entering the fraternity. Indeed, some joined fraternities mainly because they wanted to develop friendships with those who shared their sexist ideology, seeing the fraternity as a refuge from university-led ideas about equality for women. Others joined because they thought they would have more access to sexually active women (Sanday, 1990). Given the fact that many fraternity subcultures regard women as "nonpersons" or objects, it is no surprise that many members abuse these women (Schwartz, 1991).

Many of us find it hard to understand how someone can treat another human being as an object. Actually, scholars have done extensive research on this subject in other contexts. For example, how would it be possible to take Africans to America and to make them into slaves? How can you make human beings into slaves to be bought and sold? One way is to convince yourself that Africans are not only savages but cannibals, which allows you to conclude that they are not really fully human. This is exactly what was done (Turner, 1993). More recently, we have the evidence of the Holocaust, where the Germans killed millions of Jews and other peoples they did not like for one reason or another. How can a supposedly civilized people simply kill off millions of other humans? In another example, many social scientists have turned their attention to the recent period when America locked up the mentally ill and people of low mental capacity in places characterized by brutal conditions (Foucault, 1977; Goffman, 1961; Rosenhan, 1973). What we learned is that people in relatively powerful social positions find it relatively easy to brutally victimize stigmatized persons because they consider them as having little personal value, and thus being worthy of abuse (Schur, 1984). This applies to gender relations also. If the relatively powerful can convince themselves that another group (women) has little value, and that its members serve as objects of their sexual attention, then it is much easier to justify abusing these people.

Sports Teams and Violence Against Women

We have made it clear that although many authors link college fraternities with violence against women, they are not the only source of male peer support for such violence. The second most common group implicated in gang rape is sports teams (Neimark, 1991). When looking at the wider question of rapes and sexual assaults of all types, various researchers have found different numbers, but all agree on the basic proposition that there is a problem with male athletes sexually victimizing women (Eskenazi, 1991). For example, Crosset, Ptacek, McDonald, and Benedict (1996) reported, in a survey of 3 years of judicial affairs records of 10 Division I schools (five of which were perennial sports powers), that whereas male athletes made up 3.3% of the student body, they accounted for 19% of the sexual assaults. Frintner and Rubinson (1993) found even stronger results in their Midwestern study. Although male athletes were less than 2% of that student body, members of sports teams represented 22.6% of the perpetrators of forced vaginal, anal, or oral intercourse. Interestingly, athletes represented a much smaller, although still very over-represented, percentage of those who were reported committing attempted sexual assaults, sexual abuse, battery, or intimidation. Other studies, including a National Institute of Mental Health survey, have argued that athletes participate in one third of all sexual assaults on U.S. campuses (Melnick, 1992).

We know that many of the same factors that affect fraternities are important with athletes: the male bonding that leads to the objectification of women, the tight vows of secrecy that prevent exposure, and the victim blaming that allows even public cases to be ignored. One factor that is often added to the mix when athletes are considered is the coach. Nelson (1994), a former college and professional basketball player herself, argues that "when we begin to understand how male coaches and players speak and think about women and masculinity, it ceases to be surprising that college football and basketball players gang-rape women in numbers equaled only by fraternity brothers" (p. 7). She particularly takes aim at coaches who make it plain that the worst thing that a male under his charge could do is to develop any traits that would mark him as sympathetic to that dreaded enemy, women:

> Coaches who would be fired for calling athletes "nigger" employ with impunity such terms as "cunt." "Faggot" is another popular derogation. It refers not so much to sex between men as to weakness, timidity, cowardice—and femininity. . . . In response to "wimpy" performances, male coaches have been known to deposit tampons, sanitary napkins, and bras in young men's lockers. "You have debased yourself to the level of a woman" is the message. (p. 87)

Thorne-Finch (1992) explains this problem in some more depth. He argues that the way that North American team sport is taught and coached contributes not only to all of the good aspects of participation, but also to some very dangerous traditions. The most important of these dangerous traditions is to underline and force-feed to boys views of masculinity that are based as much on being "not-female" as on anything else. Little boys are commonly coached by derision. For example, they are taught to throw baseballs in the way most likely to harm their shoulders, because the alternative is to "throw like a girl." Thus, as Thorne (1993) points out, boys and girls can certainly work together and play together from the youngest ages, but most of the divisions between them are set by adults. From the sports teams organized for the youngest boys up through professional sports, one of the prized motivational moves by coaches is to accuse their charges of playing like girls or women. Messner (1994) calls the result of all of this "sexual schizophrenia," which means that all male athletes have to take part in aggressive sexual talk in the locker room, while keeping any emotional attachments they might have with females a secret.

Interestingly, this idea of pitting boys against each other in combat is not something that has had a long history in American culture. Rotundo (1993), for example, argues that the concept that being "competitive" as something positive wasn't even part of the English language until the late 1800s. It is in that era that sports moved from being good exercise to being a form of combat that breeds a forceful manhood. It was an era when the white middle class began to celebrate the primitive man, with an emphasis on camping, lodges, boy scouts, and minstrel shows.

The training of a sports team to sacrifice everything to a group goal, and to immediately accept the complete authority of the leaders, may make some athletes unable to disagree with a group's goal, even if that goal is illegal, dangerous, or immoral. The male bonding in these groups, who work, live, and play together every day for years, can be very powerful. It starts with the peer group values on athletic teams, values that encourage athletes to treat women as objects of conquest (Messner, 1992). This group bonding can be so strong that such men are willing to take part in rape, or to observe rape, or at least to take part in a cover-up, because the alternative is to go against the group. It becomes more important to be part of the group than it is to do the right thing (Neimark, 1991). This is why, many argue, so many essentially "good" kids can take part in a gang rape, or stand and watch a woman being held down and raped in a dormitory room while she screams, or just brush off hearing about such an event the next day without even considering taking any action against it. Thorne-Finch (1992) notes,

Box 4.2

Rape by Student Athletes: Katie's Story

Katie, who reports in the letter below to the student newspaper that she was raped by a star athlete now playing professionally, is an example of the frustration of many women who feel that the university does not offer them security or comfort.

To The Editor:

I was raped about a year ago at XXXX University's campus by a very public member of the student body. I never thought my life could have been turned so upside down by one person.

He did not put a gun to my head or threaten my life, but sometimes I have thought that would have been better. Then I would have had a excuse for "letting this happen." I have listened to many stories of women who have been raped, and no matter what the circumstances, the woman thinks she did something, or could have done something to prevent being raped.

Why are the lives of women so controlled and limited because we have to protect ourselves from the actions a man may perpetrate on us? All women's lives are affected by rape, whether they have been a victim or not. "Don't go out alone after dark. Carry your keys between your fingers. Don't look at him that way. Don't wear that outfit." Women hear these admonitions from the time they are young girls. Society's attitudes need to change so that men and women can stop this behavior. Young boys need to learn that "No means no. Maybe means no. Silence means no. Be responsible for your actions."

I did not ask to be raped. No woman does, yet we suffer the consequences daily, for many, many years. Meanwhile, the rapist keeps on living his life and probably keeps on raping. I have given up a lot, including my enrollment at XXXX University, just to keep my sanity.

I struggle with the fact that I did not prosecute. When I went to the hospital the next day, I did not get a rape exam, because I had not accepted that *I was raped.* Any evidence I had was gone. In court it would have been my word against this well-known member of the student body. Any chance of the school reprimanding him was highly unlikely, based on stories I have read regarding how colleges handle rapes. A letter was written to President Y at XXXX University about my incident. He replied that they were trying to raise awareness of this issue. No response was ever received from a letter written to the student's basketball coach. This type of thing is obviously no big deal to them, if they can smooth it over. Rape happens all the time, on all college campuses, to all types of women, by all types of men.

I know that I was not this rapist's only victim. I wish I could talk to the other women who have been victimized by this man. If we, as women, stand up together, abusers and rapists shall get the punishment they deserve. I know I have suffered plenty, and for what?

One thing I have learned from this experience is that I must listen to my "inner angel." When things don't seem right, don't think twice. Go with your heart.

Katie

Organized sport reinforces a notion central to traditional male culture that all male interaction—whether at the individual or national level—is adversarial and requires competitive skill and cunning to be practiced successfully. Whatever the metaphor, the notion regarding women is the same. Like enemy territory during war, they are to be conquered, and this is best done by able-bodied athletic hunks. Limp-wristed faggots need not apply. (pp. 106-107)

As we have discussed, one of the factors that makes possible the high level of sexual assault is the permission that the rest of society gives to men to engage in this behavior. Fraternity advisers, coaches, dormitory directors, and other college officials generally see a lot of "boys will be boys" in rape. Of course, once the event is defined as rape, few are able to dismiss it. What people who want to dismiss the event need to do is to change the definition of what just happened. For a woman who came to a dorm room to pick up lecture notes for an exam but was raped instead, the excuse is that she was willingly in a male dorm and should have known why she was invited. Many men are smart enough to only victimize women who are drunk, or else have agreed to have sex with another member of the team. This allows the rest of the campus to shrug it off: She came up there looking for sex, she got drunk voluntarily.

As we have said before, when the word *sex* comes up, people's moral values suddenly come to a halt. People who have campaigned for more prisons, more police, and longer sentences for criminals suddenly find it difficult to understand the difference between agreeing to a romantic sexual tryst with one man and consenting to group sex for hours while screaming and begging for mercy in a room full of strange men. We continue to hold women to blame for men's behavior.

What makes athletic teams special is that so many people have such a strong vested interest in seeing the charges dropped or bad behavior covered up. Journalists often report that police chiefs, college administrators, and others will brag about getting charges dropped. In those cases that go to trial, the jurors themselves will often acquit athletes rather than see the upcoming season ruined (Neimark, 1991). To pick one example, at the time of this writing, a judge trying to start the trial of a professional football player for drug possession was quoted by the press as complaining bitterly that he could not empanel a jury pool, because so many people said that they could not vote to convict such an important member of the team. One other interesting, and all too typical, example: a major sports magazine ran a story about how a number of players on a national championship college football team accepted cash payments and a variety of expensive presents from sleazy recruiters for agents. If this had been made public earlier, none of the players would have played in a bowl game, and the school probably would have lost the national championship. At the time, major penalties were still a possibility. The response of national sports columnists was for the most part low key and uninterested. One dismissed the entire controversy, suggesting that if schools paid athletes a weekly allowance, then athletes would not take thousands of dollars in violation of the rules. Under the best of circumstances, sports researchers argue, athletes feel that they are above the law and that rules often do not apply to them. Too often they are right. To fans, many students, professors, administrators, and some of the nation's most influential sports writers, they *are* above the law.

Of course, if athletes are allowed to rape women that they barely know, they certainly are given more leeway to assault women with whom they are intimately involved. The *Washington Post*, for example, did a count between the time that O. J. Simpson pleaded "no contest" (legally, the equivalent to pleading guilty) to spousal battery in November 1994. They found 140 other current and former pro and college football athletes reported to the police for violent behavior toward women. During that period 43 active National Football League players were accused specifically of domestic violence ("NFL Asked," 1996). What is it about North American football that makes such a high percentage of men in one profession engage in violence against their intimate partners? Lawyer Alan Dershowitz has often argued that athletes are really not more violent, but only more under the microscope of media attention. Russell (1983), however, argues that the tremendous work we do to teach aggression to athletes leads to an increase in aggressive behavior off the field. A more common answer, as mentioned above, is that athletes learn that women are acceptable commodities and objects of their physical rage, while at the same time they know full well that they too often are above the law and can get away with it. Because the NFL and the NCAA do not enforce any rules against having violent physical and sexual aggressors on teams, in many cases the worst that can happen to a good ballplayer is that he will be thrown off a team and be forced to go to another one. Telander (1989), a former college star football player and later a regular *Sports Illustrated* writer on football, argues strongly that North American sports promote the objectification of women:

> In my years in locker rooms, I have heard so much degrading talk of women by male athletes—particularly the use of women as objects to be conquered and dominated rather than as equals to be dealt with fairly—that I feel certain the macho attitudes promoted by coaches contribute (perhaps unwittingly) to athletes' problems in relating to women. (p. 88)

Certainly most athletes would claim that they were engaging in harmless joking around. Curry (1991), who has done one of the best-known ethnographies of sports locker room talk, says that most athletes he studied claimed just that, although he hastens to add that he never saw anyone publicly challenge the locker room's dominant sexism and homophobia.

What is particularly important to recall about all of this discussion is that there is no clear line from patriarchal attitudes to violence. After all, adhering strongly to an ideology of male dominance could just as easily (and often does) lead to a system of chivalry in which women may be dominated but are never assaulted sexually. Life is more complex than a simple formula that requires us to see that patriarchy causes masculinity causes violence. Earlier in this book, we discussed the fact that there are many masculinities. Different conditions, practices, beliefs, communities, and circumstances all lead to different outcomes. As we shall see in the next chapter, this is a positive viewpoint. It assumes that there can be change. If violence is caused by some unalterable single cause (e.g., masculinity), then we could only give up. If a wide variety of practices cause violence, then we have the power to identify some of them, and to attempt to make changes (Brown & Hogg, 1993).

Absence of Deterrence

The arguments in this book have all centered on the *presence* of one or more factors that make it more likely that sexual assault will occur. Thus, we have argued that in a culture marked by male dominance, in a group that provides male peer support for violence, in an atmosphere where alcohol is abused, men are more likely to assault women. Yet, there are other things we could study. One is deterrence. Are there factors that, if present, would tend to stop the behavior in question? For example, in a town where jaywalking is a serious problem, will placing a couple of police officers handing out tickets for jaywalking put a dent in the number of people who violate that law? That is at least a research question.

The question asks about the presence of deterrence. One can also look at the absence of deterrence. If there are no punishments for violating the law (if there is an absence of deterrence), will that increase the frequency of the behavior? It is our argument that on college campuses, the model we have thus far explained is not sufficient to account for the large amount of violence against women. One must further look at the lack of punishments or deterrence.

Of course, this is a difficult area of study, because we are trying to locate exactly the reason why people *don't* engage in a behavior. Criminologists for years have discussed the fact that deterrence is one of the most difficult areas to discuss, because we are measuring the *absence* of an act, rather than the *presence* of an act (Gibbs, 1975). Think about yourself. Why didn't you burglarize an apartment the last time you had the chance? Was it because of the criminal law? Because you were too scared? Because you could never face your relatives (parents, children) if you were arrested for felony burglary? Because you learned moral values in the church or synagogue or mosque as a child, which now keep you from burglary? The answer is mixed up and complicated for all of us. If you are like most of us, you don't really know why you are not committing burglaries; the answer is some combination of all of the above factors. Still, sociological and criminological researchers have begun to find that there are some times when some people who might have a tendency to commit a crime can be deterred from doing so.

Now in one way, the lack of deterrence is really exactly the same thing as male peer support, only stated backward. In many situations, we know that it is not formal punishment that keeps people from committing crime, but informal punishment from one's social group (Anderson, Chiricos, & Waldo, 1977; Pate & Hamilton, 1992). If your friends will stop talking to you, if you stand to lose your job, if your marriage partner will leave you, you just might shape up. On the other hand, we cannot assume that the threat of punishment is always a deterrent. In many times and places, a few days or even months in the county jail might even make you a hero to some of your friends (DeKeseredy & Schwartz, 1996).

This is not some wild-eyed theory we have just concocted. It is, in fact, one of the central points of most criminological theory. One of the most famous policing experiments ever run is the Kansas City, Missouri, test of deterrence more than 20 years ago. Here, districts were assigned one of three possible police coverages: normal police patrolling, a proactive patrol force that provided more than twice the usual number of police, and a reactive patrol force that only went out when called to the scene of a crime. The key is that nothing much happened: There was no change in the amount of crime, citizens' attitudes toward the police, or people's fear of arrest if they committed a crime (Kelling, Pate, Dieckman, & Brown, 1974). In other words, and a good textbook in criminal justice should cover this material in detail, such factors as increasing surveillance will not cut crime.

Unfortunately, we also have a limited amount of evidence that higher penalties will have an effect. In Chapter 5, we will take up some discussion of this issue, including our recommendations on what a college campus can do to deal with problems of woman abuse. For the time being, however, we can report that there are times when well-publicized penalties imposed on a few violators will have an effect. Furthermore, although it may not affect the community generally, some offenders themselves are able to stop committing crimes after being punished (this is known as specific deterrence). However, as an overall summary of a large amount of research, punishment is not our best answer to controlling people's behavior. Generally, although many criminologists believe that some punishments are effective, the bulk of the most sophisticated research in the field over a long period of time shows that punishment does not particularly stop, deter, or control crime (Siegel, 1993). It may exact retribution or get people off the streets, which are different issues, but it does not particularly stop, deter, or control crime.

What does seem to have some effect are informal sanctions. When people you really care about are very unhappy or even angry with you, you are more likely to reassess your behavior. Furthermore, when you have something serious to lose, such as an excellent job or a good set of human relationships, your chances of being deterred are certainly stronger than with formal punishments. Thus, on the positive side, what we would learn from criminological theory is that the best way to stop the assault of women on college campuses would be to work to develop an intellectual atmosphere where such behavior was not tolerated, where the man involved would be ashamed of himself, and where he would stand to be shunned by people who were formerly his friends (Tittle, 1980). This does not have to be a situation where such men were automatically banished, to become bitter and angry and even more abusive to other potential victims. Braithwaite and Daly (1994) show that there are mechanisms that can shame men into stopping their violence against women but at the same time provide an avenue for them to be accepted back into the community if they do so. The problem is that it is simply not true on many American college campuses that acquaintance rapists will be given the message that this behavior will not be tolerated. Quite the opposite may be true.

Still, we do not want to overstate the case. A number of important research studies have taken informal sanctions into account but still found that the threat of formal sanctions can have some effect on behavior (Hawkins & Alpert, 1989). The problem is that on most college campuses, there are neither formal nor informal sanctions for many men who engage in woman abuse (Bohmer & Parrot, 1993). *The New York Times* studied the campus disciplinary system in the United States and concluded that fraternities occupy a special place in college and university judicial systems: Not only do "thousands of criminal offenses virtually disappear each academic year," but in those cases where "student courts do mete out significant penalties, a fraternity appeal to the administration—bolstered by fraternity alumni—often results in the sanction being reduced or overturned" (Bernstein, 1996a, p. B8). Bernstein was particularly interested in a case at Miami University of Ohio, where the offender (who was witnessed raping the woman and had confessed in writing) was placed on student affairs probation as his only punishment. Three days later, a male friend of the victim, who sat by her side during the hearing to give her emotional support, was suspended from the university for possessing a beer while under-age (Bernstein, 1996c).

This lack of sanctions, Sanday (1990) argues, explains why there are large groups of men on college campuses who are actually pro-abuse and who hold numerous pro-abuse group activities. If the key issue in preventing woman abuse is to get men to worry about what would happen to their reputations if they were discovered as woman abusers, then it should be obvious why there is so much woman abuse. As a broad and general statement, most men on most campuses (not all men on all campuses) will not lose much if conduct abusive to women comes to the attention of campus officials. The reason, simply, is that on many of these campuses school officials will not seriously punish men who batter and/or sexually abuse women (Bohmer & Parrot, 1993; McMillen, 1990).

To return again to criminology, one of the most popular theories to explain criminal activity recently has been rational choice theory, which argues that offenders commit crimes because the benefits of committing the crime outweigh the risks of doing it (Clarke & Cornish, 1985). To the extent that college men rationally weigh the potential outcomes of their behavior, the rewards for abusing women may seem to outweigh the costs.

One common explanation for some campus administrations' failure to sanction men who aggress against women is that these administrations are dominated by male decision makers who lack a sensitivity to women's concerns. Some of these people are either uncomfortable with or are uninterested in formulating policies designed to reduce the number of women who are victimized by men on campus. Ironically, many schools are now writing sexual harassment policies and beginning to take seriously complaints of sexual harassment. Still, peer sexual harassment is not a subject commonly discussed on campus, and some bureaucrats and security officers still try to hide reports of sexual assault. Of course, some fraternities, universities, and campus security forces are taking appropriate and long-needed actions to prevent woman abuse and to punish offenders. However, other universities still provide institutional support for the male peer-group dynamics that perpetuate and legitimate female victimization and for the abusive behaviors of individual and group perpetrators.

Most interestingly, this is not a completely isolated case. One other area where many colleges actively support attitudes that are harmful is in the field of race relations. On many campuses, white fraternities and sororities are well-known as bastions not only of white privilege, but also of outright and active racism. It is widely supposed (for good reason) that the universities of the Deep South are the worst offenders in this regard, but many universities in the North have nothing of which to be proud. As Muir (1991) has noted, because Greek social organizations tend to operate on university property under official authority, "racism would appear to be tacitly supported, if not subsidized, by the parent institution" (p. 99). Because Greek organizations are often so powerful on campus and among alumni, "the likelihood that campus administrators will feel a personal commitment to address the issue, and have the courage to take the entailed career risk, may not be great." *The New York Times* has recently pointed out that no matter how strong colleges are in fighting other student abuses, they "continue to handle fraternity crimes with all the leniency and discretion a closed-door system of justice can afford" (Bernstein, 1996a, p. B8).

Of course, the analogy is not perfect. Both men and women are actively racist on some campuses and in some organizations. Where the analogy is to the long-term effects of campus learning, then it is a good one. As Muir suggests, because campus life is often where "connections" are made on the way to career goals, undergraduate racist organizations may help to maintain economic racial inequality. The same factors may work in gender relations, where lessons learned in all-male networks can spill over to the board room later. However, in the context of the topic of this book, what is important is that the attitudes men develop and learn on college campuses can result in some men, under strong peer influence, attacking women physically and sexually. The attack Muir makes on college administrators is just as true here: College administrators are fully aware that these attacks are taking place and that they are fostered by the very organizations they subsidize and support.

Summary

In this chapter, we have covered the main part of the revised male peer-support model. Alcohol has been seen to be a major problem on college campuses, with use increasing in recent years, especially for women. This can be a particular problem when both men and women are not aware that it is illegal, that in fact it is rape, when a man has sexual intercourse or other sexual contact with a women who is too drunk to resist or to give consent. Males learn lessons like this, and also that women can be treated as sexual objects appropriate for attack, through male peer-support groups, which might include fraternities and sports groups. Through such groups, and their extensive use of alcohol, men learn a narrow conception of masculinity, the value of group loyalty and group secrecy that protects rapists within the group, and the idea that women are appropriate objects of sexual attack.

Sports teams have similar but often somewhat different problems, with perhaps the most important one being the input of adult authorities, such as coaches, who play an important role in the degrading and objectification of women.

University authorities, to whom we turn our attention in the next chapter, have an important role to play on those campuses where there is an absence of deterrence—where men learn quickly that there is no true punishment for rape and where women quickly learn that going through campus judiciaries only makes a bad situation worse. This is particularly a problem when the university is sponsoring, promoting, and helping to pay for Greek organizations that are actively racist and sexist.

5

Prevention and Policy Implications

A central focus of this book has been that many college and university campuses provide an unsafe learning environment for women. In this chapter, we will take up some issues that are useful for people interested in making this environment safer. Of course, it is important to note that the bulk of the analysis and recommendations here are just as important for the increasingly recognized problem of male rape on campus. If, as we suggest in this book, the rape and attempted rape of women is extraordinarily underreported on college campuses, gay men suggest that the rape of men on campus is just as underreported (Scarce, 1995).

Obviously, there is a wide variety of suggestions in the literature on how to accomplish this safer atmosphere, and unfortunately many of them conflict with each other. As the journalist H. L. Mencken is reputed to have written many years ago, "For every problem, there is a solution which is simple, neat, and wrong." It is far beyond the scope of one chapter to describe and evaluate the vast array of policy proposals advanced by academics, campus administrators, criminal justice officials, faculty groups, and student organizations. Instead, where we are forced to narrow our focus, we will concentrate primarily on recommendations that are consistent with our male peer-support model. These measures involve taking an explicit *stand for women* and are designed to prevent males from sexually assaulting women on campuses and their immediate surroundings (Ellis & DeKeseredy, 1996).

We are also deeply concerned about the ways in which some types of media coverage contribute to the anti-feminist backlash and to sexual assault survivors' pain and suffering. Thus, in addition to discussing pro-feminist men's individual and collective strategies, educational campaigns, alcohol policies, codes of conduct and disciplinary procedures, and *reintegrative shaming* (Braithwaite, 1989), we will address the role of *news-making criminology*. News-making criminology is defined by Barak (1988) as "the conscious efforts of criminologists and others to participate in 'newsworthy' items about crime and justice" (p. 565).

The key argument of news-making criminology is that it is essential for pro-woman researchers not only to present their alternate messages to academic and community groups, but also to make strong attempts to reach out though the mass media (Dobash & Dobash, 1988). One of the most important lessons that sociology has to teach is that most people do not have access to the full story on most issues, and therefore must act on a more limited set of information. For example, few of us have dozens of friends who were raped, dozens more who are rapists, and more who are philosophers, lawyers, psychologists, sociologists, and criminologists, who can interpret what these people feel and think. What most people react to are representations of this reality, or news stories, "sound bites," feature films, television specials, and political speeches, which filter and interpret this information. This makes "the role of important elites and the media in disseminating ideas and 'facts' . . . frequently crucial in influencing public opinion" (Henslin, 1990, p. 61).

Before we discuss these measures, it is first necessary to evaluate one of the most common prevention strategies, *target hardening*. This approach includes measures that make it more hazardous to engage in crime (e.g., guard dogs, razor wire-topped walls) and/or more difficult and time consuming (e.g., alarms, increased lighting). Those who support target hardening contend that these initiatives and strategies, such as video security cameras, security guards, and student escorts or patrols, decrease the likelihood of sexual assault by increasing the probability of detection and capture. However, as we shall argue in the next section, these measures are by and large ineffective directly, although they may still have some value indirectly.

Target Hardening: Sexual Assault Prevention Through Opportunity Reduction

What safety measures a campus administration chooses to take (what targets to harden) depends, of course, on what the administration defines as the offender. After all, one fortifies the defenses against the enemy one expects to engage. Unfortunately, most of the safety measures implemented by campus officials thus far have served to perpetuate the widespread but outdated view that women are most likely to be victimized by strangers. If the problem is defined as stranger rapists wandering around the campus, then curbing sexual assault is mostly a matter of architectural design. For this reason, the typical measures taken across North America include increased lighting, changed landscaping (e.g., removing trees and bushes), the provision of escort services, the monitoring of public places, and the installation of alarms and security phones (Currie & MacLean, 1993). As Roiphe (1993) points out, the major accomplishment of all of this has been to ruin the natural evening beauty of many college campuses, in favor of the reflections of never-used, blue-lighted campus security telephones. The problem with these services is that women are most likely to be sexually assaulted by male intimates in private places, such as houses or apartments (Stanko, 1990).

Such services not only give women an incorrect message about the places where they should be concerned, but they also breed an unhealthy dependence. To pick one example, on one major college campus of 20,000 students, there had not been a single murder, or a single forcible or nonforcible rape of any type reported to the police in the past year. The women's studies newsletter published these crime figures without comment, and then on the same page printed a series of tips from the campus police department, which included telling women never to walk alone on campus after dark. This can lead to extraordinary sights, such as one viewed by one of the authors of this book, where more than 25 women stood around the lobby of the library for an extended period of time, waiting for the single, male 5 foot, 6 inch, 160-pound campus escort patrol officer to arrive to walk them back to their dormitories. It is hard to imagine a rapist who would attack 25 women but would back off when he discovered a man in the group. One can only speculate on how many women were convinced by the university, the police, and the women's studies program to avoid going to the library, to avoid taking classes at night, to avoid clubs, meetings, and parties at night, for fear of stranger attacks that, on this campus, almost never happen.

Scanlon (1994) endorses the argument that the greatest danger to women comes from men they know:

> In a sense, the physical landscape of the campus has become a scapegoat for the problem of violence against women. A safe world for women will not be one in which there are emergency phones on every street corner, guards at every building entrance, or 24 hours of daylight. Unless and until we make it our business to change the behavior of men, who commit approximately 89% of all violent crimes in the United States, we will not resolve the problem. (p. 32)

As suggested above, one of the easiest and most common ways that colleges and universities try to make women safer is to provide them with advice on precautions to take. Typically, these suggestions include: jog only on main, well-lit roads; don't hitchhike; never remain alone in a laundry room, mail room, or parking garage; don't use isolated bus stops; use caution in conversations with strangers; take self-defense courses; pay for your own expenses on dates so that your partner does not interpret your actions as a transaction in which you now owe him sexual gratification; and so forth. Many women are familiar with this advice and many people regard it as common sense. However, do these and other target-hardening measures work? Of course, these strategies may lessen the risk of being sexually assaulted by stereotypical strangers or some first dates. Even so, they do little, if anything, to deter the most common forms of sexual assault on campus and its immediate surroundings: date and acquaintance rape. For most women, private—not public—places pose the greatest threat to their well-being. Furthermore, as pointed out in the next section, under some circumstances, such steps can make the problem worse for many women.

There is, perhaps, one interesting exception to this line of argument. One of the things we know is that male violence forces many women to limit their activities: they take fewer night courses, participate less in study groups and campus activities, and spend less time at the library. All of these things reduce the value of the college experience for women. Extremely expensive blue lights with hotlines to the campus police and improved lighting across campus probably do absolutely nothing to improve safety for women (Steinberg, 1991). What they might do is to improve women's *perceived* safety, which might encourage them to take a more active role in campus life, and to reduce their dependence on others (Scanlon, 1994). Thus, in an indirect way, these useless devices might indeed be useful.

Of course, many administrators implement these devices because they are genuinely concerned about women's safety. Others are mainly informed by their legal staffs that they face the possibility of losing expensive lawsuits if they are sued by victimized women after the college refused to provide a safe environment. And, of course, it is always easier to change the physical environment than it is to respond to the attitudes and beliefs that perpetuate and legitimate sexual assault on the college campus. As Bohmer and Parrot (1993) point out,

> Actually, aside from the financial issues, we have found that these security issues are the easiest to resolve, because they do not require any attitudinal change on the part of college administrators. Everyone recognizes the importance of having the campus free from crime in general and such solutions as proper lighting, maintenance, and policing are simple to implement. It is those areas that require a reorientation of college administrators' attitudes that present many colleges with difficulty. This is especially true for acquaintance rape cases that occur within a party setting or in dorms where students regularly socialize, which many administrators find difficult to take seriously. (pp. 164-165)

The Limitations of Target-Hardening Strategies

One of the most pronounced limitations of target-hardening measures is that they create an exaggerated fear of male strangers and public places. This has the joint effect of convincing many women to voluntarily curtail their own freedoms and at the same time to become more dependent on their male partners. Ironically, these are the individuals who are most likely to victimize them

(Hanmer & Saunders, 1984). A number of women, including Catherine, whose story is in the Appendix, have been raped by the male friend they chose to depend upon to protect them from rapists.

Thus, target hardening may seem to place the burden on the campus, in that lights are improved and security telephones are installed but actually it places the burden on women to avoid attacks by men. By implication, women who are victimized are to blame because they failed to use target-hardening techniques. Interestingly, we have never heard of a college or university that put out an instruction sheet for men on campus:

Don't follow female joggers from behind yelling obscene things at them.

Don't force your date into sex when she has made it abundantly clear that she is not consenting.

If you feel that you lose control and may commit a crime when drunk, always be sure to drink in moderation.

Never go into a laundry room alone if there is only a lone female in it.

Although many campuses have given extensive attention to the behavior of women and how they might attract rapists, relatively less attention has been spent examining the structural, social psychological, and psychological factors that motivate men to engage in predatory sexual behavior. Thus, if a woman is victimized by a man in one or more of the situations noted above, she may hold herself responsible because she did not take what many people view as appropriate precautions. As we discussed in some depth earlier in this book, it is relatively easy for women to learn not to blame the male for being a victimizer, but rather to blame herself: "I should have never accepted his invitation to go to his apartment" (Wiehe & Richards, 1995, p. 49); "Why did I go with him? Why didn't I drive my own car? Why didn't I scream for his roommate? Why didn't I know that he was this kind of guy?" (quoted in Warshaw, 1988, p. 58).

As we noted above, target-hardening advice influences female students to curtail their individual freedom. For example, in order to avoid the possibility of being attacked, many people (including a sizeable portion of our own students) do not take night classes, stay indoors, change their style of dress, or revise their route to and from work. Bohmer and Parrot (1993) argue that many female students drop out of classes they need, quit school, or transfer to other schools for fear of being assaulted again by the men who raped them. The letter from Katie, included as Box 4.2, is an excellent example of this. These types of avoidance behaviors unfortunately only increase rather than reduce fear of sexual assault. Furthermore, they do not address the factors that motivate men to sexually assault women, because the man remains behind to potentially attack other women at the first school; it is not unusual for rapists to show a pattern of victimizing more than one woman (Allison & Wrightsman, 1993). Target hardening won't deter these men from selecting other "suitable targets," such as women who are intoxicated to the point where they cannot resist predatory sexual advances (Schwartz & Pitts, 1995). Criminologists refer to this problem as *crime displacement* (McNamara, 1994), where one individual and particular woman may be spared from repeated victimization, but the offender continues to commit the same number of crimes; just the names of the victims vary.

In sum, target-hardening strategies are riddled with limitations. They do not contribute to the safety of women in intimate contexts, and they have the potential to do more harm than good. Referred to by Koss and Harvey (1991) as *deficit-oriented approaches,* these measures: do not address the reasons why men sexually assault women on college campuses; render women powerless and make them "prisoners in their own home"; increase the power imbalance between men and women; and encourage women to view themselves as helpless. Of course, on a campus where stranger crime is an important concern, such as campuses located in high-crime areas of cities, target hardening may be fully appropriate, not only for rape, but for robbery, burglary, vandalism, and other crimes. On most campuses, unfortunately, those crimes are committed by the students themselves.

Educational Campaigns

The most widely supported intervention in the case of campus sexual assaults is some form of educational campaign. Not only does virtually every author who has studied the question end up recommending educational interventions, but student and community groups who intensively study sexual assault virtually always come to the conclusion that the first stop on the road to change is education. Generally, the argument goes, education campaigns are essential because without them, students will learn their "facts" from either gossip or the uninformed media (Bohmer & Parrot, 1993).[1]

One problem with this, as has been pointed out throughout this book, is that by the time young people reach college, it may be too late to change their attitudes, values, and behaviors. As was briefly discussed earlier, DeKeseredy and Schwartz (1994) found that many men come to college with a full armory of ideology and behaviors necessary to abuse women. As early as elementary school, students have begun to form many of their anti-woman attitudes on the Little League field, within male groups, at home, and in the classroom. It is because of such findings that many people now call not only for education at the college level, but also for early educational efforts aimed at preventing sexual assault (see, e.g., Wiehe & Richards, 1995). Some of the common responses have been elementary and high school-based educational and awareness programs, such as videos, workshops, presentations, plays, and classroom discussions. These programs help show young people what love should be, with an ultimate goal of helping to provide an atmosphere in which students show more respect for each other, and possibly changing attitudes, increasing knowledge, and changing behavioral intention, perhaps eventually lessening the amount of woman abuse in society. Many abused female teenagers want school educational programs and strongly believe that these initiatives would have helped prevent them from entering violent relationships (Fitzpatrick & Halliday, 1992).

There is growing community support for elementary and high school-based interventions, and several school boards around North America (e.g., London, Ontario) have developed prevention strategies. One problem that becomes quickly obvious, however, is that the method least likely to succeed is to do programming only when an interested teacher volunteers. A "haphazard, one-classroom-at-a-time approach" is doomed in advance, while a systemwide set of programming that has official sponsorship does have some possibility of success. Every student, teacher, and administrator should participate in programs designed to increase knowledge about woman abuse; address the forces that perpetuate and legitimate this major social problem; promote knowledge about early warning signs of abusive patterns in intimate relationships; expand definitions of abuse to include verbal, emotional, physical, and sexual victimization; provide information on community-based social support services; and develop an ongoing, systemwide commitment to preventing woman abuse and all types of violence (Jaffe et al., 1992).

Of course, our argument that education programs should start earlier than college does not mean that we are abandoning the idea that such programs should take place in college also. It is unclear at this point which methods of education are the most effective on college campuses, although group discussions in dormitories, fraternity and sorority houses; and other campus facilities may be initially useful (Schwartz, 1991). Wiehe and Richards (1995, p. 162) suggest that these group educational efforts should focus on the following goals:[2]

1. To develop a general awareness of the problem of sexual assault, and specifically an awareness that each person has the potential to be a victim or perpetrator
2. To sensitize students to the role alcohol and drugs play in creating a setting where sexual assault is more likely to occur
3. To inform students that to protect their own safety and sexual well-being, they should communicate effectively and assertively in their relationships with members of the opposite sex
4. To inform students of where to go and what they should do if they are sexually assaulted

One problem is that too many campus presentations are limited to the material above, leaving out any discussion of social structural factors such as those that have been featured throughout this book. Rather, many programs are limited to discussions of women's physical or verbal resistance to sexually assertive men, such as those based on the concept of miscommunication. If one theorizes miscommunication as the primary reason for acquaintance rape, then one teaches women to be as clear as possible in their wishes and intentions. Unfortunately, it also tells women that rape victims are responsible for their own victimization, because they obviously were not properly assertive (Rozee, Bateman, & Gilmore, 1991).

We repeatedly argue in this book that sexual assault will not stop because women take better precautions. It will stop when men stop assaulting women. For this reason, student group discussions should also address key issues such as power relations in a patriarchal society, gender role socialization, sexism in popular culture, and rape myths. Volunteers can organize and moderate these group discussions, but it is absolutely essential to have at least one full-time employee to train and coordinate peer volunteers and to coordinate other campuswide efforts (Schwartz, 1991).

Certainly it is not only male college students who need to be educated about sexual assault. Such training is needed just as badly by student affairs personnel, campus counselors, residence advisers, Greek life coordinators, medical service personnel, security officers, and those who work with athletic teams, such as coaches and trainers. These people should be sensitized to the incidence, prevalence, distribution, and key sources of sexual assault on campus. As was briefly stated at the end of Chapter 2, personnel working with students must also recognize that peer groups are an important element of young people's lives and that membership in some male peer groups and the social exchanges that occur in these all-male alliances are related to the likelihood that females will be sexually assaulted (Gwartney-Gibbs & Stockard, 1989).

Films and videos have proven to be a useful way for campus employees to begin education, and foster discussion. There are many films and videos that deal with various issues surrounding date and acquaintance rape and address the relationship between male peer-group dynamics and sexual assault.[3] For example, one that has been successfully used to examine male peer support is *Date Rape: A Question of Trust*.[4]

Another area in which faculty and other campus staff need to be trained is on the techniques to meet the physical and psychological needs of sexual assault survivors. Moreover, these people need to be trained to identify the victims of sexual assault (Bohmer & Parrot, 1993).

The Effect of Campus Rape-Prevention Programs

Given the reasons outlined above, it should be no surprise that many campuses across the country have begun to implement various forms of rape-awareness events in an attempt to help students understand the extent to which some of their belief systems are based on rape myths. Some programs are aimed at women, to help them to understand the nature of sexual assault and methods of prevention, while others are aimed at men, on the supposition that men who do not share various rape myths are less likely to be sexually aggressive. Of course, many programs simultaneously target both audiences. Unfortunately, the literature is rather sparse in describing these programs. For some reason, many of the papers written on such programs, as noted in various electronic databases, are unpublished. Of those that are published, many do not contain an evaluation component (e.g., Briskin & Gary, 1986), and others contain program evaluations that are of rather limited value. Lee (1987), for example, found that at the end of a workshop on rape, the participants filled out a rape myths questionnaire slightly differently than they had done 2 hours earlier.

Most of the few researchers who reported evaluation measures found no statistically different attitudes after hearing a presentation (Borden, Karr, & Caldwell-Colbert, 1988; Gottesman, 1977). For example, Lenihan and Rawlins (1994) reported that their date-rape prevention program did not improve the scores of 636 male and female Greek organization students who took the Rape Supportive Attitudes Survey. Frazier, Valtinson, and Candell (1994) actually found some important differences in that sorority and fraternity members who attended an acquaintance-rape prevention program endorsed fewer rape-supportive attitudes and beliefs associated with acquaintance rape than those who did not attend, when the test was given immediately after the program. However, when these students were tested again a month later, and this time compared with a control group of sorority and fraternity members who did not attend the program, there was no longer any difference between the two groups. The improved scores that showed up right after the presentation had disappeared within a month. The one program to show findings that lasted for 3 weeks was actually on physical violence during dating rather than sexual violence (Mahlstedt, Falcone, & Rice-Spring, 1993).

Based on such findings, Borden et al. (1988) argue that exposure to a lecture on the subject of rape "clearly . . . is insufficient to change attitudes" (p. 135). They were particularly surprised, they report, because their program (like others reported in the literature) had been strongly praised on campus.

Generally, it is our argument that most people taking part in these discussions have been extraordinarily hasty in rushing to judgment.

Many campus student personnel workers have put together a program that was praised by participants, and therefore just assumed that it had been wildly successful in changing attitudes. More likely, the students who least needed the program were most likely to praise it. For example, both male and female students dismayed at acquaintance rape would probably be enthusiastic about any quality program that they thought spoke to their needs or interests. Then, upon doing research and finding out that there was no change in attitudes after one presentation to an introductory psychology class at one Midwestern college (the situation in Borden et al., 1988), the authors race to argue that rape prevention programs don't work. It has been our finding in two separate studies that attitudes toward rape can indeed be changed by exposure to material on the subject that counteracts myths, and that these changes endure over time. It is possible, based on our findings, that one reason other programs may be reporting mixed results is that men and women may respond very differently to rape-prevention programs as they are currently formulated (Schwartz & Wilson, 1993).

We administered a fairly traditional test, whereby 376 entering college students, during the first few days of classes, were given a questionnaire that included a 10-item test of rape myths. About half of the students, in the third week of the term, heard a program on the nature of rape on college campuses, including coverage of rape myths, the definition of rape, the problems of alcohol on the college campus both in terms of the influence it can have on male behavior (although stressing that this does not excuse male behavior) and also of the effect it can have on increasing female vulnerability (although stressing that this does not increase female culpability). Finally, the program included rape prevention techniques, including setting limits, labeling behavior appropriately, and asking for permission before proceeding with sexual behavior. In a posttest procedure administered between 1 month and 6 weeks later (depending on the student), the experimental group that heard the program was different than an identical control group in their attitudes toward rape, in that they endorsed fewer rape myths (a finding that was statistically significant). However, it is very important to point out that the changes were much stronger and more enduring for women than for men. As some other studies have shown, the men exhibited statistically significant changes in their attitudes at the end of the program, but these changes disappeared by the time of the final test more than a month later. For the women, however, there were dramatic and significant changes immediately, which lasted throughout the testing period (Schwartz & Wilson, 1993). Similar findings were obtained by Szymanski, Devlin, Chrisler, and Vyse (1993).

However, it is still possible that some changes in the men who were exposed to the program did not show up in paper and pencil tests. For example, the students were asked at the end of the term if they had any friends who had told them that they had been sexually assaulted specifically during that fall term. Although there were no significant differences between the experimental and control group in the number who reported having such victimized friends (about 10%), there was an interesting difference in that men in the experimental group were more likely to have such a victimized friend. There were no differences for women. It is not particularly likely that the experimental group men just happened to have more victimized friends than the control group men. It is much more likely that the experimental group men became more aware of what the women they knew were saying, that they were more able to recognize the symptoms of rape, or perhaps they became more sympathetic to their friends.

Finally, all students were given a question that asked them, on a scale ranging from *very low* to *very high* to "rate your level of personal concern about sexual assault." Now, all of these students had just taken a test on rape myths twice in the same term, so they were obviously sensitized to the subject, but the experimental group rated their personal concern higher than the control group. What is particularly interesting about this statistically significant finding is that the males in the experimental group were significantly different than the males in the control group, but that there was no difference for the women. Obviously, the level of concern about sexual assault is reasonably high among all women, but programming for men can change their level of concern on the subject.

Still, one issue that has rarely been addressed in the literature is that these different programs no doubt had different agendas and topics. In fact, there has been very little work at all on the curriculum side of doing presentations. What exactly must be included in the program presented in rape-awareness programming for it to be effective (Rajacich, Fawdry, & Berry, 1992)? Surely all programs are not equally effective. This is an area that needs extensive work in the future. For example, we have noted above that rape-myths education seems to work better with women than men, and some people have argued for completely different programs for men and women (e.g., Proite, Dannells, & Benton, 1993). Schewe and O'Donohue (1993), going a step further, actually argue that when dealing with men who can be identified as being at a high risk for committing rape, a program trying to dispel rape myths is likely to fail.

Publicity Campaigns

In addition to education done in specific classroom or designed programs, colleges should implement publicity campaigns. Many people who work in this field argue that the most critical time to do this is in precollege orientation, if there is one, or in the very first few days on campus otherwise. Bluntly, a great many teenagers are away from home for the first time, under the least supervision of their life to that point, and are trying out new behaviors and ideas. Some of these behaviors can be dangerous. We have discussed earlier that one of the problems that women have is that "motivated" men on campus are looking to take advantage of women who are less able to resist attack because of intoxication. As most college students, and especially sorority women, can explain very quickly, there are some tricks and techniques that you learn very quickly at college, and especially at those colleges and universities known as party schools. These include going to major parties at fraternity houses only in groups, watching out for each other, and making sure before you leave that all of your friends are with you or adequately accounted for. Never go upstairs during a party for any reason whatsoever. Keep your drinking to a moderate level. In the first few days of college, before these lessons are learned, a great deal of sexual assault takes place on many college campuses (Kamen, 1991). Often college administrators themselves will express amazement at how many "girls" get so depressed in the first week of college and quit school. There is too often a presumption that this pattern shows that women can't stand being away from home. Much more rarely is it recognized that being raped before you have even made your first friend is one of the most alienating and depressing things that can happen to you. This does not represent a scientific sample, but for what it is worth, women in our surveys and classes who lived in the dorms virtually unanimously have recommended to us that orientations to sexual abuse be a mandatory part of precollege orientation: In one study, 87.4% of both male and female program participants said that the program should be provided during orientation to all incoming first-year students. Only 4.8% (mostly men) did not recommend that the program become mandatory, while the rest were undecided (Schwartz & Wilson, 1993).

A fairly simple, but potentially highly effective method of dealing with education is to provide packets of material on sexual abuse to all students. This material should identify and explain rape myths, why they are myths, and what kinds of attitudes are more appropriate. A strong definition of exactly what is rape should be included, so that there can be no question in the minds of either potential offenders or potential victims when something happens as to whether or not it is rape. Finally, potential victims should be given information on exactly what to do, and who to see, if it should come to pass that they become victimized by a sexual assault. Where should they go for a physical examination? Why is it absolutely essential that the physical examination take place before the victim showers or cleans herself? Who will be paying for this examination? What is the role of student judiciaries? Who should report immediately to the police, and who should go to student judiciaries, and who should go to both? What happens if you have not gone to either, or had a physical examination, but now, a week later, your depression is lifting and you really think that you would like to make some sort of charges; is it too late? Whether you press charges or not, where can you go on this campus for some counseling, where you can be absolutely and totally assured of confidentiality and a counselor sensitive to the specific needs and concerns of sexual assault survivors? It is often too late to get this material into people's hands *after* they have been victimized. They should have it, even if it is unread and sitting in a desk drawer, before they need it.

Finally, the most difficult thing for many campuses to do is to report sexual assaults through campus newspapers and radio and television. An all-too-typical response by campus security to sexual assault is to make believe that it did not happen, hoping that publicity can be avoided (Schwartz, 1983). Media publicity, the theory goes, only leads to more trouble, with students upset, phone calls from parents, and the risk of lower enrollment as parents pull their daughters out of schools where they stand a risk of sexual assault. Some campus officials state that they don't want their colleges to be labeled "date rape U," and therefore it is better that "the students live happily in ignorance" (Schwartz, 1991, p. 313).

Although hiding crime is occasionally effective, over time it is much more likely to have two other effects. First, it feeds campus rumor mills. If students widely know, or at least believe, that the campus administration as a matter of policy regularly hides reports of sexual crimes on campus, then there is no way for the administration in a crisis to show that any particular rumor is false. If a rampant rumor spreads throughout campus that there have been 10 rapes in the Engineering Building this semester already (and these types of rumors are common on any large campus), this poses a problem for the administration, particularly if there is no truth to the rumor. Any attempt by the campus security force or the administration to deny a report or rumor will be taken by students as just another example of their typical cover-up techniques. The best way for students to gain confidence that their administrators are telling the truth is for their administrators to make a *practice* of telling the truth. If nothing else, in most years, most of the time, the administration will gain the support of the student newspaper and the student government in spreading the word.

An important second problem with hiding crime is the resulting reduced confidence that women on campus will have in the campus security force. It gives the strong impression that the campus police or security force is trivializing the problems of women. We have noted in this book several times that women are unlikely to report sexual assaults to the campus police. Reducing their confidence in the force, and increasing their fear that there will be a cover-up, is certain to make women even less likely to report.

Alcohol Policies

Certainly we have made it abundantly plain in this book that alcohol consumption on college campuses is extremely high, and among many groups (such as women) getting progressively higher. We have rejected any notion that alcohol use *causes* sexual aggression against women, but we have noted a number of different ways in which it is related. Some men use alcohol to specifically give them permission to claim that their inhibitions have been lowered, so that they can go out and do things (victimize women) that they would not otherwise do. In the context of a major party, with the support of their male peers, many men will commit a rape or a gang rape that they would not do without such alcohol-fueled male peer pressure. Many men feel that it is not a crime to force a woman into sexual intercourse or other sexual acts if she is too drunk to resist; thus, a woman who voluntarily gets drunk to the point that she is unable to resist one of these men may be increasing her chances of actually being victimized (Norris, Nurius, & Dimeff, 1996). This is not to argue that such victimizations are the fault of drunken women; it is to say that there are men on every college campus who go out looking for women against whom they can commit criminal acts. Thus, a large empirical literature shows that "alcohol use serves to increase the chances that a rape will occur" (Allison & Wrightsman, 1993, p. 255).

If campus administrators need some other reason to work on new alcohol policies, it might be the suggestion of Sanday (1996a), who points out that we may be making a mistake in simply treating alcohol abuse as a constant figure on the college campus. She obtained Koss's original survey data, and was able to compare 30 campuses across the country on the percentage of males who said that they drank more than five or six cans of beer or other alcoholic beverages on the nights they went out. The percentages ranged from 6% to 71%. Her conclusion (1996a): "Because all studies . . . are unanimous on the effect of drinking, this information, perhaps more than any other, is suggestive of variation in the rape-prone nature of campus environments" (p. 201). The obvious implication is that if we can do something to cut back on alcohol abuse on our own campuses, it may follow that we will be cutting back on sexual assault also.

So, what can be done about this problem? Bohmer and Parrot (1993) suggest that alcohol should be prohibited on campus in order to reduce sexual assault. This policy could easily be implemented, and in fact, many colleges throughout North America have shut down student pubs, prohibited campus parties that involve alcohol consumption, and banned alcohol from dormitories and campus apartments. Because alcohol use is a major correlate of date and acquaintance rape, many people are likely to believe that these measures will help make female students' lives safer. However, to the best of our knowledge, there is no empirical evidence showing that women on alcohol-free campuses are safer than those on campuses where alcohol is not restricted. For example, Schwartz and Pitts (1995) found that 17.1% of their entire sample had been raped when they were unable to defend themselves because of intoxication, and *another* (there is no overlap between these categories) 19.4% of all of the women in their sample had been victims of attempted rape while intoxicated. If a woman was a victim of both, she was only counted once. Thus, more than a third of all of these college women had been sexually victimized in a situation where she had been extremely drunk. What is interesting in this context is that this all took place on a college campus that is technically alcohol-free. The student pub had been converted into a coffee shop, and there is a strongly enforced rule against having alcohol in the dorms (this was a heavily residential campus) or any other campus building. Obviously, simply passing a rule against drinking is not a solution here.

Of course, part of the problem is that a substantial number of college women who are sexually assaulted are attacked off campus (Elliot et al., 1992), where they can often drink freely. Just because people cannot drink on campus does not mean that they won't go to off-campus pubs, bars, and dance halls. Some colleges have begun to try to deal with this problem by extending their campus alcohol codes to include violations by students in off-campus environments (Bohmer & Parrot, 1993). Unfortunately, it is unlikely that this will have much more effect than on-campus bans. Bartenders (mostly students and members of the university community) and tavern owners are not likely to report their patrons to campus officials for fear of losing business. Students who engage in destructive or criminal behavior in the bar may be reported, but it is hard to imagine simple drinking being reported. Some bars, especially those in small college towns, depend on students for their economic survival. If you open up a bar near the dormitories in a college town where 75% of the students are below the legal drinking age, and name it something obviously student oriented like "The College Inn," it is rather apparent that your business will ultimately depend on illegal business. In such towns, there is virtually always a cottage industry in fake identification cards. Another easy method of evading the law in many areas is to throw the parties in a dormitory, fraternity or sorority house, or apartment building, or to hold yard parties or a "street party." All that an entire group needs is one person of legal drinking age to go to the local beer distributor to purchase one or more kegs of beer, which can then be set up to serve anyone at the party. There are distributors who make much of their money from illegal under-age student drinking located near most campuses, and not surprisingly they are often honored members of the college's society of private donors.

Certainly some state governments aggressively police such bars to try to arrest under-age drinkers and the holders of fake identification cards, but typically a state will have 10 or 15 liquor control agents to police all of the bars in the entire state, plus all of the other events where beer or liquor is illegally sold. Law enforcement barely makes a dent in the highly profitable business of getting students drunk.

Part of the problem is that few people see drinking as a behavior worthy of informing, "squealing," or complaining. Rather, it is a situation that to most people perfectly fits the definition of a *victimless crime*, where there is not a clear-cut victim or offender. Schur (1974) would describe under-age drinking as "the exchange between willing partners of strongly desired goods and services. The 'offense' in such a situation, then, consists of a consensual transaction—one person gives or sells another person something he or she wants" (p. 6). Thus, there hardly seems to be an incentive to call the police when you cannot even really identify the crime. As we mentioned earlier in this book, few students think that they have a problem with drinking, and fewer still have negative attitudes toward drinking.

This is not to say that we are opposed to colleges taking steps to lower the currently high levels of alcohol consumption and under-age drinking. As we have said, we do know that alcohol abuse is part of a lifestyle that also seems to breed sexual assault. We also know that alcohol abuse affects students' academic performance and that it is an extremely dangerous drug: 25,000 people die each year from cirrhosis of the liver, which is directly caused by alcohol abuse, while tens of thousands of lives (including those of many college students) are taken each year in alcohol-related car accidents (DeKeseredy & Schwartz, 1996). We are generally aware that many colleges have been more influenced by a fear of losing lawsuits (Gonzalez, 1994) than a felt need to reduce drinking or sexual assaults, but that does not mean that the effort should not be made. Interestingly, few colleges that have begun to hold rape awareness seminars have seen fit to make alcohol and substance abuse awareness a major part of this programming (Abbey, Ross, McDuffie, & McAuslan, 1996).

One technique that has only begun to be addressed has been to look for more responsible drinking, or to aggressively attempt to convince students that it is possible to have a good time without throwing up afterward. Goodwin (1989), for example, suggests from his work that there is a nucleus of fraternity and sorority members who are not heavy drinkers and do not approve of the extensive abuse around them. He suggests that these people might be recruited to develop techniques for holding exciting and interesting alcohol-free parties and other events.

Similarly, Beck et al. (1995) suggest that messages about responsible attitudes toward drinking today fail to address the developmental needs of college-age people. They recommend that

> a variety of prevention approaches must be developed which differentially address the various segments of the college drinking population (e.g., males vs. females, high vs. low intensity), the different contexts in which they drink, and must also recognize the systemic opportunities for alcohol misuse which are created within the college environment. (p. 1112)

Rabow and Duncan-Schill (1995) make the same argument a bit more clearly: "A successful emphasis would seem to require focus upon the host (students), along with the environment (norms, culture) and less upon the agent (alcohol)" (p. 61). Furthermore, as Scott and Ambroson (1995) point out, the differences between campuses and patterns of behavior on various campuses can be so great that simply borrowing models from another campus is a strategy doomed to failure. Programs must be developed to meet the particular needs of each particular campus.

Of course, no matter how important dealing with alcohol abuse might be, many sober people sexually assault women. Programs such as eliminating alcohol use on campus by themselves do little, if anything, to address the broader social forces that perpetuate and legitimate sexual assault. A man may stop drinking, but this does not mean that he will no longer be exposed to sexist media, patriarchal teachers, and pro-abuse male peer groups. Certainly, education and awareness programs should sensitize people to the ways in which alcohol is associated with sexual assault, beatings, and other crimes on campus. However, alcohol policies, workshops, and awareness programs should only be used in conjunction with the other strategies advanced in this chapter. Campus officials should be extremely cautious about discussing alcohol without addressing other key determinants of sexual assault. As Schwartz and Pitts (1995, p. 28) point out, the solution is not to keep men and women away from alcohol and bars; rather, sexual assault will not be eradicated in North America without major social, economic, and legal change.

Codes of Conduct and Disciplinary Procedures

University administrations, which, coincidently or not, are generally dominated by male decision makers, are often very uncomfortable with or are uninterested in developing codes of conduct and disciplinary strategies to deal specifically with sexual assault. In fact, some administrations still try to hide reports of sexual assault. As stated in Chapter 1, when a college or university campus rarely takes serious punitive action against sexual assault perpetrators, these men quickly develop the feeling that they are above the law. And so they are.

A first step is for colleges to establish a written protocol for dealing with sexual assault cases. It is not sufficient just to have a general code that allows students to be disciplined for unruly behavior, or whatever. Nor is it sufficient just to have a document somewhere that lists certain behaviors as offenses. Rather, there is a need for a protocol that can be widely distributed that tells people exactly what to do in case of a reported sexual assault. Bohmer and Parrot (1993) recommend that such a policy be explicit about naming and describing where the college policies are located that list which sexual behaviors are offenses on campus.

Furthermore, such a protocol must explicitly list the procedures to follow when a report is made. The key is to have everyone at the university in positions of authority acting in the same way, based on the same set of presumptions (Koss, 1992). It might be best to have several highly trained and sensitive individuals always on call, so that one can be brought in to take over the investigation of every single reported assault on campus. Or other campuses might prefer to train a wide range of student personnel, residence life, and faculty representatives to carry out the required steps of the protocol.

Procedures listed in a protocol might include who to notify, how to do this notification, and how to involve the victim in giving consent for certain of the notifications to be made. For example, should the city police be notified? Who makes that determination and on what grounds? This should not be a separate decision for every residence hall director to make on her or his own, but should be based on a standard, well worked out policy. Is it essential that the campus police be notified? Who does that notification? Actually, depending on the college, state, and country you are in, there are some legal requirements about reporting that must be taken into account.

Bohmer and Parrot (1993) make some other suggestions about what would be part of a good protocol. They suggest making explicit the procedures for keeping the names of both the victim and the offender confidential and for referring the victim to either on-campus or off-campus counseling. All in all, such a protocol can be made up into a brochure that can be given immediately to anyone who reports a sexual assault. She or he can then be quickly apprised, in writing, of what will happen, how it will happen, victim rights, accused offender rights, and anything else that a victim should know.

One of the more widely debated problems among rape counselors is what to do next. Not uncommonly, a hearing is scheduled at some time convenient to the administration—perhaps as long as months away, and in the meantime there is no action. If the offender is smart, he can gain delay after delay until he graduates and the college drops the issue. One problem with delay is that, for example, if a woman is raped in a co-ed dorm by a man who lives on the same floor, she must continue to live right down the hallway from her rapist, and see him every morning on the way to the bathroom. She may be in a class with him, or find him following her home from the library. One of the most common suggestions is that one or the other should be moved to provide for victim safety, whether that safety is physical or psychological. In some cases, that can be accomplished by moving the woman to another dorm and switching some of her classes. Unfortunately, this is a difficult situation that requires some sensitivity and perhaps political savvy. Why should *she* be moved? She is the victim in this case, and now she is being punished again by being forced to move. Yet, on the other hand, before there is a judicial hearing of some sort, there must be some presumption of innocence of the man. After he is found guilty, there should be no problem moving him, or even expelling him from school. It is the period before that, however, that requires a careful assessment and knowledge of what the victim wants and what is best for her.

One way to deal with this problem, of course, is to speed up any campus judicial hearings, to make the time between report and finding as short as possible. Unfortunately, as campus judicial proceedings begin to imitate official criminal justice procedures more and more, the process is similarly becoming more and more cumbersome. Any student or administrative group looking into such procedures would do well to consult Bohmer and Parrot (1993), who include extensive discussion of the technical details of who should serve on judiciary panels, who should be allowed to testify before them, what rights to give both victims and defendants, and what to put into various brochures and protocols.

Penalties

One of the complaints from student groups that has received national attention recently has been the extremely light penalties that many colleges have given out to those found guilty of sexual assault (Bernstein, 1996c). This can be a very difficult area to discuss, particularly when the people trying to provide a safer atmosphere for women are also people who do not have much faith in the ability of the criminal justice system to curb criminal behavior through harsh penalties. It is entirely possible, however, that the problem of campus sexual assault is somewhat different from what is faced by many criminal justice agencies. As we have seen here, some of what we are dealing with is a group of people who believe that they are above the law. If there is going to be a group in society that is amenable to being influenced, it is this group.

We will talk about reintegration below, but the subject of deterrence is relevant here. There are two different types of deterrence. In *specific deterrence*, the goal of the system is to convince the individual and specific defendant not to commit the crime again. If a person believes that he can commit such crimes because he won't be punished but in fact is now being punished, he will either need to reevaluate his behavior or learn some amazing mental gymnastics to continue. In *general deterrence*, the goal is not to deal with the person being punished so much as to send out a message to the wider community. Let us say, for example, you join a fraternity and are taught in great detail that it is acceptable behavior to work a yes out of a woman by getting her to pass out from alcohol intoxication and then removing her clothes and having sexual intercourse with her helpless body. In Chapter 4, we found in the newsletter of the ABC fraternity that you might even be written up as a hero for engaging in such behavior, rather than punished for it. Let us suppose, however, that several of your friends have recently been expelled for such behavior, and the university has shut down three fraternities so far for having members who did exactly what you did. Certainly you would stop bragging about your behavior. Would you also think about not doing it if it meant that getting caught would result in your being expelled and your fraternity losing its charter?

Colleges and universities need to assess carefully what the purpose of a judiciary hearing might be. If the case involves a high-level felony rape and the victim feels that an appropriate response by society is in order, then there may be no important role by the campus other than perhaps a ride to the city police station and the provision of counseling services. The unfortunate truth is, however, that many women (and male victims too) do not wish to involve the criminal justice system. They may feel that the penalties are too high, or that the price that the victim has to pay in public humiliation is too much to bear. Campus judiciaries offer some of these victims an option, where the goal tends to be: (a) to get the offender to stop committing these offenses, and/or (b) to provide a safe environment for the survivor. Both of these goals are served by the most obvious penalty: expulsion. As Bohmer and Parrot (1993) point out, however, even this is not foolproof, as the friends of the offender might continue to harass the women for some period of time.

There are a number of other penalties that hold out some promise of providing a safer environment for women. Ehrhart and Sandler (1985, p. 11) suggest a few, although there are a great many more that can be tailored to any individual situation (e.g., being permanently barred from entering certain campus buildings).

- Probation for a specified time
- Individual and group counseling
- Denial of campus housing
- A requirement that the perpetrators inform their parents
- Placement of a letter in the offenders' permanent file
- Participation in community service
- A letter of apology to the victims

Of course, there is no reason why just one of the above needs to be chosen. Several, or even all of them might be applied to any particular case.

Furthermore, there is no reason to keep such sanctions confidential. Many college administrators, sensitive to defendants' legitimate rights, have tried to keep secret the penalties assessed in individual cases. In fact, although federal law requires college campuses to publish reported crimes at off-campus fraternity houses, *The New York Times* reports, "that provision is widely ignored" (Bernstein,

1996a, p. B8). The problem with secrecy, at least in our experience, is that the campus rumor mill will presume that cases never heard about again were dropped without penalty. However bad reality sounds to the campus public affairs officer, the campus rumor mill generally is circulating a story worse for the college than the truth (Schwartz, 1983). In this case, hiding the outcome has a poor effect in many ways. Women (and in some cases male) potential victims become convinced that student judiciaries is a joke, that it does not take these cases seriously, that offenders have their cases dropped, and that the administration does not care about the safety of women. Thus, even fewer cases are reported to the authorities. From the point of view of men, who hear exactly the same stories, it may be a sign that the university legitimizes their behavior and is giving them permission to sexually assault women on campus. They learn from the campus grapevine that they are indeed above the law. Penalizing rapists and then keeping it secret negates the entire point of general deterrence.

What we have said about individual deterrence applies just as well to groups. A central argument of this book has been that male social networks often encourage and justify sexual assault on the college campus. Throughout this book, we have struggled with the extensive arguments made in the literature that fraternities are fertile breeding grounds of sexual victimization. They are also sometimes referred to as "rape cultures" in which the social exchanges between members are riddled with patriarchal practices and discourses (Schwartz, 1991). As we have said, the data on this may be confusing for two reasons. First, there are other groups on campus just as dangerous to women as fraternities. These might include sports teams, especially where they live in sports dorms; certain dormitory groups; or even just groups of men who live together in apartments. Second, there is no good reason not to believe that some fraternity houses do not promote the objectification and sexual commodification of women, or at least that they do not do so more than the typical male grouping on a college campus. It very well may be the case that everyone is right: that on any particular campus, some fraternities are extreme problems while others are not. So fraternities *are* the problem, or fraternities are *not* the problem, depending on the angle at which you look at them.

One thing for certain is that *some* fraternities are a serious problem. Perhaps only in private, but the administrator in charge of the

Greek system at virtually any campus with fraternities can almost certainly raise your hair with horror stories. What should be the response of a university when the problem turns out to be that this fraternity is especially active in promoting the sexual exploitation and victimization of women? What should we do with ABC fraternity in Chapter 4? Of course, there are a broad range of potential penalties. Ehrhart and Sandler (1985, p. 12) contend that fraternities that include individuals who sexually assault women should be subject to at least one of the following punishments. Which do you think are likely to have an effect? Do you think that some of these are a waste of time?

- Disbanding of the chapter
- Loss of campus housing
- Prohibition of social activities for a specified time
- Prohibition of alcohol at fraternity events
- Prohibition of fraternity members from holding office in student government or having any campus position of leadership and status
- Prohibition of service projects for a specified period of time
- A requirement for community service such as participation in rape prevention programs for all fraternity members
- Restriction of female guests to the downstairs area of the fraternity during social events
- A requirement that every fraternity develop and record its official position on sexual violence and develop its guidelines to ensure that the policy will be enforced

Prevention

All of the sanctions above are real; they have been and continue to be imposed on fraternities at various campuses across the country. If the point of the exercise is deterrence, such sanctions hold some promise of providing a reasonably clear message that those who sexually abuse women can be officially designated as deviant by campus officials. However, more and more people are now asking "Why close the barn door after the horses have left?" Of course, those who sexually assault women should be made to realize that what they did is a major violation of criminal law. Nevertheless, shouldn't we devote much more attention to preventing the pain and suffering caused by sexual assault rather than mainly limiting our focus to restorative approaches to this problem?

Obviously, survivors need social support; but every attempt should be made to prevent men from ever attacking women. Punitive measures, then, can only be seen as useful as part of a multiagency approach to curb sexual assault. We have covered other parts of this approach, such as wide education campaigns, target hardening, and alcohol policies, but none of these adequately addresses the patriarchal forces that motivate men to sexually assault women. As we have said throughout, programs that discuss such forces must be part of any programming on the college or university campus.

One of the problems we need to face is that punitive measures have the potential to do more harm than good. According to Braithwaite and Daly (1994), such measures "may do more to cement over cracks in patriarchal structures then prise them open. Current practices leave patriarchal masculinities untouched and victims more degraded and defeated; and to continue with more of the same policies may make things worse" (p. 210). For this and other reasons, some progressive criminologists offer alternative models. One that has been particularly popular in various locations throughout the world has been the notion of reintegrative shaming of offenders and reintegrative caring for victims. It is to this measure that we now turn.

Reintegrative Shaming

Australian criminologist John Braithwaite has developed an extremely important set of arguments, ultimately based on the problem that most punishment does not work. Our punishment models are often based on stigmatizing a person and driving him out of the group. Whatever the value this might have for general deterrence, it usually serves to *keep* the person outside the group, bitter and at best unchanged. Braithwaite (1989) has argued that a better form of punishment would be modeled after the way an ideal family treats its children. We let the child know that we love her or him, administer the punishment, but make sure that the child knows that with a change in behavior she or he is fully welcome to come back into the family and resume his or her former status.

Although it has been unclear what relevance this has had to violence against women, recently Braithwaite and Daly (1994) have tried to deal with this. The problem they identify should be familiar to readers of this book: most rapists are not made accountable for their actions; if they are prosecuted they have probably been committing rape for years, so that it is an entrenched pattern of behavior by now; and women who engage the criminal justice process are revictimized by that experience.

Although space is not available here to explain a model that is extremely complex, the essential idea is that the traditional system accomplishes little. The men are embittered. The women are embittered. The crimes do not stop. Braithwaite and Daly (1994) base their ideas on the community conference, the preferred technique in the New Zealand juvenile justice system for close to a decade. The goal is to promote an environment where the offender (who is mainly encouraged to take part by the possibility of a lesser punishment) is encouraged strongly by peers and family to face up to his problems of aggressive masculinity. Although the goal is to shame him, it is a reintegrative shaming where there is always room for him to come back into society. The victim is herself supported by a strong network of friends and family, to bolster her self-esteem and her willingness to go through with the process. This cannot be mediation, of course, where the more powerful figure simply wins the best agreement. Rather, it is an attempt to convince the abuser that the community disapproves of his behavior.

The goal, then, is to deal directly with the problem identified in this book: male peer support for violent behavior against women. While no one is naive enough to think that this method will solve all cases instantly, it is an attempt to break down models of support for such violence, and to give communities such as pro-feminist men an opportunity to impress upon the offender an alternative set of supports. Conferences are aimed at giving the victim more control, and more voice, partially by avoiding proceedings (like campus judiciaries) that end up in contests where each side attempts to portray the other as complete liars, absolutely amoral, or at least demons incarnate. The community conference aims to break down the excuses and rationalizations the offender has, not to paint him as a demon, but to slowly show him that he does not really have excuses for his behavior.

Obviously, this is a new model for North America. However, because we already know that heavy penalties have little effect except to send rapists away to commit their crimes elsewhere, that student judiciaries are almost universally attacked by victim advocate groups, and mediation advocates have not been able to create atmospheres that eliminate power inequalities that affect outcomes, following this model, based heavily on Maori culture in New Zealand, would seem to offer an excellent avenue at least for a trial.

Men's Strategies

Ideally, all men should struggle to reduce female victimization in public and private contexts. Unfortunately, very few male campus administrators, professors, and students are currently committed to this effort. Many men are uncomfortable talking about men giving up power and are much more attracted to backlash arguments about political correctness, academic freedom, and individual rights that are at heart attempts to maintain male dominance (Hornosty, 1996).

In this environment, one of the questions that arises is what the role of men might be in effecting change. Should we sit on the sidelines, watching football games, and wait for women to do all of the work? One group of men, who call themselves pro-feminist men, argue that men must take an active role in making change. These men place the responsibility squarely on men for male conduct that physically, sexually, and psychologically victimizes women: "Since it is men who are the offenders, it should be men—not women—who change their behavior" (Thorne-Finch, 1992, p. 236). Indeed, this may sound like a rather simplistic point, but it is an essential one to bring forward again and again: Sexual assault on the college campus will not stop until men stop sexually assaulting women.

Unfortunately, some women's groups have been "burned" so often that they question whether any men's groups can be counted upon as useful allies. Campus anti-rape groups nationally are often split on whether to accept the help of college men. Part of the problem is that many men who want to be a part of programming still hold and express attitudes that undercut the entire point of educational campaigns. Another cause for suspicion is that, after all, the entire unlikely point of pro-feminist men's groups is to organize to give up some of men's power (Christian, 1994). Yet, there are reasons for women and men to work together on this problem. One argument is made by hooks (1992):

Men who actively struggle against sexism have a place in feminist movement. They are our comrades. . . . Those women's liberationists who see no value in this participation must rethink and reexamine the process by which revolutionary struggle is advanced. Individual men tend to become involved in feminist movement because of the pain generated in relationships with women. Until men share equal responsibility for struggling to end sexism, the feminist movement will reflect the very sexist contradictions we wish to eradicate. . . . In particular, men have a tremendous contribution to make . . . in the area of exposing, confronting, opposing, and transforming *the sexism of their male peers* [italics added]. (pp. 570-571)

What exactly is it that men can do to "chip away" at the overall society that promotes hegemonic masculinity, callous disregard for the position of women, the objectification of women, and the support of men who sexual abuse women? Hundreds, maybe thousands, of strategies could be suggested here, so the individual and collective areas of activity described below are just a few examples of how male members of the college community can attempt to lower the alarmingly high rates of sexual assault described in Chapter 1.

Individual Strategies

Strategies by individual male members of college communities might be modified to fit a particular local situation, or might be variations of suggestions made by others. Two writers who have examined lists of possible strategies and made some recommendations are Thorne-Finch (1992, pp. 236-237) and Warshaw (1988, pp. 161-164). Some strategies adopted from them are:

- Put a "Stop Woman Abuse" bumper sticker on your car and declare your home, classroom, recreational center, or workplace a Woman-Abuse-Free Zone.
- Confront woman abusers, whether they are your friends or strangers. If you witness a man physically, sexually, or psychologically hurting a woman, directly intervene. If you fear for your personal safety, then seek the help of others or call the police. If it is a friend, let him know that his behavior is unacceptable.

- Confront male friends, classmates, coworkers, teachers, strangers, and others who make sexist jokes and who engage in sexist conversations.
- Speak out when possible against sexual assault, perpetuating myths about women that lead to sexual assault, or the actions of friends of yours that you feel facilitate the abuse of women.
- Never force and/or pressure a woman to have sex.
- Fight the myth where you can, including in your own life, that a drunk woman "deserves" to be sexually assaulted.
- Don't assume that you know what a woman wants; accept the fact that "no means no."
- Take what opportunities you have to talk to women about their lives and feelings.
- Support and participate in rape-awareness programs on campus.

Individual Sports Strategies

Sabo and Messner (1994) have developed a set of strategies that deal with the relationship of sports to masculinities, some of which are particularly relevant here. They include (pp. 214-218):

- Resist locker-room sexism. This not only includes refusing to laugh at sexist jokes and challenging the objectification of women in locker-room talk, but also bullying tactics used against other men.
- Teach young athletes nonsexist values and practices. Parents and community members can help children to recognize gender stereotypes and to question practices such as making fun of an athlete because he "throws like a girl."
- Fight sexism in sports media. Sometimes campus media are much worse than community media, and it is worthwhile to phone or write to object to images of female athletes as sex objects, or male athletes as dumb jocks.

Collective Strategies

Men should also work with groups on campus to curb sexual assault and other symptoms of gender inequality. May and Strikwerda

(1994) make the argument that men as a group benefit in many ways from rape, even if all men are not rapists:

> If patriarchy is understood as something which is based on common interests, as well as common benefits, extended to all or most men in a particular culture, then it may be that men are collectively responsible for the harms of patriarchy in a way which distributes out to all men, making each man in a particular culture at least partially responsible for the harms attributable to patriarchy. (p. 145)

Interestingly, the Fraternity Violence Education Program, discussed below, takes the opposite position: that only some men are rapists but that it is in men's interest to deal with this problem because it affects them also (Mahlstedt, n.d.).

Below are some modified examples of collective actions suggested by Thorne-Finch (1992) and DeKeseredy (1996b; 1996c):

- Lobby campus administrators to provide better support services for female survivors of sexual assault and other forms of woman abuse.
- Lobby campus officials to provide pro-feminist therapy groups for abusive male students. Such sessions could be run by faculty members and/or campus counselors.
- Insist that woman abuse prevention courses be required for all male students.
- Hold "town hall" meetings to discuss progressive ways in which men can help stop woman abuse.
- Struggle for the removal of pedagogical "aids" (slides, movies, cartoons) that perpetuate and trivialize woman abuse, if professors on your campus are using them.
- Insist that all students, regardless of their scholarly interests, take progressive courses on gender relations.
- Produce and distribute literature that debunks woman abuse myths.

These lists do not exhaust the possible strategies. To avoid duplicating what others are doing, Thorne-Finch (1992) recommends contacting other groups (he includes a list in the appendix of his book) to determine what type of work is needed. Campus counselling services are also excellent sources of information and often seek volunteers, and on many campuses, the residence life staff are well-informed on these issues.

Strategies With Fraternities

Although many campuses have mandatory or voluntary sessions on acquaintance rape with fraternity members, few have developed a specific curriculum designed for fraternity members, or have published these materials. One exception is the Fraternity Violence Education Project (FVEP) at West Chester University in Pennsylvania. Under the leadership of Deborah Mahlstedt of the Department of Psychology, and a group of fraternity officers, FVEP has developed a series of activities designed to reduce sexual violence caused by fraternity members (Mahlstedt et al., 1993).

The program is centered around developing a group of peer educators from current fraternity members. Mahlstedt offers a course for these men (Fraternity Violence Education Seminar) to give them basic information and skills, although she is very up front about the fact that there is also a reward (3 credits) for those involved. The basic idea is to "grow" this group from among fraternity members, and to slowly become a visible presence on campus, offering leadership on this issue (Mahlstedt, n.d.).

Will the strategies outlined here eliminate sexual assault and make colleges and universities safer for women? It really is impossible to answer this question at this very early stage. Before being sure of the answer, it will be necessary to first introduce such strategies on all North American colleges. The struggle to do so will be difficult, because the number of pro-feminist men pales in comparison to the number of their counterparts. Furthermore, a major obstacle is the fact that many men do not want to give up the power and privilege granted to them in a male-dominant society. As we have noted earlier, many men do not even want to recognize that they benefit from living in a male-dominated and rape-supportive culture. Any progress is sure to be slow, and any activists in this area who do not want to burn out quickly will need to learn from other movements to celebrate small victories along the way to solving the overall problem of woman abuse on college campuses.

News-Making Criminology

In this section, we call for a type of progressive struggle that moves well beyond the "hallowed halls" of college campuses: news-making criminology. Although a growing number of people are now taking sexual assault on campuses seriously, these people may only constitute a minority of the general population. A substantial number of people either dismiss or attack the data described in Chapter 1; many women who publicly reveal their brutal experiences are ignored. Even today, their reports are often interpreted as products of either fantasy, "vindictive artifice," or political correctness.

At the time of writing, the whole North American woman abuse discourse was "characterized by a general atmosphere of mistrust and a well-organized backlash against feminism" (Levan, 1996, p. 350). For example, throughout the continent, many women's shelters, rape crisis centers, and batterers' programs have been or are at great risk of being shut down because of funding cuts. Moreover, an enormous and highly appreciative audience exists within the popular media for people without expertise, experience, or data who mock and taunt female survivors of various types of woman abuse on college campuses and in other contexts (e.g., the household and workplace) (Schwartz & DeKeseredy, 1994b). In Chapter 1, we discussed the most prominent of the "people without data," such as Neil Gilbert, Katie Roiphe, and John Fekete. For a number of reasons, the kind of media attention given to various conservative attempts to deny the abuse taking place on college campuses can enhance the pain and suffering of woman abuse survivors and prevent the implementation of the policies described in this chapter.

Perhaps Stanko (1995) is right to point out that feminist researchers should see the backlash as a sort of proof that their analyses are now becoming mainstream enough for the conservatives to take extremely seriously; that Gilbert, Roiphe, and Fekete's denial of the evidence of widespread sexual assault on college campuses shows that feminist researchers have successfully challenged the ideological hegemony of the "safe family," "ivory tower," or loving relationship. Unfortunately, the widely publicized backlash perspectives on male-to-female victimization have garnered the most public support (Renzetti, 1994). These attacks are also likely to give patriarchal government officials and college administrators a "scholarly excuse" to both trivialize the data reported in Chapter 1 and to reduce funding to services aimed at curbing woman abuse (DeKeseredy, 1996a). Consequently, many female college students will continue to suffer in silence and to study and socialize in a "chilly" academic climate.

As we stated at the beginning of this chapter, it is essential that those intent on making learning environments safer avoid limiting their presentations of data or policy proposals to academic forums or community groups. They need to disseminate their arguments through the mass media, an approach referred to as news-making criminology (Barak, 1988, 1995). This strategy is often vaguely distasteful to academics raised in an atmosphere of supposedly value-free positivism, even when they intellectually reject their training (Brownstein, 1991). Academics are often taught that their job is just to announce the facts, then stand back and allow the politicians and activists to debate and use these "facts." Unfortunately, the world of understanding is largely a symbolic one where reality is constructed and negotiated (Goodwin, 1983). The struggle to define the "typical case," often called by sociologists *typification*, is an essential one. The group that is most successful in setting up the facts that are recognized in the minds of politicians and the general public as being typical examples of the problem is going to be the group most likely to have an affect upon the development of the solution (Best, 1990; Schwartz & DeKeseredy, 1993).

For example, if we mention that a woman was raped yesterday at a fraternity house, some image will pop into your head. That image might be that she was probably some drunken slut who sexually teased some poor guy all night, willingly went upstairs with him, and then woke up this morning filled with remorse for her actions, which she decided to deal with by charging him with rape. If that is what pops into your mind, no doubt you have little intention of racing to the student affairs office to demand disciplinary action against the male. On the other hand, you might automatically assume that we are dealing here with an innocent college student who was forced into sexual acts against her will by yet another of the almost outlaw sexually coercive fraternity men that roam our campus, committing felony crimes at will. One of the reasons that the battle within the media is so important is that it helps us to "frame" our views in advance. If Neil Gilbert, Katie Roiphe, John Fekete, and others are successful in convincing people that claims of sexual assault on campus are some sort of feminist plot to reinterpret traditional male-female relations to give women the permanent upper hand, then any attempts to work on this problem are doomed in advance.

Although many progressive scholars are aware of misleading images in the media, most limit themselves to papers at conferences about the problem of sexual assault. Few point to methods of using the media to present more accurate portrayals (Surette, 1992). Strategies derived from news-making criminology, however, may enable academics such as ourselves to share our critiques with a large audience. People involved in the struggle to end sexual assault on campus and other violent symptoms of gender inequality should develop relationships with progressive reporters who are more likely to report alternative interpretations of gender issues and other social problems (Barak, 1988). Making links with reporters involves letting them know that academic researchers are available for comment on breaking national or local news, or being willing to work on the types of newspaper op-ed pieces and other stories that have been traditionally unproductive in terms of academic career credentials. Interestingly, however, many universities today have begun to see the op-ed piece as a way to get the names of the faculty (and, of course, the university) widely known. Many university news bureaus not only are willing to help with newspaper op-ed pieces on virtually any topic of public policy, but they also are very competent in helping to place such pieces in newspapers around the country. In an electronic age, it is faster and easier to place such pieces than ever before.

Summary

The primary purpose of this chapter was to review several ways of curbing sexual assault on the college campus. Target hardening, rape awareness educational campaigns, alcohol policies, codes of conduct, and disciplinary procedures may have some positive effect for some people, but overall, they should not be viewed as adequate solutions because they do not address the broader forces that motivate men to sexually assault women. Are the other policy proposals better? We think so; however, before we can determine their effectiveness, it is first necessary to implement these and other progressive approaches in all North American colleges. The struggle to do so will be difficult because they call for empowering women and challenging the patriarchal status quo in some way or form, initiatives that are no doubt at odds with the conservative climate in which we live today.

We reviewed Braithwaite and Daly's (1994) attempt to bring reintegrative shaming to the problem of violence against women, and concluded that it is worth a trial. Efforts to deeply stigmatize men promise only to displace the problem elsewhere, rather than stopping or solving it.

Furthermore, we argued that the battle to frame or typify the issue is an essential one to gaining any influence into determining what the solution will be. Unfortunately, the media in recent years have mainly been the preserve of conservative critics who claim that the problem of sexual assault on campus is a feminist invention. It is for this reason that news-making criminology is important as a lesson in how experts in this field can help to determine the nature of news coverage of violence against women on college campuses.

Some critical scholars, occasionally referred to as "idealists," contend that sexual assault on campus and other forms of woman abuse will not be eliminated until there is a fundamental change in the structure of colleges and society as a whole. To a certain extent, we agree with this position. Nevertheless, a major social transformation is not likely to occur in the near future, and thus various short-term strategies are required now. It is essential to achieve short-term goals as a way of maintaining momentum and commitment, because women's safety on college campuses is a "never ending and constantly evolving issue" (Ledwitz-Rigby, 1993, p. 93).

Notes

1. See DeKeseredy and Schwartz (1994) for a comprehensive review of the North American survey research on woman abuse in high school dating relationships.

2. Wiehe and Richards's (1995) suggestions focus specifically on acquaintance rape, and we have tailored them to deal with the multidimensional nature of sexual assault on college campuses.

3. A reasonably current list of some of the visual aids that would be helpful in presentations can be found in Wiehe and Richards (1995).

4. Produced by Pixie Bigelow Productions, this video is available from Magic Lantern Communications Ltd., 775 Pacific Road, Suite 38, Oakville, Ontario, Canada L6L 6M4, (800) 263-1717.

Appendix

Catherine's Story

What follows is an edited interview with one woman, who was raped as a 20-year-old third-year student, followed by some journal entries she made at roughly the same time. There are several things that make this woman's story particularly useful. First, she suffered the type of intrusion that most people trivialize as fairly minor. In this case, she was drunk and passed out, and a man who was a close friend took her to bed and had intercourse with her. Although those who have never had this happen to them may argue that this was fairly minor, Catherine's reactions may show you a different side.

Second, this is a highly educated woman, a committed feminist, and a rape activist. Still, it took her weeks to figure out that what happened to her was rape.

Third, she discusses the empty and bitter feelings she had at the reactions of her friends. There are many lessons to learn here about how to react to the grief of a friend or lover.

Finally, she ruminates on the uselessness of the student judiciary system, and takes on Jason herself, convincing him that he did something really terrible to her. This, of course, appalls her friends even more.

If date rape were a minor event that perhaps only the sexually naive or the badly injured suffered from, then Catherine is one of the last people to have poor reactions. She has taken classes in rape victimization, led her campus's Take Back the Night march, and been active in both campus politics and local community politics. But date rape doesn't just affect the weak and naive. Listen to her own words in this interview a couple of months after the rape.

Amazingly enough, one of the things that she must deal with is that she is a volunteer in campus rape-awareness programs, as is Jason, the man who raped her. In some passages that might be confusing below, she talks about the added problem of working with her rapist in date-rape awareness classes.

Q: I'd like to start by asking you to describe the ways that the rape has affected you.

Catherine: The most obvious way is that it has very much hindered my progress on my thesis, which is on date rape. It's a date-rape survey. And I started my thesis before this happened; the rape happened in November, and I started my research in September, and I had planned on doing my research long before that. I got a grant to do it with my adviser. And afterward, after the rape and then after I started thinking about it and realizing what had happened to me and all—this is after really the ball got rolling in my own head—it became increasingly difficult for me to, to face my work. So I pretty much abandoned it for several weeks and couldn't even deal with it. Now, I'm back on track, fortunately, but I think, I think that is the most . . . obvious and tangible way it has affected me. Other than that, well, I broke up with my boyfriend. I couldn't deal with that situation, because I didn't see that he was very helpful or supportive and so it's affected me socially, I guess. I think it has affected me indirectly. I'm much less organized and uhm, I seem to forget things a lot lately. You know this is pretty . . . I consider it to be pretty recent, and so I'm still dealing with a lot of things. I've also had really bad dreams. I've had a really hard time sleeping. So, in those sort of indirect ways I think my life is kind of . . . I feel like I have less control over my life, you know, as far as sleeping when I want to sleep, and remembering my appointments, and things like that and, you know, working on the work that I need to do to get out of here and graduate. So I feel that I have lost control over a large part of, over a lot of my life. And I'm trying to get some of that back. I'm working on little projects; I'm teaching myself how to play the guitar and I'm lifting weights and things like that, just little things to put more structure in my life. But I would say generally a lack of control.

Q: Does that mean you are thinking about what happened, somewhere in your head, most of the time?

Catherine: Well, at the beginning of the quarter when I really started dealing with the issue. . . . Pretty much over Christmas break I didn't even think about it, didn't realize what happened to me was rape, all that crap that I thought that I was way beyond, being a feminist and being informed and all that. . . . But right at the beginning of the quarter it was more direct. It was more like I was thinking about things all the time like that and I was obsessing about it and, you know, crying about it. Now I don't find myself actually, consciously thinking about it but it's somewhere back there. It's affected me and I can't reach it. But I . . . I'm the kind of person who normally takes on lots of projects and has control over lots of things, and I usually do extremely well in those sorts of environments, and since that has happened, I'm sort of going through this phase right now where I just can't do that. I find myself incapable of doing the same kinds of things I used to be doing. And I don't, it's not that I necessarily find myself thinking right now, you know, when I was supposed to be somewhere else, "Gee, I was raped." But I guess maybe it's depression and things like that, that have come up, that have distracted me.

Q: OK, well that makes me interested in when you talk about how it has affected you, you don't mention your feelings.

Catherine: Uhm, well, I don't think I'm ready to deal with my feelings about it in a direct way. I don't remember what happened to me because my rape was an acquaintance rape and I was completely drunk and passed out and that sort of thing. So, I don't have actual feelings about that event because I don't think I was there. It was a "friend"—in quotes— who raped me, and I have feelings about that. I have feelings about him and our friendship and feelings about the way other people have treated me. But no, I haven't really confronted them a lot. I'd say mostly not, mostly I haven't confronted them.

Q: Well, are you willing to talk at all about the period of time that you were crying about it?

Catherine: Sure. Well, the first . . . I think of it in sort of chapters and the first chapter was "I think what happened to me was rape." And I kind of chuckle about it because, you know, I'm studying this and I've talked about stuff for years and it doesn't make any difference. And so my first chapter was kind of feeling out my friends and saying, "What do you . . . What you do think happened here?" you know. And the reactions I got from them, my friends who call themselves feminists, [were] very negative. They were very negative. They were . . . One of my friends said, "Catherine, you'd sleep with anyone when you're drunk" and things like that. And so initially when I was crying, I was crying about "Gee, I feel abandoned, you know. Why, why don't I feel that support there that I thought would be there?" You know, my friends who consider themselves feminists and who support women's issues and who are very "radical," uhm . . . don't seem to be very supportive when it really comes down to the wire. And they are friends with this person as well, and I think that might have been part of it. But that was mostly what I was crying about in the beginning. Gosh, my feelings about the person who raped are really . . . confused. And I don't remember crying too much about that. I remember feeling really vulnerable, feeling like people didn't believe, like I was a liar, or that I wasn't trustworthy, not understanding my own depression about things. I cried when I talked to my boyfriend. He . . . I . . . I said, "It sounds to me like you're jealous of what happened because I slept with someone else." He said, "Maybe a little." And . . . I cried about that. So I guess . . . still I haven't cried about "the rape." I've cried about all the other things, the second rape, the victimization that's happened to me since then.

Q: So most of your hurt seems to focus around the stuff you didn't get from people.

Catherine: Yeah. Yeah. Definitely. I still know this per— . . . I work with this person in one of my student organizations and it's kind of an interesting situation. We've kept in contact and I've talked with him at length about this many, many, many times and he said to me, you know, finally, "Yes, I did rape you." And I cried then, when he said that you know. It was, it was like it really happened when he said that. And we still kept talking because he's really remorseful and all that business and, you know, I kept trying to encourage him to come to [the student health center] and talk to someone, that kind of thing. And I think I've cried a couple of times mostly because I felt like I lost a friend who. . . . He was . . . I called him my best friend before this happened. In fact, to even prove to me, you know, that he's trying so hard, he called his parents and told them in front of me. He said, you know, "I raped my best friend, Catherine, and I wanted to tell you about it." And his parents reacted very negatively. They said, you know, they asked what happened, so I wrote them a letter and I told them—a five-page letter and I described what happened. And they said, "Well, your friend's obviously an alcoholic" because I was drunk at the time, and "obviously an alcoholic and she just doesn't want to take responsibility for her actions" and on and on and on. And so I cried about that, you know. That was really hard for me because I haven't talked to my parents about it, and so [his parents] were really the only parental figures involved at all and they were very unsupportive. And in fact . . . the . . . "rapist" . . . uhm, even tried to convince his parents that yes, that's what happened, "Yes, that's what I did." So, he's come a lot farther, really far. His parents haven't, his friends haven't, my friends haven't . . . and really I feel less hostility towards him about it than I do the rest of the people now, which I think is pretty ironic.

Q: Yeah. Yeah. Can you talk to me about the dreams?

Catherine: Yeah, they're not about him but they're about. . . . They're really vague. But they are fear dreams, stalking kinds of things. Uhm, there aren't people in them really but they're just . . . lots of fear. I feel like I'm running, I'm running from something. They usually happen right before this. . . . They're kind of in a REM stage before I really fall asleep. And I have a really hard time going to sleep now. I don't sleep very much at night. I sleep during the day. And when I sleep at night, I turn the light on. I do all sorts of things to sort of trick myself into calming down and sleeping because, you know, I have to keep functioning.

Q: Like?

Catherine: Like sleeping during the day, like keeping the door open, things like to try to make the environment seem less threatening, not be dark with the door closed by myself. Things like that. I just feel this sense of fear when I sleep. I can remember one specific dream, my uncle was in it actually. He's not someone I know well at all, but my uncle kept trying to kiss me in this dream. It was very terrifying, and I don't know what that means, but I keep thinking "Jesus, this is bringing on every victimization experience I must have ever had" or you know. I think it's like opening a very humongous can of worms.

Q: Are those kind of nightmares a new experience for you?

Catherine: Yes.

Q: And have they been pretty steady since November?

Catherine: Yeah. . . . Not since November, since January. November was when it happened, January was the recognition of what happened.

Q: So since January?

Catherine: Yeah.

Q: And how often?

Catherine: Oh, probably at least . . . four nights a week. So, I don't sleep much at all. It's kind of ironic, I might as well. . . . You're going to read my journal anyway, and like I kept thinking what am I going to say because you know this person. . . . It's Jason. And I was thinking when he was doing that work, how ironic it was that he was sitting there on one side and you were sitting on the other and I wanted nothing to do with it because I just couldn't deal with that. And it's interesting, I had an experience with the man in charge of it that really pissed me off. The student had initially contacted me to help with this thing. Well, subsequently we decided Jason would do it because I just didn't want to deal with it. No way in hell was I going to have to deal with that in the midst of all of this. And so by this time I pretty much trust . . . trusted Jason to do it well, because he's been, you know, flagellating himself mentally for months now, and he's really come to terms with, with how to treat women. But when I went over to talk with the person in charge, which I do quite often in my capacity as student volunteer, he had a very hard time turning it over to me. He said, "I want to make sure you don't have any personal interest in this," you know. And I said, "What do you mean personal interest?" He said, "Well, I want to make sure you're not biased in any way, blah, blah, blah, . . . " and I said "Do you mean because I'm a woman, I'm a feminist, is that why you won't just let me do this?" He went . . . "Well, . . . holy cow, you're right. You have every right to do this, go ahead." And during that whole experience, I kept thinking, "Jesus, you know, here is . . . you know, if anybody's biased, it would be Jason," which he didn't know, but here's Jason with a similar problem to what the whole thing was about, and uh, having to deal with that was very difficult. And you know, the person in charge is a great guy, and I think he's learned a lot in the past couple of years from you, but he's, he's got a long way to go. And so that was really hard. And things like that seem to keep popping up now that I'm a survivor. There just seem to be things all the time that are in my face like that. It's really weird.

Q: It's hard.

Catherine: Yeah.

Q: Well, are there are other . . . I mean, when we start to talk about this stuff, obviously there is a lot more than "it's interrupted my thesis."

Catherine: Uh huh.

Q: Are there other ways that it's shown up for you?

Catherine: I guess I don't know how to describe . . . and that's why . . . I mean, it's affected my entire life, you know; every minute that I'm awake and then when I try to sleep it's there. But it's so abstract, it's difficult for me to describe. My thesis is an obvious tangible way. My boyfriend is an obvious tangible way. But I guess I just can't . . . I don't know how to . . . I'll try. A general sense of depression, a loss of control. I feel very lost, but it's something that is with me every minute, so, you know, it's sort of . . . I'm getting used to it now.

Q: Describe to me what the depression is like.

Catherine: It's like . . . being on the verge of tears a lot for no reason. Feeling very lonely, very alone. And I think my particular experience has really contributed to that. I feel like I've really been abandoned. Although my friends have come around since then, it doesn't make any difference. Feeling stigmatized, like when I had that experience with that whole thing I was just telling you about, I really wanted to tell him, "Screw you, you know, it's these men who are biased. It's not women who, who know, you know, what it's like to be victimized, that are biased. It's these men who know what it's like to be victimizers that are looking out for themselves." But I feel too stigmatized to say that, to say, "I know what these women have been through." It's . . . I haven't been able to tell my adviser about it because of the embarrassment and the stigma, even though I know he's a feminist and he's wonderful and, you know, he taught me about the issue of violence against women. But I feel like if I tell him this is why I abandoned my thesis, things would be different, that he'd treat me differently. It's just, I feel very fragile, like my position in the world is very precarious.

Q: That's a very good description for not knowing quite how to do it. . . . When you think about all of that, what is it that feels most significant about it?

Catherine: Something that I didn't mention, but that is pretty significant, and this is weird, because I haven't really talked about this, in this way, to anyone, so it's just all being articulated for the first time so . . . I . . . I guess there is also a sense of rage and injustice, particularly because I feel that I spend most of my life trying to help other people, trying to make this world a better place, and that's really the source of my getting up in the morning and going to bed at night. And I don't know, I feel like everything's against me for doing that. I feel very, I feel like. . . . It's a great injustice that people like me and the other women I know have to go through this. Because for the most part, we're wonderful and we all want to change the world and make it a better place. And even our friends, who call themselves liberals or, and run in the same circles, are working against us, and that's . . . that's very difficult. I feel like, I have felt about . . . I've felt like giving up. And I don't mean giving up in the sense that I don't want, I want to stop helping people but giving up in the sense that I don't want to get up in the morning. I just don't ever want to get up again . . . so, that's pretty damn significant I think.

Q: So where do you find the energy to get up?

Catherine: I don't know, but I do it. I have no idea . . . other than what gets me up every day and that's, you know, every day's an opportunity to interact with people and to make some kind of a difference.

Q: Has the wanting to give up ever become more than "just don't want to get up?"

Catherine: Yeah. Like you mean, suicidal thoughts? Yes. Yes. I can remember walking home a couple of times, I live on the west side, so it's down the hill. I can remember walking home and crossing the street and very seriously thinking about continuing to walk in the street and you know, not actually making it to the sidewalk. And I guess you could definitely call that a suicidal thought, because cars come and that's the whole idea. And I. . . . It's not been a very melodramatic kind of like "I'm going to kill myself" kind of thing but just "I want to keep walking and want this car to hit me." I got in a car accident a couple of weeks ago with my sister, it wasn't very serious. The other car was totaled but everyone walked away. And I remember feeling a tiny bit of disappointment that I got up and, you know, everything was fine.

Q: Does that scare you?

Catherine: Yeah, Yeah. It does. But I think I'm dealing with as much as I can deal with as I go on. And there's so much there that I haven't dealt with. And even those things, I sort of put aside and eventually I'll probably feel more upset about than I do now. It doesn't scare me like "Oh my God, Oh my God, you know, that's so horrible and how could you think that" but it's just, I have this sort of anxious feeling that doesn't really go anywhere. . . . And I keep thinking this is normal, I'm supposed to feel this way. You know, so many people who have been through this. . . .

Q: Well, one of the questions that is, you know, in my mind for you specifically is what has it been like for you having all these facts about "the experience" in comparison to living the experience?

Catherine: It's a totally different experience; reading and knowing. I thought I had a handle on it all, you know. Both my sisters have been raped, and, you know, more friends than not have been, and you read and read and read and read. And I really thought, you know, "I know what's it like. I can intellectualize and I can think about this." It's just so . . . It's so different. It's like putting on a pair of glasses that actually work. And now I'm really getting into my thesis because now when I read women's answers, uhm, to some of my questions, I say "Aha! I know exactly what you mean" and. . . . There's just no comparison. Although I have to say if I were not prepared in the way that I was, then things would have been a lot worse for me. It was hard enough for me to come to the conclusion that I'd been raped, even with all the education about it. Had I not, if I didn't have that knowledge, you know, maybe 3 years ago in high school, I would never have come to that conclusion at all. And yet I would have felt the same way, I think, about it and maybe even worse because I wouldn't have something to point to, something to move on from, something to get over.

Q: Well, have there been changes in how you feel about yourself?

Catherine: Umm hmm! Yeah, I think a lot about my relationships with men, and I think that this has really forced me to examine those. I've always had relationships that were sort of unbalanced. I've always been the one to not want commitment, to have lots of dates and never want to settle into, you know, something serious. But on the other hand, I've always had serious relationships, so I've had both, which is very interesting and difficult. But I used to think that I was really emotionally and psychologically independent, and I don't think that anymore. I think that's something I need to work on. I think it. . . . A lot of it had to do with the way my boyfriend reacted, and I had to break up with him. You know, I told him I needed some time to be by myself and this has been really good for me because I've realized that "shit, I'm really a lot more dependent upon . . . upon . . . knowing what men think of me and how I relate to them than I used to think." . . . And I wonder why it is that I had so many male friends, like Jason, when I'm such a feminist and I should be having all these female friends, which I don't. Well, I'm trying to foster that. Also, I started lifting weights, I think because I. . . . It's made me feel really helpless, not really that that would have made any difference at all. No self-defense class in the world would have made any difference there, but that's not really what it's about. I think it's more psychological helplessness. But now I feel psychologically stronger now that I have biceps. . . . And also, you know, I think I mentioned this a few minutes ago, that I feel less sure of my position in the world, maybe less idealistic, less ready to take it all on.

Q: We've talked about some of these but I'd like to know . . . your descriptions of how the things you've talked about in terms of feeling less secure about your place, feeling abandoned, alone, all of it, how does that show up in how you relate with your friends?

Catherine: OK, well, I'm pretty much an internal kind of person anyway, but I'm also very talky with my friends about things and I've stopped doing that. My roommates, Patty and Karen, were the first people I told, and in fact, I told them the day, the day after it happened. But I didn't say I was raped. I said, "Do you think it's appropriate that Jason has sex with people who are unconscious, or who are barely conscious?" And their reactions were very . . . Karen especially, Karen said, "Uh! I just don't want to even think about this anymore or talk about this," and walked out of the room. And so, I don't relate that well with them anymore. Uh, and you know, we still live together and on the surface everything is fine, but I don't spend any time with them. I don't go out with them or hang out like we used to. . . . I spend a lot more time by myself. My sister Ann has been wonderful from day one and always will be, and because of that I think, I think I'm a lot closer to her. From the beginning, she said, "This is whatever you define it as. If you feel that you were raped, then you were. I'm not going to put any expectations on you. If you want to spend time with Jason even, I don't care what you do as long as you're doing what you want to do." Speaking of that, I also feel pressure from my feminist friends, who feel guilty about the way they first reacted, to no longer speak to Jason anymore, which I find amazing. My friend Lisa initially just really blew me off when I told her what happened. And now she is up in arms that I still speak to Jason, and, you know, and I keep thinking to myself, you know, out of all the people in my life who've really tried to change and really tried, or . . . to come to grips with this, Jason is the one. Jason felt horrible and cried and cried and it was a horrible experience for him. And he dealt with it day after day and talked about it and he's really made some major changes in his life. My other friends have merely reacted upon, I don't know, selfish tendencies, I'm not sure. But initially they were very resistant, and then when it started seeming like a political issue that they needed to jump on, they did it. And now they're even, some of my friends are even saying, "I think you're spending too much time doing this or this or this. I think you need to go to the health service. I think you need to do" . . . and it's more of a control thing. And the other day I said, finally, "Just leave me the hell alone. I'm going to do what I want to do. I'm tired of everyone telling me what to do. I'm tired of people being supportive when it's convenient for them." So I guess it's really been "detrimental"—in quotes—to my friendships, although it's been educational and been interesting. And my other sister, Lynn, I talked about it with her as well, and she was great. So my sisters are wonderful friends and it's been good for us.

Q: I know you've mentioned that you haven't talked about it with your parents, but do you notice any change with them even though you haven't told them?

Catherine: No, because . . . for one thing, I don't spend very much time with them, and also I'm very good at hiding the things that are wrong. And also I think that my parents are willfully oblivious to things that go wrong in their daughters' lives. My sister Ann was gang raped in high school, uhm, and after that experience she became an alcoholic, a drug user, she even at one point broke down and asked for psychological assistance, and they pretty much ignored the entire thing. So if they are capable of doing that, then they're surely capable of ignoring what may be very subtle in my behavior. But they are very cool people, but generally not supportive. Nice people, bad parents.

Q: OK, and the last group is. . . . I had a question about your partner, but you sort of talked about what happened with him.

Catherine: Yeah.

Q: And then the last category is about men in general.

Catherine: Well, I used to date a lot. I haven't dated anyone since. . . . I mean, I broke up with my boyfriend and I haven't dated anyone, don't want to. Would rather go out with women. Although, I think I'm unfortunately more heterosexual than is really convenient.

Q: When you mean "go out with women," do you mean in a romantic sense?

Catherine: Yeah, I would like to do that, and right now I really don't want much to with men, as far as romantic situations. But like I said, I think I'm too heterosexual to go out with women.

Q: I'm curious to know if that—sort of on an intellectual level—thinking about that, is a new option for you, or if that is something that was present before?

Catherine: Uhm, well, I've always been really . . . open minded . . . and I had a fling with one friend last year, but it's never, I never really took it seriously. I never really thought that's something I would think about, you know. I'm just so open minded, and I'm . . . you know, I'm such a radical. And of course, you know, all my friends are gay, "why not?" that kind of thing. I never really seriously considered it, ever. Now, however, I'm finding myself wishing that I was attracted to women more than I really, you know. . . . I like having affectionate relationships but right now I just don't want anything to do, in that way, with men. So . . . yeah, intellectually speaking, I would definitely. . . . All my friends are gay, or bisexual mostly, but I never took it seriously . . . I never really thought. . . .

Q: So there has been a change in . . . ?

Catherine: Yeah, I think I've taken it more seriously. I've actually considered, "maybe I should have a relationship with a woman." Whereas I never really thought that before.

Q: If you were going to describe the rape, living through that, and living past it, to somebody who had no idea, how could you do that so that they might understand what your experience has been?

Catherine: You mean my psychological experience, or do you want to know more specifics about the rape?

Q: What has it been like for you?

Catherine: OK. . . . Oh, gosh, I guess I would tell them. . . . It's like nothing I would have ever expected. It's like having all your foundations, all the things that you stand on, all the things that support you, crumble instantly, including your past, your family, your . . . paradigm that you work out of, your belief system, your social support. I guess I would say it's like being cut off from everything . . . past . . . future . . . friends. . . . Yeah, I'd say it's like being very alone.

Q: We've talked some about talking with other people, but I'd like to do that in a little more detail in terms of what that has been like for you.

Catherine: OK, well, I mentioned the one friend who said, "Catherine, you'd sleep with anyone when you're drunk." And I mentioned my one friend Karen who got very ardent and didn't want to talk about it at all. And my friend Patty was less hostile but not supportive when I first talked about it. And because of that, she's feeling very guilty now I think—guilt or whatever—feminist guilt and she's now, uh . . . I feel like it's an intrusion actually. She asks me about it all the time; how am I feeling, and you know, "how are things?" and "I think you're spending too much time with Jason" and "I think you ought to go to the health service" and things like that. I'm obviously not very happy about that. . . . I've had a lot of people, I've not told that many people, but of the people I've told, if they're women and feminists, they've been mostly not supportive and then . . . overcompensating, I'd say. I told two important men in my life, one is a friend that I've had since seventh grade, his name is Dan. Another one is an ex-boyfriend, we went out for 4 years. I told them both, and they were very supportive at the time but then, uhm, then it's been silence as if I never told them, as if I never told them.

Q: That gives me a sense of what . . . of how other people have responded to you, but what's that been like for you?

Catherine: Come on Catherine! Uhm. . . . Well, I guess, for the most part, I've been real angry, real angry, in fact, just pissed off. In fact, in fact, Susan said, mentioned, the other day, "you know, Catherine you just seem very angry lately" because my jokes are getting really sarcastic and I was kind of being very angry. And I thought about that and decided "yes, I am angry" but something else also, I carry around with me: Anger. I'm just pissed, you know. I want to just say, "Fuck you all!" As far as Dan and Chris, I'm angry about that. I feel like . . . I don't know, I guess just like they're just all acting quite inappropriately, and I know they don't know how to act, intellectually, but that doesn't make me feel any better.

Q: Well, tell me what you wanted from people that you didn't get from them?

Catherine: Uhm . . . from the women that I told—and this excludes my sisters because they were wonderful—I wanted them to believe me first of all, most importantly. I wanted them to say, "Catherine, isn't that rape?" or "What you're describing sounds very inappropriate, yes, you're right." I'd say that is absolutely the most important thing. And from Dan and Chris—who pretty much acted like that anyway; "yes, you're right," which is kind of ironic—I guess I wanted, I wanted to feel like I could talk about it with them afterward, that they were open to that. But they don't seem to be. And I probably feel the same about both groups. It's probably, probably because of the way the women acted in the first place, you know. Then when they ask me questions, I feel like they're not doing it because they care; they're doing it because they feel guilty. But overall, most importantly, I just wanted them to believe in me and to not make me do all the work. The work being "was I raped? Yes." You know, that is a tremendous burden, and it would have been very nice if they had said, "Go for it, Catherine, you feel this way and that's your right. You have a right to feel this way."

Q: So a sense of support?

Catherine: Yes, absolutely. And now that is over, and I had to come to that conclusion almost by myself, I feel like they weren't with me all the way, so . . . and they weren't with me when it counted, so I don't want them to be with me now. And I especially don't want people to be telling me what to do.

Q: Well, when you talk about your sisters being terrific, what was it that they did that was good?

Catherine: Well, uhm . . . both of them right away said, "Catherine, you're right to think of it, that what he did was wrong. You're absolutely right." And both of them understood when I didn't cut him out from my life and write his name in the bathroom walls and that sort of thing. In fact, you know, Ann's been—Lynn lives further away, I live with Ann—and she's been great. And even saying, "I'm proud of you. I know the reason why, you know, you're still friends with him, and it's because you care about the world, and, you know, you want to teach him, you know, to be better. And I think that's great." So she, she never judged me about what is appropriate behavior. She never tried to tell me or take control of my life, or, you know, send me over to the health service when she couldn't deal with me or anything. She treated me like, you know, with respect, you know, an adult, fully capable of dealing with this. And she's believed me 100% all the way. If I went in and told her today, "I changed my mind I wasn't raped at all," I don't think she'd believe that but she'd say, "Catherine what you think, you know, happened to you, happened to you, and, you know, you need to deal with those feelings, but it's how you feel about the event that counts." You know. And Lynn was the same way. Lynn went a little further

even and said, "The legal definition of rape, blah, blah, blah." . . .
And they're both intelligent enough to note that, knowing that,
knowing that this person raped me they still respect my decision
about still maintaining contact with him. In fact, Jason even
comes over to my house and you know, shows me guitar things,
and Ann's nice to him, not because she's not sticking up for me
and being loyal, but because she believes in me, she believes in
what I'm doing. And so, I guess, gosh . . . you know . . . everything; believing in me, trusting me, supporting me, respecting
me, and not thinking about themselves, not thinking about what's
P.C., or what's appropriate, or "this is my friend too and do I want
to get involved in this."

Q: Are there things that you haven't been able to talk about with
people, that you've just kept inside?

Catherine: My feelings. Obviously. How I really feel inside. I talk a
lot about the external world and "this pisses me off" and things
like that, but I don't talk a lot how about how Catherine's feeling
inside her own head. My boyfriend, who I love a lot, you know,
we've been going out for two and a half years. It's been very hard
for me to even think about it, let alone talk about it, him not being
supportive and the implications that has for our relationship.
Also the actual event. I mean, I've still been talking about "the
incident" not "the rape." And I have a hard time saying "Jason"
and "rapist" in the same sentence, things like that.

Q: Well, that's quite a segue for my next question, which is, can, can
you, you describe what happened. . . .

Catherine: Yes. The first time I did it was in a five-page letter to
Leonard and that was pretty detailed, so I think I can do it now.
We were at a party. I was not on a date with Jason. We were with
all the other volunteers; Lisa . . . Jason . . . my friend Marie . . . I
think you know all these people, Marie, Lisa, Jason, and Mike
and myself. We had been to Seven Sauces and had downed four
bottles of wine, which sloshed me over. We went back to Marie's
and . . . we drank lots more, a lot, and I drank a lot. We were there
for a couple of hours and Jason was on one side of the room and
I was on the other side of the room. I was just minding my own
business getting sloshed, and when it came time for everyone to
leave, and Lisa said, "Jason, take her home, take her directly
home, do not stop at your house. She's far too drunk to be making

any decisions about, you know, intimacy or anything." And Marie told me later that she also thought about, about having me sleep on the couch there, but then she said, "Oh, what difference does it make?" By this time, I was really really drunk and most of what I'm going to tell is not from my own memory but what I've pieced together from other people, mostly Jason, but other people too. Jason and I live on the same side of town, so he was going to walk me home, but my house is two blocks further than his house. And apparently it took him an hour to get me home because I kept falling down and passing out. I was really drunk. Oh, in addition to changing other things about myself, I've stopped drinking. I don't trust anyone to be drunk around. But I had had way too much and went beyond just, you know, happy drinking, I was completely bombed. And so, apparently I fell down several times along the way and when I woke up the next morning I had a big bruise on my face from when I fell to prove it. So it took him an hour to get me to his house, and he decided . . . He tells me. . . . He thought . . . It would have taken him too long to get me to my house. And we got to his house. I passed out on the porch for 10 minutes and, as if that weren't indication enough . . . And he got me inside . . . and carried me upstairs to his room . . . uhm . . . And he says that I started kissing him, which may or may not be true but it really doesn't matter much at this point. So he took that as an indication, and he doesn't say much about what happened for the next hour but . . . uhm . . . And he knew I was extremely drunk. And I asked him the next day, "Look, couldn't you tell that I wasn't going to remember this the next morning and how many indicators, things . . . you know . . . ?" He said that I kept getting up to leave, trying to go home . . . uhm . . . and I was too drunk to go home and "it was much more safe for me to be there." So . . . and I do remember actually getting up and then falling down on his floor, like three or four times, and he kept putting me back in his bed. And he said that, that, we had sex for about an hour. The first half an hour he thought that I was, that I had been sobered up but then I started repeating questions that I had just asked him, and it was clear that nothing was going in my head and staying there. And so, apparently, he realized this. . . . He told me that he realized this and I asked him, "So Jason, what about the next half an hour?" And he just looked at me like, you know, "I'm an asshole." So, I woke up the next morning. . . . Also, apparently, things were pretty violent. We both had bruises the next day, and I said "Where the hell did I get these?" That was after I asked, "Why the hell am I in your bed with no clothes on?" And he said, "Well, you know, we were pretty wild, you know, getting all aggressive and stuff." I had no idea . . . whether or not . . . to believe him that I was participating in that . . . but I told him that, you know. "Jason, if you had to, I mean, if you had to carry me practically, carry me upstairs to your bed, I passed out several times, you know, why did you think I was . . . enough to participate in anything violent, you know, that I was, you know, making a decision, you know, to be thrown around?" And he said, "Well, you know, I have bruises too, you know, see and it was obviously mutual." And I don't know what to think about that. But anyway, I woke up the next day with a splitting hangover and I didn't remember a thing. I remembered slowly and I'm remembering a little bit more but don't think I'll remember most of it. And . . . Oh, I also . . . Jason said, "You don't remember anything that happened do you?" At the time, I wasn't actually very aggressive about it, I said "What am I doing here?" You know, I wasn't like "What the hell am I doing here?" I should have been. And I said . . . Jason said, "You don't remember any of this do you?" And I said "No, not . . . none of it. I remember being at Seven Sauces and I remember being at Marie's and that's all I remember." And he actually acted hurt, you know, that I didn't remember this experience. It hurt his male ego, you know, that it wasn't memorable. Which I couldn't believe. And then he said, "Well, you're lucky that I'm such a nice guy that I used a condom." And those things really hurt me. When I think about the rape, I think about those things because I remember them and those were . . . "How could you say that to me?" You know, "I'm lucky that you used a condom on someone that obviously was not, that you knew was not capable of even knowing to think about something like that. . . . I'm lucky?! And your ego is hurt?! You know, that I didn't remember?! I think you should have been thinking, wondering, things like, is she going to call the police? Not, you know, my ego's hurt." And . . . I walked home, and I was a mess. My face was all cut up from where I had fallen and I was really sick. I think I was sick for 2 days because I had had so much alcohol, and you know because, unfortunately I don't throw up when I'm too drunk. So I might have had blood alcohol poisoning because I was shaking for 2 straight days. So, I pretty much had to go to bed. And right when I got home, that's when I had this encounter with Patty and Karen about "Do you think it's appropriate for someone to have sex with someone who is so drunk?" And Karen said, "Oh, I don't even want to talk about this." And that was my first encounter with . . . with my experience. That was the indication of all the things to come. . . . So, that's what happened.

Q: When you . . . I mean, I realize that when you recount an experience it's easy to remove yourself from it. But are there things that you think are important to say about the things that happened to you and how it makes you feel?

Catherine: Yes . . . uhm . . . but again, I'm recounting this all on sort of an intellectual level, and I don't know if I can get closer to how I feel. . . . But I, you know. . . . The things that I kept saying to Jason when we had these talks, night after night after night, about what happened, you know. . . . I kept saying, you know, "How, how could you do that knowing . . . you knowing that I was incapable?" And his response had been, only, "I didn't know, I didn't know, I didn't know." And, you know, I didn't believe that, and I kept saying, "What do you mean, you didn't know? You had to carry me upstairs. I passed out, you know, several times. I was practically, you know. . . . You might have been calling the hospital, I was so drunk. How could you not know?" And it bothers me so much that people lie to themselves. And he lied to himself and me that he didn't know, because eventually he said, "Yes, you know, of course there was at least that half hour where I had realized that you were totally gone, that you weren't even there." And that bothers me. The fact that. . . . In fact, he didn't tell me about me getting up and trying to go home. It was only a couple of weeks ago that I remembered it myself. And I guess some things are too embarrassing to talk about. And I said, "Jason" . . . I asked him, "Jason, can I ask you a question about what happened?" And he said, "Of course." I asked, "Did I get up and try to leave?" And he said, "Yes," and I said "How many times?" He said, "Several." And I remember that now. I remembering getting up and leaving . . . trying, trying to leave, and I wasn't saying at the time, "you're raping me, I'm leaving." I was saying, "I want to go home. I want to go home." And I guess . . .

I just can't believe, you know, that someone who's actually a nice person, you know, compared to the rest of these people . . . which I guess makes him not so nice, but. . . . You know, someone who considers himself sensitive would have sex with someone who kept trying to leave and was not even capable of getting out the door! You know, those sorts of things make me extremely angry. The condom comment. I cannot get over it. I . . . Every time I think about it I get angrier, you know. I'm . . . All of a sudden I'm lucky that Jason was gracious enough to use a condom, you know, (a) as if it isn't both people's responsibility, and (b) you know, obviously, if he, if he, really wants to say I was lucky that he did that, then he knew enough to know that I was incapable of thinking of those things myself. And also that, you know, what, it's women's responsibility? It's like, you got away . . . you would have gotten away with something?! You know, "Cool, I didn't have to use a condom." What the hell is that?! That I'm lucky I didn't have to have an abortion after my rape?! . . . That upsets me a lot. I remember . . . walking home by myself. I keep thinking about that, that I had to walk home by myself. It was really cold, and I was freezing. And I was really hung over. I felt really sick but I wanted to go home and . . . that I . . . the fact that I had to walk home by myself really pisses me off. You know, I don't know why that's stuck in my head, but that, you know, here I was feeling horrible, and feeling sick, and very bewildered about my experience, and Jason stayed in bed and I got up and walked. And . . . for some reason, I kept thinking about telling him, you know, despite him being so supportive. . . . He's always very, very giving and he was always very nice about, you know, always, making sure that I got to walk with someone, even during the day. And I keep thinking of the story that I told Jason afterward, that when Charles and I first started going out, we didn't kiss until the fifth date. And then I kept . . . We were, you know, have a bunch of wine . . . and we both are really into red wine and pasta and stuff because we're both Italian. . . . And I would come on to him and he would absolutely have nothing to do with me if I was even slightly drunk, if I even had one drink, you know, until it was certain, you know. So we didn't have sex for months after we starting going out. And I keep telling that to Jason like, you know, "that's how you're supposed to act." But then I guess I assume men were supposed to like that, the men

that I trusted, the men I knew, were like that. And he seemed so
parental that night when we were at Heather's house and when
we were at Seven Sauces, about "Catherine, I think you're drinking too much," and you know, you know, things like that made
me trust him, you know, "Here, take care of me" and you know,
I could maybe not have to walk home by myself, and so I wouldn't
have to worry. And obviously he wasn't trustworthy. I would
have been much better to just walk home alone. And I've heard
that many times but didn't really think about it and really, you
know, in my life; that it's safer for a woman to actually walk home
than to find someone to walk with her. . . .

Q: Are there other things that you want to say that we haven't talked
about?

Catherine: I think I might have already said this, but I think . . . if I
were telling someone how to behave after someone tells them
they've been raped, I would say two things. Number one, believe
and number two, don't judge. And right now what I'm dealing
with is, you know, all these people telling me what's appropriate
right now for me, you know, how to deal with this. My boyfriend
wants to get back together but he's, he's got this idea in his head
that now that—now that he's believing that I was raped—now
he can tell me not to have anything to do with Jason and all this
crap. And I guess I would just tell people to stop judging, stop
trying to control, especially when it's out of guilt.

Q: The last area has to do with you—important things about who
you are—and some basic things like how old you are, where you
are in school, that sort of thing. So can you tell me some about
you?

Catherine: Oh, an open-ended demographic question! . . . Uhm . . .
Well, who am I? I'm a feminist, still. I'm socialist, still. I say that
because I've been so jaded by this experience. And I think I'm
still quite a bit of an idealist. . . . It's funny, I can talk about rape
but I can't talk about myself. I guess that's what depression is, I
don't know. . . . I'm at a midwestern university [laughs], a public
institution. I'm a junior, but I'm graduating this year. I'm a
psychology major, and I hate quantitative research, and I'll never
do it again . . . Oh gosh. . . .

Q: How old are you?

Catherine: I'm 21, I was 20 when I was raped, but I'm 21 now. I'll be 22 next year . . . What else?

Q: Anything else you want to say about you?

Catherine: I'm a survivor. And now I guess I really understand what that means.

Journal Entries

2/24 6:49 p.m.

Minutes after initial interview.

I feel very unsure about my place in the world whenever I think about the rape or its aftermath. The hour and 1/2 session with my counselor was very difficult for me because when I talk about it I feel even more precarious, fragile, as if my lungs aren't capable of breathing the air, my feet aren't capable of walking me around, and my back isn't strong enough to carry such burdens. I feel sad.

What would feel helpful right now? I don't know.

2/27 11:24 p.m.

I haven't written not because I have had nothing to say but because there is almost too much to say. The rape has been with me, is with me, and it seems will be for some time. It's not the actual event that keeps coming up; it is the peripheral issues that have come to have a prevalent place in my daily existence. For example, dealing with other people about it has been extremely difficult. My friend and housemate Patty has taken on maternal roles toward and with me. Her maternal concern, however, is completely uninvited. She questions how I spend my time, where and when I go out, and whether or not I drink a beer while I'm there. I feel as if she is trying to compensate for her rather unsupportive first reaction to the issue. But right now I don't need to be controlled; I am not a child, and being raped doesn't take away my need for self-sufficiency—in fact, it heightens it. Control is a major issue for me right now. I need to feel like I can make decisions for myself and that I can survive in the world without someone holding my hand. I perceive a certain precariousness about my position in the world and I need to face it and overcome it.

Patty and other people in my life also assume that I trust them. I do not. I have lost faith that many (most) of my close friends are capable of responding to any crisis in my life with any degree of thoughtful consideration. It is especially my feminist friends who have let me down. They who are so well-versed in nonvictim-blaming rape theory were the first to criticize me and the last to believe me. Two exceptions are (of course) Ann and Lynn, my sisters.

3/3 1:15 p.m.

In class and I keep thinking about stigma. It's diversity week on campus, in which gay/lesbian/bisexual students "come out" in an effort to be visible and thereby help fight the stigma of homosexuality. Women who have been raped feel stigmatized too, but what can we do? Social forces seem even more determined to silence us than to silence the gay community.

How have I been stigmatized? By whom? I feel stigmatized more by societal silence about rape than by my friends and acquaintances who have directly labeled me, disbelieved me, judged me. I feel stigmatized because I can't tell my professors why my grades have been slipping, why I have missed so many classes. Even if they would understand, they'd say "poor _____, she's had it rough," they'd treat me like a victim (best case scenario), they'd encourage me to go to the health service to get my head checked.

I am not poor or pitiful, I'm not crazy. I'm just depressed and pissed. I want people to accept that, and to direct their concern to the men who do these things and to leave me the hell alone.

3/5 1:00 p.m.

My friend Lisa told me today that she feels like she's "given (me) so much this quarter" in the way of moral support and I haven't given anything back. After thinking about this for a few minutes, I told her I haven't anything to give her right now. It's true. I feel so drained emotionally; physically, that all I can do is keep plugging away. Keep studying and trying to make up all the work I missed.

3/5 5:15 p.m.

Another story in [student newspaper] about a woman being attacked on campus. For every stranger-rape incident there must be

10 date rapes. How amazing it would be to see those in [student newspaper]—would people start to wonder, finally, what the hell is wrong?

3/9 5:30 p.m.

Working on my thesis, finally getting control of all the work I must do. It's astonishing to think that after all I've been through, I must finish this work on date rape, or I don't graduate. But things are better in that regard. I'm beginning to view my thesis as a way to say what needs to be said, as the first step in the process toward contributing to other women, other survivors.

3/10

I keep wondering if I did the right thing with Jason. As I see it, my three options were: first, never confronting the issue; second, pressing charges through the judiciary process; and three confronting him but not pressing charges. I did the latter, for a couple of reasons. (The first option I wouldn't even consider now.) I didn't press charges in part because I didn't think that such action would ameliorate my situation. What hurts me so much is that I trusted him and he broke that trust. Nothing will change that. Also, I've seen what women go through in the judiciary system. They have to defend their charges, they're asked very personal questions, and they have to do this in front of many people. (the hearing board, the judiciary director, the defendant, his character witnesses, his parents, etc.). I talked to Jason about this, and he says he would have admitted the charges to avoid all that. I think I believe him. But then would I feel any better if he were suspended from school? Hell no!

3/12

Talked to my thesis adviser about why I've been so slow. He was great—his reaction was exactly what I needed. He didn't act like I was a poor victim that needed to be rushed over to the health service for psychological counseling, or assume that I'm now incapable of doing work on the issue, but he was also not flippant. He actually looked quite sad, very understanding, and he still treated me like an adult, and somewhat of a colleague.

3/15

Just spoke to my counselor. When I told her how great my adviser was about the whole thing, she said, "he'd better be!" What a great reminder that understanding is something I should expect and not be so *grateful* for. This is everyone else's problem, too!

References

Abbey, A. (1991). Acquaintance rape and alcohol consumption on college campuses: How are they related? *Journal of American College Health, 39,* 165-169.

Abbey, A., & Harnish, R. J. (1995). Perception of sexual intent: The role of gender, alcohol consumption, and rape supportive attitudes. *Sex Roles, 32,* 297-313.

Abbey, A., Ross, L. T., McDuffie, D., & McAuslan, P. (1996). Alcohol and dating risk factors for sexual assault among college women. *Psychology of Women Quarterly, 20,* 147-169.

Ageton, S. (1983). *Sexual assaults among adolescents.* Lexington, MA: Lexington Books.

Alder, C. (1985). An exploration of self-reported sexually aggressive behavior. *Crime and Delinquency, 31,* 306-331.

Allison, D. (1995). *Two or three things I know for sure.* New York: Dutton.

Allison, J. A., & Wrightsman, L. S. (1993). *Rape: The misunderstood crime.* Newbury Park, CA: Sage.

Anderson, L., Chiricos, T., & Waldo, G. (1977). Formal and informal sanctions: A comparison of deterrent effects. *Social Problems, 25,* 103-114.

Arias, I., & Beach, S. R. H. (1987). Validity of self-reports of marital violence. *Journal of Family Violence, 2,* 139-149.

Baer, J. S. (1994). Effects of college residence on perceived norms for alcohol consumption: An examination of the first year of college. *Psychology of Addictive Behavior, 8,* 43-50.

Baer, J. S., Kivlahan, D. R., & Marlatt, G. A. (1995). High-risk drinking across the transition from high school to college. *Alcoholism, Clinical & Experimental Research, 19,* 54-61.

Baker, P. (1992). Maintaining male power: Why heterosexual men use pornography. In C. Itzen (Ed.), *Pornography: Women, violence, and civil liberties* (pp. 124-144). New York: Oxford University Press.

Baldwin, W., & Cain, V. S. (1980). Social class and help-seeking behavior. *Family Planning Perspectives, 12,* 34-43.

Barak, G. (1988). News-making criminology: Reflections on the media, intellectuals, and crime. *Justice Quarterly, 5,* 565-588.

Barak, G. (Ed.). (1995). *Media, process, and the social construction of crime: Studies in news-making criminology.* New York: Garland.

Barnes, G. E., Greenwood, L., & Sommer, R. (1991). Courtship violence in a Canadian sample of male college students. *Family Relations, 40,* 37-44.

Baron, L., & Straus, M. (1989). *Four theories of rape.* New Haven, CT: Yale University Press.

Barrett, M. (1985). *Women's oppression today: Problems in Marxist feminist analysis.* London: Verso.

Bart, P. B., & Moran, E. G. (Eds.). (1993). *Violence against women: The bloody footprints.* Newbury Park, CA: Sage.

Beauchesne, E. (1995, August 18). Canada best place to live—with a catch. *Ottawa Citizen,* pp. A1-A2.

Beck, K. H., Thombs, D. L., Mahoney, C. A., & Fingar, K. M. (1995). Social context and sensation seeking: Gender differences in college student drinking motivations. *International Journal of the Addictions, 30,* 1101-1115.

Belknap, J. (1989). The sexual victimization of unmarried women by nonrelative acquaintances. In M. A. Pirog-Good & J. E. Stets (Eds.), *Violence in dating relationships: Emerging social issues* (pp. 205-218). New York: Praeger.

Bem, S. (1974). The measurement of psychological androgyny. *Journal of Consulting and Clinical Psychology, 42,* 155-162.

Berkowitz, A. (1992). College men as perpetrators of acquaintance rape and sexual assault: A review of recent research. *Journal of American College Health, 40,* 175-181.

Berkowitz, A. D., Burkhart, B. R., & Bourg, S. E. (1994). Research on college men and rape. In A. D. Berkowitz (Ed.), *Men and rape: Theory, research, and prevention programs in higher education* (New Directions for Student Services, No. 65, pp. 3-20). San Francisco: Jossey-Bass.

Bernstein, N. (1996a, May 6). Behind some fraternity walls, brothers in crime. *New York Times,* pp. A1, B8.

Bernstein, N. (1996b, February 11). Civil rights lawsuit in rape case challenges integrity of a campus. *New York Times,* pp. A1, 32.

Bernstein, N. (1996c, May 5). With colleges holding court, discretion views with fairness. *New York Times,* pp. A1, 16.

Best, J. (1990). *Threatened children: Rhetoric and concern about child-victims.* Chicago: University of Chicago Press.

Boeringer, S. D. (1996). Influences of fraternity membership, athletics, and male living arrangements on sexual aggression. *Violence Against Women, 2,* 134-147.

Boeringer, S. D., Shehan, C. L., & Akers, R. L. (1991). Social contexts and social learning in sexual coercion and aggression: Assessing the contribution of fraternity membership. *Family Relations, 40,* 58-64.

Bohmer, C., & Parrot, A. (1993). *Sexual assault on campus: The problem and the solution.* New York: Lexington.

Bohrnstedt, G. W. (1969). Conservatism, authoritarianism, and religiosity of fraternity pledges. *Journal of College Student Personnel, 10,* 36-43.

Borden, L. A., Karr, S. K., & Caldwell-Colbert, A. T. (1988). Effects of a university rape prevention program on attitudes and empathy toward rape. *Journal of College Student Development, 29,* 132-136.

Boumil, M. M., Friedman, J., & Taylor, B. E. (1993). *Date rape: The secret epidemic.* Deerfield Beach, FL: Health Communications.

Bowker, L. (1983). *Beating wife-beating.* Lexington, MA: Lexington Books.

Boxley, J., Lawrance, L., & Gruchow, H. (1995). A preliminary study of eighth grade students' attitudes toward rape myths and women's roles. *Journal of School Health, 65,* 96-100.

Brain, P. F. (1986). Multidisciplinary examinations of the "causes" of crime: The case of the link between alcohol and violence. *Alcohol and Alcoholism, 21,* 237-240.

Braithwaite, J. (1989). *Crime, shame, and reintegration.* New York: Cambridge University Press.

Braithwaite, J., & Daly, J. (1994). Masculinities, violence, and communitarian control. In T. Newburn & E. A. Stanko (Eds.), *Just boys doing business? Men, masculinities, and crime* (pp. 189-213). New York: Routledge.

Briskin, K. C., & Gary, J. M. (1986). Sexual assault programming for college students. *Journal of Counseling and Development, 65,* 207-208.

Brosius, H., Weaver, J. B., & Staab, J. F. (1993). Exploring the social and sexual "reality" of contemporary pornography. *The Journal of Sex Research, 30,* 161-170.

Brown, D., & Hogg, R. (1993). Masculinity, sport, and the swinging arm. *Polemic, 4,* 83-87.

Brownstein, H. H. (1991). The social construction of public policy. *Sociological Practice Review, 2,* 132-140.

Buchwald, E., Fletcher, P. R., & Roth, M. (Eds). (1993). *Transforming a rape culture.* Minneapolis: Milkweed Edition.

Burrell, L. F. (1992). Student perceptions of alcohol consumption. *Journal of Alcohol and Drug Education, 37,* 107-113.

Burston, B. W., Jones, D., & Roberson-Saunders, P. (1995). Drug use and African Americans: Myth versus reality. *Journal of Alcohol and Drug Education, 40*(2), 19-39.

Burt, M. R. (1980). Cultural myths and supports for rape. *Journal of Personality and Social Psychology, 38,* 217-230.

Burt, M. R., & Albin, R. (1981). Who is a rape victim? Definitional problems in sexual victimization. *Victimology, 6,* 15-28.

Calhoun, L., Selby, J., & Warring, L. (1986). Social perception of the victim's causal role in rape: An exploratory examination of four factors. *Human Relations, 29,* 517-526.

Caplan, G. (1974). *Social systems and community mental health.* New York: Behavioral Publications.

Carlin, D. R. (1994, February 25). Date rape fallacies: Can there be purely voluntary acts? *Commonwealth, 121*(4), 11-12.

Cassel, J. C. (1976). The contribution of the social environment to host resistance. *American Journal of Epidemiology, 104,* 107-123.

Cassidy, L. (1995). The influence of victim's attire on adolescents' judgments of date rape. *Adolescence, 30,* 319-323.

Center on Addiction and Substance Abuse. (1994). *Rethinking rites of passage: Substance abuse on America's campuses.* New York: Columbia University.

Chappell, D., Geis, G., Schafer, S., & Siegel, L. (1977). A comparative study of forcible rape offenses known to the police in Boston and Los Angeles. In D. Chappell, R. Geis, & G. Geis (Eds.), *Forcible rape: The crime, the victim, and the offender* (pp. 227-244). New York: Columbia University Press.

Chodorow, N. (1978). *The reproduction of mothering.* Berkeley: University of California Press.

Chomak, S., & Collins, R. L. (1987). Relationship between sex-role behaviors and alcohol consumption in undergraduate men and women. *Journal of Studies on Alcohol, 48,* 194-201.

Christian, H. (1994). *The making of anti-sexist men.* London: Routledge.

Clarke, R., & Cornish, D. (1985). Modeling offenders' decisions: A framework for research and theory. In M. Tonry & N. Morris (Eds.), *Crime and justice* (Vol. 6, pp. 147-187). Chicago: University of Chicago Press.

Clarke, R. V., & Felson, M. (1993). Introduction: Criminology, routine activity, and rational choice. In R. V. Clarke and M. Felson (Eds.), *Routine activity and rational choice* (pp. 1-14). New Brunswick, NJ: Transaction.

Clawson, M. A. (1989). *Constructing brotherhood: Class, gender, and fraternalism.* Princeton, NJ: Princeton University Press.

Cohen, L. E., & Felson, M. (1979). Social changes and crime rate trends: A routine activities approach. *American Sociological Review, 44,* 588-608.

Cohen, S., & Wills, T. A. (1985). Stress, social support, and the buffering hypothesis. *Psychological Bulletin, 98,* 310-357.

Connell, R. W. (1992). Drumming up the wrong tree. *Tikkun, 7,* 31-36.

Connell, R. W. (1995). *Masculinities.* Berkeley: University of California Press.

Copenhaver, S., & Grauerholz, E. (1991). Sexual victimization among sorority women: Exploring the link between sexual violence and institutional practices. *Sex Roles, 24,* 31-41.

Cowan, G., & Dunn, K. F. (1994). What themes in pornography lead to perceptions of the degradation of women? *The Journal of Sex Research, 31,* 11-21.

Crawford, C. M. (1995). Alcohol consumption patterns among undergraduates: The impact of family income. *Journal of Alcohol and Drug Education, 40*(3), 1-9.

Cressey, D. R. (1953). *Other people's money.* Glencoe, IL: Free Press.

Cross, W. F. (1993). *Differentiation of sexually coercive and noncoercive college males.* Unpublished doctoral dissertation, Ohio University.

Crosset, T. W., Ptacek, J., McDonald, M. A., & Benedict, J. R. (1996). Male student-athletes and violence against women: A survey of campus judicial affairs offices. *Violence Against Women, 2,* 163-179.

Crossman, L. L. (1994). *Date rape and sexual aggression in college males.* Paper presented at annual meeting of Southwest Educational Research Association, San Antonio, TX.

Curran, D. J., & Renzetti, C. M. (1996). *Social problems: Society in crisis* (4th Ed.). Boston: Allyn & Bacon.

Currie, D. H., & MacLean, B. D. (1993). Woman abuse in dating relationships: Rethinking women's safety on campus. *The Journal of Human Justice, 4,* 1-24.

Curry, T. J. (1991). Fraternal bonding in the locker room: A pro-feminist analysis of talk about competition and women. *Sociology of Sport Journal, 8,* 119-135.

Davis, T. C., Peck, G. Q., & Storment, J. M. (1993). Acquaintance rape and the high school student. *Journal of Adolescent Health, 14,* 220-224.

Deighton, L. (1990). *Spy sinker.* New York: HarperCollins.

DeKeseredy, W. S. (1988a). Woman abuse in dating relationships: The relevance of social support theory. *Journal of Family Violence, 3,* 1-13.

DeKeseredy, W. S. (1988b). *Woman abuse in dating relationships: The role of male peer support.* Toronto: Canadian Scholars' Press.

DeKeseredy, W. S. (1990a). Male peer support and woman abuse: The current state of knowledge. *Sociological Focus, 23,* 129-139.

DeKeseredy, W. S. (1990b). Woman abuse in dating relationships: The contribution of male peer support. *Sociological Inquiry, 60,* 236-243.

DeKeseredy, W. S. (1992). Wife assault. In V. F. Sacco (Ed.), *Deviance: Conformity and control in Canadian society.* Toronto: Prentice Hall.

DeKeseredy, W. S. (1994). Addressing the complexities of woman abuse in dating: A response to Gartner and Fox. *Canadian Journal of Sociology, 19,* 75-80.

DeKeseredy, W. S. (1995). Enhancing the quality of survey data on woman abuse. *Violence Against Women, 1,* 158-173.

DeKeseredy, W. S. (1996a). The Canadian national survey on woman abuse in university/college dating relationships: Biofeminist panic transmission or critical inquiry? *Canadian Journal of Criminology, 38,* 81-104.

DeKeseredy, W. S. (1996b). Left realism and woman abuse in dating. In B. D. MacLean (Ed.), *Crime and society: Readings in critical criminology* (pp. 183-206). Toronto: Copp Clark.

DeKeseredy, W. S. (1996c). Making an unsafe learning environment safer: Some progressive policy proposals to curb woman abuse in university/college dating relationships. In C. Stark-Adamec (Ed.), *Violence: A collective responsibility* (pp. 71-94). Ottawa: Social Science Federation of Canada.

DeKeseredy, W. S. (in press). Measuring sexual abuse in Canadian university/college dating relationships: The contribution of a national representative sample survey. In M. D. Schwartz (Ed.), *Rape methodology.* Thousand Oaks, CA: Sage.

DeKeseredy, W. S., Burshtyn, H., & Gordon, C. (1992). Taking woman abuse seriously: A critical response to the Solicitor General of Canada's crime prevention advice. *International Review of Victimology, 2,* 157-167.

DeKeseredy, W. S., & Hinch, R. (1991). *Woman abuse: Sociological perspectives.* Toronto: Thompson.

DeKeseredy, W. S., & Kelly, K. (1993a). The incidence and prevalence of woman abuse in Canadian university and college dating relationships. *The Canadian Journal of Sociology, 18,* 137-159.

DeKeseredy, W. S., & Kelly, K. (1993b). *Sexual abuse in university and college dating relationships: The contribution of male peer support.* Ottawa: Health and Welfare Canada, Family Violence Prevention Division.

DeKeseredy, W. S., & Kelly, K. (1993c). Woman abuse in university and college dating relationships: The contribution of the ideology of familial patriarchy. *The Journal of Human Justice, 4,* 25-52.

DeKeseredy, W. S., & Kelly, K. (1995). Sexual abuse in Canadian university and college dating relationships: The contribution of male peer support. *Journal of Family Violence, 10,* 41-53.

DeKeseredy, W. S., & Schwartz, M. D. (1993). Male peer support and woman abuse: An expansion of DeKeseredy's model. *Sociological Spectrum, 13,* 393-413.

DeKeseredy, W. S., & Schwartz, M. D. (1994). Locating a history of some Canadian woman abuse in elementary and high school dating relationships. *Humanity and Society, 18,* 49-63.

DeKeseredy, W. S., & Schwartz, M. D. (1996). *Contemporary criminology.* Belmont, CA: Wadsworth.

Dobash, R. E., & Dobash, R. (1988). Research as social action: The struggle for battered women. In K. Yllo & M. Bograd (Eds.), *Feminist perspectives on wife abuse* (pp. 51-74). Beverly Hills, CA: Sage.

Durkheim, E. (1951). *Suicide: A study in sociology.* Glencoe, IL: Free Press.

Dutton, D. G., & Hemphill, K. J. (1992). Patterns of socially desirable responding among perpetrators and victims of wife assault. *Violence and Victims, 7,* 29-40.

Eccles, A., Marshall, W. L., & Barbaree, H. E. (1994). Differentiating rapists and nonoffenders using the rape index. *Behavior Research & Therapy, 32,* 539-546.

Ehrhart, J. K., & Sandler, B. R. (1985). *Campus gang rape: Party games.* Washington, DC: Project on the Status and Education of Women, Association of American Colleges.

Eisenstein, Z. (1980). *Capitalist patriarchy and the case for socialist feminism.* New York: Monthly Review Press.

Eitzen, D. S., & Baca Zinn, M. (1994). *Social problems* (6th ed). Boston: Allyn & Bacon.

Elliot, S., Odynak, D., & Krahn, H. (1992). *A survey of unwanted sexual experiences among University of Alberta students* (Research report prepared for the Council on Student Life, University of Alberta). Edmonton: University of Alberta, Population Research Laboratory.

Ellis, D. (1988). Post-separation woman abuse: The contribution of social support. *Victimology, 13,* 439-450.

Ellis, D., & DeKeseredy, W. S. (1996). *The wrong stuff: An introduction to the sociological study of deviance* (2nd ed.). Toronto: Maxwell Macmillan.

Engs, R. C., & Hanson, D. J. (1985). The drinking patterns and problems of college students: 1983. *Journal of Alcohol and Drug Education, 31*, 65-83.

Eskenazi, G. (1991). Male athletes and sexual assault. *Cosmopolitan, 210*(2), 220-223.

Estrich, S. (1987). *Real rape: How the legal system victimizes women who say no.* Cambridge, MA: Harvard University Press.

Fairstein, L. A. (1993). *Sexual violence: Our war against rape.* New York: William Morrow.

Faludi, S. (1991). *Backlash: The undeclared war against American women.* New York: Crown.

Farr, K. A. (1988). Dominance bonding through the good old boys sociability group. *Sex Roles, 18*, 259-277.

Fekete, J. (1994). *Moral panic: Biopolitics rising.* Montreal: Robert Davies.

Feltey, K. M., Ainslie, J. J., & Geib, A. (1991). Sexual coercion attitudes among high school students: The influence of gender and rape education. *Youth and Society, 23*, 229-250.

Fenstermaker, S. (1989). Acquaintance rape on campus: Responsibility and attributions of crime. In M. A. Pirog-Good & J. E. Stets (Eds.), *Violence in dating relationships: Emerging social issues.* New York: Praeger.

Fine, G. A. (1987). *With the boys: Little League baseball and preadolescent culture.* Chicago: University of Chicago Press.

Finkelman, L. (1992). *Report of the survey of unwanted sexual experiences among students of U.N.B.-F. and S.T.U.* Fredericton: University of New Brunswick, Counseling Services.

Fitzpatrick, D., & Halliday, C. (1992). *Not the way to love: Violence against young women in dating relationships.* Amherst, Nova Scotia: Cumberland County Transition House Association.

Foucault, M. (1977). *Discipline and punish.* New York: Pantheon.

Franks, D. D. (1985). Role-taking, social power, and imperceptiveness: The analysis of rape. *Studies in Symbolic Interaction, 6*, 229-259.

Frazier, P., Valtinson, G., & Candell, S. (1994). Evaluation of a coeducational interactive rape prevention program. *Journal of Counseling & Development, 73*, 153-158.

Friedrichs, D. O. (1995). *Trusted criminals: White-collar crime in contemporary society.* Belmont, CA: Wadsworth.

Frintner, M. P., & Rubinson, L. (1993). Acquaintance rape: The influence of alcohol, fraternity membership, and sports team membership. *Journal of Sex Education & Therapy, 19*, 272-284.

Gallagher, R. P., Harmon, W. W., & Lingenfelter, C. O. (1994). CSAO's perceptions of the changing incidence of problematic college student behavior. *NASPA Journal, 32* (Fall), 37-45.

Garrett-Gooding, J., & Senter, R. (1987). Attitudes and acts of sexual aggression on a university campus. *Sociological Inquiry, 57*, 349-371.

Gavey, N. (1991). Sexual victimization prevalence among New Zealand university students. *Journal of Consulting and Clinical Psychology, 59*, 464-466.

George, W. H., Gournic, S. J., & McAfee, M. P. (1988). Perceptions of post-drinking female sexuality: Effects of gender, beverage choice, and drink payment. *Journal of Applied Social Psychology, 18,* 1925-1317.

Giacopassi, D. J., & Dull, R. T. (1986). Gender and racial differences in the acceptance of rape myths within a college population. *Sex Roles, 15,* 63-75.

Gibbs, J. P. (1975). *Crime, punishment, and deterrence.* New York: Elsevier.

Gilbert, N. (1991). The phantom epidemic of sexual assault. *The Public Interest, 103,* 54-65.

Gilbert, N. (1992, May). Realities and mythologies of rape. *Society, 29,* pp. 4-10.

Gilmartin-Zena, P. (1987). Attitudes toward rape: Student characteristics as predictors. *Free Inquiry in Creative Sociology, 15*(2), 175-182.

Gilmartin-Zena, P. (1988). Gender differences in students' attitudes toward rape. *Sociological Focus, 21,* 279-292.

Gilmartin-Zena, P. (1989). Attitudes about rape myths: Are women's studies students different? *Free Inquiry in Creative Sociology, 17,* 65-72.

Gilmore, D. D. (1990). *Mankind in the making: Cultural concepts of masculinity.* New Haven, CT: Yale University Press.

Gleason, N. (1993). College women and alcohol: A relational perspective. *Journal of American College Health, 42,* 279-289.

Globetti, G., Stern, J. T., Marasco, F., & Hoeppner, S. H. (1988). Student residence arrangements and alcohol use and abuse. *Journal of College and University Student Housing, 18,* 28-33.

Goettsch, J. M., & Hayes, M. A. (1990). Racism and sexism in Greek events. *NASPA Journal, 28,* 65-70.

Goffman, E. (1961). *Asylums.* Garden City, NY: Doubleday Anchor Books.

Gonzales, G. M. (1990). A comparison of alcohol use and alcohol-related problems among caucasian, black, and Hispanic college students. *NASPA Journal, 27,* 330-335.

Gonzalez, G. (1994). Can colleges reduce student drinking? *Planning for Higher Education, 22,* 14-21.

Goodwin, G. (1983). Toward a paradigm for humanist sociology. *Humanity & Society, 7,* 219-237.

Goodwin, L. (1989). Explaining alcohol consumption and related experiences among fraternity and sorority members. *Journal of College Student Development, 30,* 448-458.

Gottesman, S. T. (1977). Police attitudes toward rape before and after a training program. *Journal of Psychiatric Nursing and Mental Health Services, 15,* 14-18.

Gwartney-Gibbs, P. A., & Stockard, J. (1989). Courtship aggression and mixed-sex peer groups. In M. A. Pirog-Good & J. E. Stets (Eds.), *Violence in dating relationships: Emerging social issues.* New York: Praeger.

Hall, R. (1985). *Ask any woman: A London inquiry into rape and sexual assault.* London: Falling Wall Press.

Handler, L. (1995). In the fraternal sisterhood: Sororities as gender strategy. *Gender & Society, 9,* 236-255.

Hanmer, J., & Saunders, S. (1984). *Well-founded fear: A community study of violence to women.* London: Hutchinson.

Harmon, P. A., & Check, J. V. P. (1988). *The role of pornography in woman abuse.* North York, Ontario: LaMarsch Research Programme on Violence and Conflict Resolution.

Harney, P. A., & Muehlenhard, C. L. (1991). Rape. In E. Grauerholz & M. A. Koralewski (Eds.), *Sexual coercion.* New York: Lexington.

Harris, M. (1989). *Our kind: Who we are, where we came from, where we are going.* New York: Harper & Row.

Hawkins, R., & Alpert, G. P. (1989). *American prison systems.* Englewood Cliffs, NJ: Prentice Hall.

Heilbrun, A. B., Jr., & Loftus, M. P. (1986). The role of sadism and peer pressure in the sexual aggression of male college students. *Journal of Sex Research, 22*(3), 320-332.

Henslin, J. M. (1990). *Social problems* (2nd ed.). Englewood Cliffs, NJ: Prentice Hall.

Henslin, J. M. (1994). *Social problems* (3rd ed.). Englewood Cliffs, NJ: Prentice Hall.

Herek, G. M. (1987). On heterosexual masculinity: Some psychological consequences of the social construction of gender and sexuality. In M. S. Kimmel (Ed.), *Changing men: New directions in research on men and masculinity* (pp. 68-82). Beverly Hills, CA: Sage.

Hey, V. (1986). *Patriarchy and pub culture.* London: Tavistock.

Hills, S. (1984). Crime and deviance on a college campus: The privilege of class. In M. D. Schwartz & D. O. Friedrichs (Eds.), *Humanistic perspectives on crime and justice* (pp. 60-69). Hebron, CT: Practitioner Press.

hooks, b. (1992). Men: Comrades in struggle. In M. S. Kimmel & M. A. Messner (Eds.), *Men's lives* (pp. 561-571). New York: Macmillan.

Hornosty, J. M. (1996). A look at faculty fears and needed university policies against violence and harassment. In C. Stark-Adamec (Ed.), *Violence: A collective responsibility* (pp. 31-56). Ottawa: Social Science Federation of Canada.

House, J. S. (1981). *Work stress and social support.* Reading, MA: Addison-Wesley.

Hughes, M. J., & Winston, R. B., Jr. (1987). Effects of fraternity membership on interpersonal values. *Journal of College Student Personnel, 28*(5), 405-411.

Hunnicutt, D. M., Davis, J. L., & Fletcher, J. (1991). Preventing alcohol abuse in the Greek system on a community campus. *NASPA Journal, 28,* 179-184.

Itzin, C., & Sweet, C. (1992). Women's experience of pornography: UK magazine survey evidence. In C. Itzin (Ed.), *Pornography: Women, violence, and civil liberties* (pp. 222-235). New York: Oxford University Press.

Jaffe, P., Sudermann, M., Reitzel, D., & Killip, S. (1992). An evaluation of a secondary school primary prevention program on violence in intimate relationships. *Violence and Victims, 7,* 129-146.

Janoff-Bulman, R. (1979). Characterological versus behavioral self-blame: Inquiries into depression and rape. *Journal of Personality and Social Psychology, 37,* 1798-1809.

Janoff-Bulman, R. (1982). Esteem and control bases of blame: "Adaptive" strategies for victims versus observers. *Journal of Personality, 50*, 180-192.

Jefferson, T. (1994). Theorizing masculine subjectivity. In T. Newburn & E. Stanko (Eds.), *Just boys doing business: Men, masculinities, and crime* (pp. 10-31). London: Routledge.

Jensen, R. (1995). Pornographic lives. *Violence Against Women, 1*, 32-54.

Johnson, R. (1996). *Hard time: Understanding and reforming the prison* (2nd ed.). Belmont, CA: Wadsworth.

Johnson, J. M., & Ferraro, K. J. (1988). Courtship violence: Survey vs. empathic understandings of abusive conduct. In N. Denzin (Ed.), *Studies in symbolic interaction* (Vol. 9, pp. 175-186). Greenwich, CT: JAI Press.

Kalof, L. (1993). Rape-supportive attitudes and sexual victimization experiences of sorority and nonsorority women. *Sex Roles, 29*, 767-780.

Kalof, L., & Cargill, T. (1991). Fraternity and sorority membership and gender dominance attitudes. *Sex Roles, 25*, 417-423.

Kamen, P. (1991). *Feminist fatale: Voices from the twentysomething generation.* New York: Donald Fine.

Kanin, E. J. (1957). Male aggression in dating-courtship relations. *American Journal of Sociology, 63*, 197-204.

Kanin, E. J. (1967). An examination of sexual aggression as a response to sexual frustration. *Journal of Marriage and the Family, 29*, 428-433.

Kanin, E. J. (1984). Date rape: Unofficial criminals and victims. *Victimology, 9*, 95-108.

Kanin, E. J. (1985). Date rapists: Differential sexual socialization and relative deprivation. *Archives of Sexual Behavior, 14*, 219-231.

Karuza, J., & Carey, T. O. (1984). Relative preference and adaptiveness of behavioral blame for observers of rape victims. *Journal of Personality, 52*, 249-260.

Kaufman, M. (1995). The construction of masculinity and the triad of men's violence. In M. S. Kimmel & M. A. Messner (Eds.), *Men's lives,* (3rd ed., pp. 13-25). Boston: Allyn & Bacon.

Kelling, G., Pate, T., Dieckman, D., & Brown, C. (1974). *The Kansas City preventive patrol experiment: A summary report.* Washington, DC: Police Foundation.

Kelly, K. D., & DeKeseredy, W. S. (1994). Women's fear of crime and abuse in college and university dating relationships. *Violence and Victims, 9*, 17-30.

Kelly, L. (1987). The continuum of sexual violence. In J. Hanmer & M. Maynard (Eds.), *Women, violence, and social control* (pp. 46-60). Atlantic Highlands, NJ: Humanities Press International.

Kennedy, L., & Dutton, D. G. (1989). The incidence of wife assault in Alberta. *Canadian Journal of Behavioral Science, 21*, 40-54.

Kessler, R. C., & McLeod, J. D. (1985). Social support and mental health in community samples. In S. Cohen & S. L. Syme (Eds.), *Social support and health* (pp. 219-240). Toronto: Academic Press.

Kilgannon, S. M., & Erwin, T. D. (1992). A longitudinal study about the identity and moral development of Greek students. *Journal of College Student Development, 33*, 253-259.

Kilpatrick, D., Saunders, B., Amick-McMullan, A., Best, C., Veronen, L., & Resnick, H. (1989). Victim and crime factors associated with the development of crime-related post-traumatic stress disorder. *Behavior Therapy, 20,* 199-214.

Kimmel, M. S. (1987). Rethinking "masculinity": New directions in research. In M. S. Kimmel (Ed.), *Changing men: New directions in research on men and masculinity* (pp. 9-24). Beverly Hills, CA: Sage.

Klein, H. (1992a). College students' attitudes toward the use of alcoholic beverages. *Journal of Alcohol and Drug Education, 37*(3), 35-52.

Klein, H. (1992b). Self-reported reasons for why college students drink. *Journal of Alcohol and Drug Education, 37*(2), 14-28.

Koss, M. P. (1985). The hidden rape victim: Personality, attitudinal, and situational characteristics. *Psychology of Women Quarterly, 9,* 193-212.

Koss, M. P. (1988). Hidden rape: Sexual aggression and victimization in a national sample in higher education. In A. W. Burgess (Ed.), *Rape and sexual assault: Vol. 2.* New York: Garland.

Koss, M. P. (1989). Hidden rape: Sexual aggression and victimization in a national sample of students in higher education. In M. A. Pirog-Good & J. E. Stets (Eds.), *Violence in dating relationships: Emerging social issues* (pp. 145-168). New York: Praeger.

Koss, M. P. (1992). Rape on campus: Facts and measures. *Planning for Higher Education, 20,* 21-28.

Koss, M. P., & Cook, S. L. (1993). Facing the facts: Date and acquaintance rape are significant problems for women. In R. J. Gelles & D. R. Loseke (Eds.), *Current controversies on family violence* (pp. 104-119). Thousand Oaks, CA: Sage.

Koss, M. P., & Gaines, J. A. (1993). The prediction of sexual aggression by alcohol use, athletic participation, and fraternity affiliation. *Journal of Interpersonal Violence, 8,* 94-108.

Koss, M. P., & Gidycz, C. A. (1985). Sexual experiences survey: Reliability and validity. *Journal of Consulting and Clinical Psychology, 53,* 422-423.

Koss, M. P., Gidycz, C. A., & Wisniewski, W. (1987). The scope of rape: Incidence and prevalence of sexual aggression and victimization in a national sample of higher education students. *Journal of Consulting and Clinical Psychology, 55,* 162-170.

Koss, M. P., & Harvey, M. R. (1991). *The rape victim: Clinical and community interventions* (2nd ed.). Newbury Park, CA: Sage.

Koss, M. P., Leonard, K., Beezley, D., & Oros, C. J. (1985). Non-stranger sexual aggression: A discriminant analysis of the psychological characteristics of undetected offenders. *Sex Roles, 12,* 981-992.

Lamanna, M. A., & Riedmann, A. C. (1985). *Marriages and families.* Belmont, CA: Wadsworth.

Laner, M. R., & Thompson, J. (1982). Abuse and aggression in courting couples. *Deviant Behavior, 3,* 229-244.

Lasch, C. (1977). *Haven in a heartless world: The family besieged.* New York: Basic Books.

Layden, T. (1995). Better education. *Sports Illustrated, 82*(13), 68-83.

Layng, A. (1995). Evolution explains traditional gender roles. In J. S. Petrikin (Ed.), *Male/female roles* (pp. 17-23). San Diego: Greenhaven Press.

Ledwitz-Rigby, F. (1993). An administrative approach to personal safety on campus: The role of a President's Advisory Committee on Woman's Safety on Campus. *The Journal of Human Justice, 4*, 85-94.

Lee, L. A. (1987). Rape prevention: Experiential training for men. *Journal of Counseling and Development, 66*, 100-101.

Leggett, M., & Schwartz, M. D. (1996). *The aftermath of campus sexual assault.* Paper presented at the annual meetings of the Academy of Criminal Justice Sciences, Las Vegas, NV.

LeMasters, E. E. (1975). *Blue-collar aristocrats: Life-styles at a working-class tavern.* Madison: University of Wisconsin Press.

Lenihan, G. O., & Rawlins, M. E. (1994). Rape supportive attitudes among Greek students before and after a date rape prevention program. *Journal of College Student Development, 35*, 450-455.

Levan, A. (1996). Violence against women. In J. Brodie (Ed.), *Women and Canadian public policy* (pp. 319-354). Toronto: Harcourt Brace.

Levant, R. (1994). *Male violence against female partners: Roots in male socialization and development.* Paper presented at the American Psychological Association meetings, Los Angeles.

Levine, E. M., & Kanin, E. J. (1986). Adolescent drug use: Its prospects for the future. *Journal of Family Culture, 1,* 4.

Levine, E. M., & Kanin, E. J. (1987). Sexual violence among dates and acquaintances: Trends and their implications for marriage and family. *Journal of Family Violence, 2*(1), 55-65.

Levinson, D. (1989). *Family violence in cross-cultural perspective.* Newbury Park, CA: Sage.

Lichtenberg, J. W. (1993). *Sexual coercion and aggression on campus: Characteristics of offenders.* Paper presented at annual meeting of the American Psychological Association, Toronto.

Lichtenfeld, M., & Kayson, W. A. (1994). Factors in college students' drinking. *Psychological Reports, 74,* 927-930.

Lisak, D., & Roth, S. (1988). Motivational factors in nonincarcerated sexually active men. *Journal of Personality and Social Psychology, 55*(5), 795-802.

Lloyd, S. (1991). The dark side of courtship: Violence and sexual exploitation. *Family Relations, 40,* 14-20.

Longino, H. (1995). Pornography, oppression, and freedom: A closer look. In S. Dwyer (Ed.), *The problem of pornography* (pp. 34-47). Belmont, CA: Wadsworth.

Lottes, I. L., & Kuriloff, P. J. (1994). Sexual socialization differences by gender, Greek membership, ethnicity, and religious backgrounds. *Psychology of Women Quarterly, 18,* 203-129.

Lyman, P. (1987). The fraternity bond as a joking relationship. In M. S. Kimmel & M. A. Messner (Eds.) *Men's lives* (3rd ed., pp. 86-96). Boston: Allyn & Bacon.

MacIvor, H. (1995, April). The biopolitical agenda. *The Literary Review of Canada,* pp. 20-21.

MacKinnon, C. (1993). *Only words.* Cambridge, MA: Harvard University Press.

Madigan, L., & Gamble, N. (1989). *The second rape: Society's continued betrayal of the victim.* New York: Lexington.

Mahlstedt, D. (n.d.). *Getting started: Setting-up a FVEP on your campus.* West Chester, PA: West Chester University.

Mahlstedt, D., Falcone, D., & Rice-Spring, L. (1993). Dating violence education: What do students learn? *Journal of Human Justice, 4,* 101-117.

Makepeace, J. M. (1986). Gender differences in courtship violence victimization. *Family Relations, 35*(3), 383-388.

Malamuth, N. M., Sockloskie, R. J., Koss, M. P., & Tanaka, J. S. (1991). Characteristics of aggressors against women: Testing a model using a national sample of college students. *Journal of Consulting & Clinical Psychology, 59,* 670-681.

Malaney, G. D. (1990). Student attitudes toward fraternities and sororities. *NASPA Journal, 28,* 37-42.

Margolis, G. (1992). Earlier intervention: Confronting the idea and practice of drinking to drunkeness on college campuses. *Journal of College Student Psychotherapy, 7,* 15-22.

Martin, P. Y., & Hummer, R. A. (1989). Fraternities and rape on campus. *Gender and Society, 3,* 457-473.

Martin, S. (1980). *Breaking and entering.* Berkeley: University of California Press.

Matza, D. (1964). *Delinquency and drift.* New York: John Wiley.

May, L., & Strikwerda, R. (1994). Men in groups: Collective responsibility for rape. *Hypatia, 9,* 134-151.

McCandless, N. J. (1994). Sex-role differentiation: Exploring race differences. *Free Inquiry in Creative Sociology, 22,* 144-148.

McMillen, L. (1990). An anthropologist's disturbing picture of gang rape on campus. *Chronicle of Higher Education, 37,* A3.

McNamara, R. (1994). *Crime displacement: The other side of prevention.* East Rockaway, NY: Cummings & Hathaway.

Mead, G. H. (1934). *Mind, self, and society.* Chicago: University of Chicago Press.

Melnick, M. (1992, May/June). Male athletes and sexual assault. *Journal of Physical Education, Recreation, and Dance,* pp. 32-35.

Mercer, S. (1988). Not a pretty picture: An exploratory study of violence against women in high school dating relationships. *Resources for Feminist Research, 17,* 15-23.

Merton, A. (1985, September). Return to brotherhood. *Ms. Magazine, 14,* 60-64, 121-122.

Messerschmidt, J. (1993). *Masculinities and crime: Critique and reconceptualization of theory.* Lanham, MD: Rowman & Littlefield.

Messner, M. (1992). *Power at play: Sports and the problem of masculinity.* Boston: Beacon Press.

Messner, M. A. (1994). Women in men's locker room? In M. A. Messner & D. F. Sabo (Eds.), *Sex, violence, & power in sports: Rethinking masculinity* (pp. 42-52). Freedom, CA: The Crossing Press.

Messner, M. A., & Sabo, D. F. (1990). Toward a critical feminist reappraisal of sport, men, and the gender order. In M. A. Messner & D. F. Sabo (Eds.), *Sport, men, and the gender order: Critical feminist perspectives* (pp. 1-15). Champaign, IL: Human Kinetics Books.

Miller, J., & Schwartz, M. D. (1992, November). *Lewd lighters and dick-ee darts: The commodification of women through sexual objects.* Paper presented at the annual meetings of the American Society of Criminology, New Orleans.

Miller, J., & Schwartz, M. D. (1995). Rape myths and violence against street prostitutes. *Deviant Behavior, 16*(1), 1-23.

Miller, L. D. (1973). Distinctive characteristics of fraternity members. *Journal of College Student Personnel, 14,* 126-128.

Mills, C. W. (1940). Situated actions and vocabularies of motive. *American Sociological Review, 5,* 904-913.

Morgan, D. H. J. (1992). *Discovering men.* London: Routledge.

Morris, J. R. (1991). Racial attitudes of undergraduates in Greek housing. *College Student Journal, 25,* 501-505.

Muehlenhard, C. L., & Linton, M. A. (1987). Date rape and sexual aggression in dating situations: Incidence and risk factors. *Journal of Counseling Psychology, 34,* 186-196.

Muehlenhard, C. L., Sympson, S. C., Phelps, J. L., & Highby, B. J. (1994). Are rape statistics exaggerated? A response to criticism of contemporary rape research. *The Journal of Sex Research, 31,* 144-146.

Muir, D. E. (1991). "White" fraternity and sorority attitudes toward "blacks" on a deep-South campus. *Sociological Spectrum, 11,* 93-103.

Murdoch, D., Pihl, D. O., & Ross, D. (1990). Alcohol and crimes of violence: Present issues. *International Journal of the Addictions, 25,* 1065-1081.

Neimark, J. (1991). Out of bounds: The truth about athletes and rape. *Mademoiselle, 97*(5), 196-199, 244-246.

Nelson, M. B. (1994). *The stronger women get, the more men love football: Sexism and the American culture of sports.* New York: Harcourt Brace.

NFL asked to start campaign against violence. (1996, January 26). *Columbus Dispatch,* p. 5F.

Nogrady, C. (1992). *Rape myth acceptance: A feminist analysis and empirical investigation within a college population.* Honors tutorial college thesis, Ohio University.

Norris, J., & Cubbins, L. (1992). Dating, drinking, and rape: Effects of victim's and assailant's alcohol consumption on judgments of their behavior and traits. *Psychology of Women Quarterly, 16,* 179-191.

Norris, J., Nurius, P. S., & Dimeff, L. A. (1996). Through her eyes: Factors affecting women's perception of and resisistance to acquaintance sexual aggression threat. *Psychology of Women Quarterly, 20,* 123-145.

Orcutt, J. D., & Faison, R. (1988). Sex role attitude change and reporting of rape victimization, 1973-1985. *Sociological Quarterly, 29,* 589-604.

Pate, A. M., & Hamilton, E. E. (1992). Formal and informal deterrents to domestic violence. *American Sociological Review, 57,* 691-697.

Pierson, R. R. (1991). Violence against women: Strategies for change. *Canadian Women's Studies, 11,* 10-12.

Pirog-Good, M. A., & Stets, J. E. (Eds.). (1989). *Violence in dating relationships: Emerging social issues.* New York: Praeger.

Pitts, V. L., & Schwartz, M. D. (1993). Promoting self-blame among hidden rape survivors. *Humanity & Society, 17,* 383-398.

Pollard, J. (1993). *Male-female dating relationships in Canadian universities and colleges: Sample design, arrangements for data collection, and data reduction.* Toronto: Institute for Social Research.

Pollard, P. (1992). Judgements about victims and attackers in depicted rapes: A review. *British Journal of Social Psychology, 31,* 307-326.

Proite, R., Dannells, M., & Benton, S. L. (1993). Gender, sex-role stereotypes, and the attribution of responsibility for date and acquaintance rape. *Journal of College Student Development, 34,* 411-417.

Rabinowitz, F. E., & Cochran, S. V. (1994). *Man alive: A primer of men's issues.* Pacific Grove, CA: Brooks/Cole.

Rabow, J., & Duncan-Schill, M. (1995). Drinking among college students. *Journal of Alcohol & Drug Education, 40,* 52-64.

Rajacich, D., Fawdry, M. K., & Berry, M. L. (1992). An institutional response to date rape. *The Canadian Journal of Higher Education, 22,* 41-59.

Rapaport, K., & Burkhart, B. R. (1984). Personality and attitudinal characteristics of sexually coercive college males. *Journal of Abnormal Psychology, 93,* 216-221.

Reese, F. L., & Friend, R. (1994). Alcohol expectancies and drinking practices among black and white undergraduate males. *Journal of College Student Development, 35,* 319-323.

Renzetti, C. (1994). On dancing with a bear: Reflections on some of the current debates among domestic violence theorists. *Violence and Victims, 9,* 195-200.

Richardson, D., & Campbell, J. (1988). Alcohol and rape: The effect of alcohol on attributions of blame for rape. *Personal and Social Psychology Bulletin, 8,* 468-476.

Richardson, L. (1988). *The dynamics of sex and gender: A sociological perspective* (3rd ed.). New York: Harper & Row.

Richmond-Abbott, M. (1983). *Masculine and feminine: Sex roles over the life cycle.* New York: Random House.

Rivera, G. F., Jr., & Regoli, R. M. (1987). Sexual victimization experiences of sorority women. *Sociology and Social Research, 72*(1), 39-42.

Roark, M. (1987). Preventing violence on college campuses. *Journal of Counseling and Development, 65*(7), 367-371.

Roiphe, K. (1993). *The morning after: Sex, fear, and feminism on campus.* Boston: Little, Brown.

Rosenhan, D. L. (1973). On being sane in insane places. *Science, 179,* 250-258.

Rotundo, E. A. (1993). *American manhood: Transformations in masculinity from the revolution to the modern era.* New York: Basic Books.

Rozee, P., Bateman, P., & Gilmore, T. (1991). The personal perspective of acquaintance rape prevention: A three-tier approach. In A. Parrot & L. Bachhofer (Eds.), *Acquaintance rape: The hidden crime* (pp. 337-354). New York: John Wiley.

Russell, D. E. H. (1984). *Sexual exploitation: Rape, child sexual abuse, and sexual harassment.* Beverly Hills, CA: Sage.

Russell, D. E. H. (1992). *Rape in marriage* (2nd ed.). Bloomington: Indiana University Press.

Russell, G. W. (1983). Psychological issues in sports aggression. In J. H. Goldstein (Ed.), *Sports violence* (pp. 157-182). New York: Springer-Verlag.

Sabo, D., & Messner, M. (1994). Changing men through changing sports: An 11-point strategy. In M. A. Messner & D. F. Sabo (Eds.), *Sex, violence, & power in sports* (pp. 214-218). Freedom, CA: The Crossing Press.

Sanday, P. R. (1990). *Fraternity gang rape.* New York: New York University Press.

Sanday, P. R. (1996a). Rape-prone versus rape-free campus cultures. *Violence Against Women, 2,* 191-208.

Sanday, P. R. (1996b). *A woman scorned: Acquaintance rape on trial.* New York: Doubleday.

Sarason, I. G., & Sarason, B. R. (1985). *Social support: Theory, research, and applications.* The Hague, The Netherlands: Martinus Nijhof.

Scanlon, J. (1994). The truly well-lit path: Efforts toward a rape-free college campus. *Initiatives, 56,* 31-40.

Scarce, M. (1995). *Through the cracks: Male rape on campus.* Ohio State University Department of Health Promotion, Columbus, OH.

Schaeffer, A., & Nelson, E. (1993). Rape-supportive attitudes: Effects of on-campus residence and education. *Journal of College Student Development, 34,* 175-179.

Schafran, L. H. (1995, September 11). Blinded by rape myths. *National Law Journal, 18,* A21-A22.

Schewe, P. A., & O'Donohue, W. (1993). Sexual abuse prevention with high-risk males: The roles of victim empathy and rape myths. *Violence and Victims, 8,* 339-351.

Schreiber, L. (1995). Brain structure does not explain male/female differences. In J. S. Petrikin (Ed.), *Male/female roles* (pp. 57-65). San Diego: Greenhaven.

Schuh, J. H., Triponey, V. L., Heim, L. L., & Nishimura, K. (1992). Student involvement in historically black Greek letter organizations. *NASPA Journal, 29,* 274-282.

Schur, E. M. (1974). A sociologist's view: The case for abolition. In E. Schur & H. A. Bedau (Eds.), *Victimless crimes: Two sides of the controversy* (pp. 3-52). Engelwood Cliffs, NJ: Prentice Hall.

Schur, E. M. (1984). *Labeling women deviant.* New York: Random House.

Schur, E. M. (1988). *The Americanization of sex.* Philadelphia: Temple University Press.

Schwartz, M. D. (1982). The spousal exemption for criminal rape prosecution. *Vermont Law Review, 7,* 33-57.

Schwartz, M. D. (1983). Sexual assault on college campuses. In D. Mechlem, K. Haley, & J. Vondress (Eds.), *Critical issues in campus policing.* Cincinnati: Criminal Justice Publications.

Schwartz, M. D. (1988). Ain't got no class: Universal risk theories of battering. *Contemporary Crises, 12,* 373-392.

Schwartz, M. D. (1989). Family violence as a cause of crime: Rethinking our priorities. *Criminal Justice Policy Review, 3,* 115-132.

Schwartz, M. D. (1991). Humanist sociology and date rape. *Humanity and Society, 15,* 304-316.

Schwartz, M. D. (1995). Date rape. In A. Thio & T. Calhoun (Eds.), *Readings in deviant behavior.* New York: HarperCollins.

Schwartz, M. D. (1996). The study of masculinities and crime. *The Criminologist, 21,* 1-5.

Schwartz, M. D., & Clear, T. R. (1980). Toward a new law on rape. *Crime and Delinquency, 26,* 129-151.

Schwartz, M. D., & DeKeseredy, W. S. (1993). The return of the battered husband syndrome through the typification of women as violent. *Crime, Law, and Social Change, 20,* 249-265.

Schwartz, M. D., & DeKeseredy, W. S. (1994a). *Male peer support, pornography, and the abuse of Canadian women in dating relationships.* Paper presented at the annual meeting of the American Society of Criminology, Miami, FL.

Schwartz, M. D., & DeKeseredy, W. S. (1994b). People without data attacking rape: The Gilbertizing of Mary Koss. *Violence Update, 5,* 5, 8, 11.

Schwartz, M. D., & Nogrady, C. (1996). Fraternity membership, rape myths, and sexual aggression on a college campus. *Violence Against Women, 2,* 148-162.

Schwartz, M. D., & Pitts, V. L. (1995). Exploring a feminist routine activities approach to explaining sexual assault. *Justice Quarterly, 12,* 9-31.

Schwartz, M. D., & Wilson, N. (1993). We're talking but are they listening? Student retention of sexual assault programming. *Free Inquiry in Creative Sociology, 21*(1), 3-8.

Scott, C. G., & Ambroson, D. L. (1995). The importance of individualizing and marketing campus prevention and intervention programs to meet the needs of specific campus audiences. *Journal of Alcohol & Drug Education, 40,* 21-36.

Scully, D. (1990). *Understanding sexual violence: A study of convicted rapists.* Boston: Unwin Hyman.

Scully, D., & Marolla, J. (1985). Riding the bull at Gilley's: Convicted rapists describe the rewards of rape. *Social Problems, 32,* 251-263.

Seckman, M. A., & Couch, C. J. (1989). Jocularity, sarcasm, and relationships. *Journal of Contemporary Ethnography, 3,* 327-344.

Shelton-Keller, A., Lloyd-McGarvey, E., West, M., & Canterbury, R. J. (1994). Attachment and assessment of blame in date rape scenarios. *Social Behavior & Personality, 22,* 313-318.

Shenkman, R. (1989). *Legends, lies, & cherished myths of American history.* New York: Harper & Row.

Sherry, P., & Stolber, V. (1987). Factors affecting alcohol use by college students. *Journal of College Student Personnel, 28,* 350-354.

Shotland, R. L. (1992). A theory on the causes of courtship rape: Part 2. *Journal of Social Issues, 48,* 127-143.

Siegel, L. (1993). *Criminology* (4th Ed). St. Paul, MN: West.

Silverman, R., & Kennedy, L. (1993). *Deadly deeds: Murder in Canada.* Scarborough, ON: Nelson.

Simpson, M. (1994). *Folk erotica: Celebrating centuries of erotic Americana.* New York: HarperCollins.

Smith, M. D. (1983). *Violence and sport.* Toronto: Butterworths.

Smith, M. D. (1987). The incidence and prevalence of woman abuse in Toronto. *Violence and Victims, 2,* 173-187.

Smith, M. D. (1990a). Patriarchal ideology and wife beating: A test of a feminist hypothesis. *Violence and Victims, 5,* 257-273.

Smith, M. D. (1990b). Socioeconomic risk factors in wife abuse: Results from a survey of Toronto women. *Canadian Journal of Sociology, 15,* 39-58.

Smith, M. D. (1991). Male peer support of wife abuse: An exploratory study. *Journal of Interpersonal Violence, 6,* 512-519.

Smith, M. D. (1994). Enhancing the quality of survey data on violence against women: A feminist approach. *Gender & Society, 18,* 109-127.

Smith, T. S. (1964). The emergence and maintenance of fraternal solidarity. *Pacific Sociological Review, 7,* 29-37.

Spain, D. (1992). The spatial foundations of men's friendships and men's power. In P. Nardi (Ed.), *Men's friendships* (pp. 59-73). Newbury Park, CA: Sage.

Spence, J., Helmreich, R., & Stapp, J. (1974). The Personal Attributes Questionnaire. *JSAS Catalog of Selected Documents in Psychology, 4,* 43.

Stanko, E. A. (1990). *Everyday violence: How women and men experience sexual and physical danger.* London: Pandora.

Stanko, E. A. (1995). The struggle over commonsense feminism, violence, and confronting the backlash. In B. Gillies & G. James (Eds.), *Proceedings of the fifth symposium on violence and aggression* (pp. 156-172). Saskatoon, Saskatchewan: University Extension Press, University of Saskatchewan.

Steinberg, T. N. (1991). Rape on college campuses: Reform through Title IX. *Journal of College and University Law, 18,* 39-71.

Stombler, M. (1994). "Buddies" or "Slutties": The collective sexual reputation of fraternity little sisters. *Gender & Society, 8,* 297-323.

Straus, M. A., Gelles, R. J., & Steinmetz, S. K. (1981). *Behind closed doors: Violence in the American family.* New York: Anchor Books.

Sudermann, M., & Jaffe, P. (1993). *Violence in teen dating relationships: Evaluation of a large-scale primary prevention program.* Paper presented at the annual meetings of the American Psychological Association, Toronto.

Sugarman, D. B., & Hotaling, C. T. (1989). Dating violence: Prevalence, context, and risk markers. In M. A. Pirog-Good & J. E. Stets (Eds.), *Violence in dating relationships: Emerging social issues.* New York: Praeger.

Surette, R. (1992). *Media, crime, & criminal justice: Images and realities.* Pacific Grove, CA: Brooks/Cole.

Sutherland, E. H., & Cressey, D. R. (1978). *Criminology* (10th ed.). Philadelphia: J. P. Lippincott.

Szymanski, L. A., Devlin, A. S., Chrisler, J. C., & Vyse, S. A. (1993). Gender role and attitudes toward rape in male and female college students. *Sex Roles, 29,* 37-57.

Tampke, D. R. (1990). Alcohol behavior, risk perception, and fraternity and sorority membership. *NASPA Journal, 28,* 71-77.

Telander, R. (1989). *The hundred yard lie.* New York: Simon & Schuster.

Thorne, B. (1993). *Gender play: Girls and boys in school.* New Brunswick, NJ: Rutgers University Press.

Thorne-Finch, R. (1992). *Ending the silence: The origins and treatment of male violence against women.* Toronto: University of Toronto Press.

Tittle, C. (1980). *Sanctions and social deviance.* New York: Praeger.

Toby, J. (1975). Violence and the masculine ideal: Some qualitative data. In S. M. Steinmetz & M. A. Straus (Eds), *Violence in the family.* New York: Dodd, Mead.

Tong, R. (1984). *Women, sex, and the law.* Totawa, NJ: Rowman & Allanheld.

Turner, P. A. (1993). *I heard it through the grapevine: Rumor in African American culture.* Berkeley: University of California Press.

Turner, R. J. (1983). Direct, indirect, and moderating effects of social support upon psychological distress and associated conditions. In H. P. Kaplan (Ed.), *Psychological stress: Trends in research and theory* (pp. 105-155). Toronto: Academic Press.

Tyler, L., & Kyes, K. B. (1992). *Alcohol, sex, and contraceptive use among college seniors.* Paper presented at the annual meeting of the Southeastern Psychological Association, Knoxville, TN.

United Nations. (1995). *Human development report 1995.* Toronto: Oxford University Press.

Ursel, J. (1984). Toward a theory of reproduction. *Contemporary Crises, 8,* 265-292.

Vachss, A. (1993). *Sex crimes: Ten years on the front lines.* New York: Random House.

Waller, W. (1937). The rating and dating complex. *American Sociological Review, 2,* 727-734.

Walston, B. S., Alagna, S. W., DeVellis, B. M., & DeVellis, R. F. (1983). Social support and health. *Health Psychology, 4,* 367-391.

Ward, C. A. (1995). *Attitudes toward rape: Feminist and social psychological pespectives.* London: Sage.

Ward, S., Chapman, K., Cohen, E., White, S., & Williams, K. (1991). Acquaintance rape and the college social scene. *Family Relations, 40,* 65-71.

Warshaw, R. (1988). *I never called it rape.* New York: Harper & Row.

Weis, K., & Borges, S. (1973). Victimology and rape: The case of the legitimate victim. *Issues in Criminology, 8,* 71-115.

Wesley, F., & Wesley, C. (1977). *Sex-role psychology.* New York: Human Sciences Press.

White, J., & Sorenson, S. (1992). A sociocultural view of sexual assault: From discrepancy to diversity. *Journal of Social Issues, 46,* 187-195.

Whitehead, A. (1976). Sexual antagonisms in Herefordshire. In D. Barker & S. Allen (Eds.), *Dependence and exploitation in work and marriage* (pp. 169-203). London: Longman.

Wiehe, V. R., & Richards, A. L. (1995). *Intimate betrayal: Understanding and responding to the trauma of acquaintance rape.* Thousand Oaks, CA: Sage.

Wilder, D. H., Hoyt, A. E., Doren, D. M., Hauck, W. E., & Zettle, R. D. (1978). The impact of fraternity and sorority membership on values and attitudes. *Journal of College Student Personnel, 19,* 445-449.

Worth, D. M., Matthews, P. A., & Coleman, W. R. (1990). Sex role, group affiliation, family background, and courtship violence in college students. *Journal of College Student Development, 31,* 250-254.

Index

About the Authors

Martin D. Schwartz is Professor of Sociology at Ohio University. He has written more than 60 articles, chapters, edited books, and books on a variety of topics in such journals as *Criminology, Deviant Behavior, Justice Quarterly,* and *Women and Politics.* A former president of the Association for Humanist Sociology, he has never been convicted of a major felony. He is the co-author of *Contemporary Criminology* and *Corrections: An Issues Approach,* now in its fourth edition; the editor of *Researching Sexual Violence Against Women: Methodological and Personal Perspectives;* and the co-editor of *Race, Class, and Gender in Criminology: The Intersections.* He serves as deputy editor of *Justice Quarterly* and has received the lifetime achievement award from the American Society of Criminology's Division on Critical Criminology.

Walter S. DeKeseredy is Professor of Sociology at Carleton University. He has published dozens of journal articles and book chapters on woman abuse and left realism. He is the author of *Woman Abuse in Dating Relationships: The Role of Male Peer Support;* with Ronald Hinch, co-author of *Woman Abuse: Sociological Perspectives;* with Desmond Ellis, co-author of the second edition of *The Wrong Stuff: An Introduction to the Sociological Study of Deviance;* with Linda MacLeod *Woman Abuse: A Sociological Story* (forthcoming). In 1995 he received the Critical Criminologist of the Year Award from the American Society of Criminology's Division on Critical Criminology. In 1993 he received Carleton University's Research Achievement Award. currently he is co-editor of *Critical Criminology: An International Journal* and serves on the editorial board of *Women & Criminal Justice.*

Printed in the United States
59411LVS00003B/193